A SHORT HISTORY OF
MODERN RUSSIA

A SHORT HISTORY OF
MODERN RUSSIA

by

Richard Freeborn

HODDER AND STOUGHTON

PRINTED IN GREAT BRITAIN FOR HODDER AND STOUGHTON LTD.,
ST. PAUL'S HOUSE, WARWICK LANE, LONDON, E.C.4, BY
HAZELL WATSON AND VINEY LTD., AYLESBURY, BUCKS

Contents

Chapter VI 1917–1936

Chapter VII 1936–1953

Epilogue 1953–1964

Conclusion

Select Bibliography

Index

Maps

Introduction

A SHORT history is bound to lack that "buzz of implication" to which Lionel Trilling has referred in speaking of one's awareness of the present.* It must inevitably be a digest not of the implications but of the most salient facts around which the implications buzzed in their time. To this extent, lacking chiefly the sound of the past, the present has to condescend, not arrogantly but with a proper confidence in its own continuing vitality, to the history which it serves to perpetuate. What the writer of a history must always regret, presumably, is either the lack or the extreme faintness of that "buzz of implication" which was the living present of history. But what the present writer regrets especially is that, in compiling this short history from many secondary sources, he may seem to have condescended too much to the most salient facts and too little to the often high-pitched buzzing which surrounded them in their time and continues to surround them in the many expert general or specialised histories of Russia. What he has attempted to do is to provide a short history of modern Russia from the Napoleonic invasion to the era of Khrushchev which may be of interest both to the general reader and to the student who seeks a brief historical background to the literature of the period. It is in the literature of modern Russia that the implications of Russian historical development buzzed most fiercely. If this short history can help to demonstrate, however slightly, the connection between the historical and the literary developments, then its primary aim will have been achieved.

A few words must be said in justification of the term "modern". The decision to begin this history with the Napoleonic invasion has been taken in the belief that this event marks the emergence of Russia as a great world Power in the modern sense. The Russian victory over Napoleon gave Russia for the first time a decisive role to play in the councils of Europe and therefore of the world. Perhaps still more important for an understanding of Russia's present position in the alignment of world Powers, Russia emerged after the Napoleonic invasion as an opponent of Great Britain. This opposition has grown, with the predominance of the United States in the twentieth century, into an opposition between the English-speaking and Russian-speaking peoples—in

* Trilling, L., *The Liberal Imagination*, L. 1955, 206.

other words, into one of the most important aspects of the contemporary world situation. The limits set upon this history have been governed partly by this consideration.

But the term "modern" in relation to Russia has also been taken to mean that period of Russian history during which opposition to Tsarism began to assume a revolutionary character. The revolutionary movement which culminated in the overthrow of Tsarism in 1917 is not the specific concern of this history, but it is obvious that modern Russian history must have as its centrepiece the revolution which brought into being the Soviet Russia of the present day. The Napoleonic invasion in many ways provided the impetus to the revolutionary movement which gathered momentum throughout the nineteenth century; and for this reason it has seemed appropriate to make this event the starting-point for a short history of modern Russia.

The term "Russia" has been taken to mean the state governed in the nineteenth century by the Emperors of the house of Romanov and since 1917 by the Bolshevik, or Communist, Party. Although modern Russia has always been multi-national in character, this history is concerned exclusively with the Russian people and makes no more than passing reference to the other nationalities who formed part of the pre-1917 Russian Empire and now form part of the Soviet Union.

A Prologue offers a brief digest of Russian history to the beginning of the nineteenth century and an Epilogue provides a review of developments during the era of Khrushchev, from 1953 to 1964.

In transliterating from the Russian, I have used accepted anglicised forms in the majority of cases, but in transliterating the Russian ё I have used the form yo in several proper names (Potyomkin, Pugachyov, Mogilyov, for example, rather than Potemkin, Pugachev, Mogilev); an exception in this respect is Khrushchev (pron. Khrushchyov). In the case of certain pre- and post-revolutionary institutions, I have used transliterated forms of the singular and plural, e.g. *zemstvo*, pl. *zemstva*; *kolkhoz*, pl. *kolkhozy*; *sovkhoz*, pl. *sovkhozy*. In giving dates, I have used the Julian (Old Style) Calendar—eleven days behind the Gregorian (New Style) Calendar in CXVIII, twelve days in CXIX and thirteen days in CXX—for all events occurring within the borders of Russia, or in Russian-occupied territory, before February 1st 1918.

This history owes much to the generous advice, careful criticism of the text and stimulating comment which I have received from my colleague, Mr J. S. G. Simmons. The range and devotion of his scholarship deserve better reward than this short history can hope to offer. He is responsible for none of its shortcomings. I am indebted to Dr George

Katkov for advice on some of the changes which have occurred in Soviet Russia since Stalin's death. I must acknowledge a warm debt of gratitude to Mr Mark Lovell for editorial suggestions of the utmost value. My thanks are also due to Miss Mary Potter of the School of Geography, Oxford University, for her kindness in drawing the maps.

PROLOGUE

800 – 1800

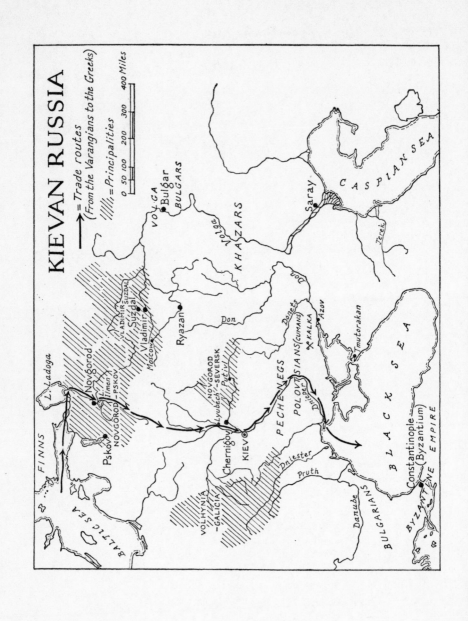

KIEVAN RUSSIA

= Trade routes
(From the Varangians to the Greeks)

///// = Principalities

0 50 100 200 300 400 Miles

FINNS

BALTIC SEA

L. Ladoga

Novgorod

L. Ilmen

NOVGOROD-PSKOV

Pskov

VLADIMIR-SUZDAL

Suzdal

Vladimir

Moscow

Ryazan

VOLGA

Bulgar

BULGARS

Volga

KHAZARS

Don

Don

Saray

CASPIAN SEA

Terek

NOVGOROD-SEVERSK

Putivl

Lyubech

Chernigov

KIEV

Donets

Donets

PECHENEGS

POLOVTSIANS (CUMANS)

KALKA

Azov

Tmutorakan

Dnieper

Dnieper

BLACK SEA

VOLHYNIA-GALICIA

Dniester

Pruth

BULGARIANS

Danube

Constantinople
(Byzantium)

BYZANTINE EMPIRE

Kievan and Moscovite Russia

KIEVAN RUSSIA probably first came into existence in the latter half of the ninth century A.D. According to the Russian Primary Chronicle, in 862 a Varangian called Ryurik and his two brothers and their respective retinues were invited to rule over the Slavs. Many historians have concluded from this that the "Russians", being described as "Varangians" (Norsemen, Normans), were of Scandinavian extraction. But attempts to prove the Scandinavian origins of the Russians have met serious difficulties. More recently, especially in Soviet studies, attempts have been made to demonstrate that the Russians were of Slav origin, deriving their name possibly from the River Ros, a tributary of the Dnieper. Although, until such time as more conclusive evidence becomes available, there is always likely to be controversy over this point, there can be little doubt that Ryurik and his followers were warriors. Oleg, who succeeded Ryurik as ruler of Novgorod, attacked Kiev in 882, captured it, set himself up as Prince of Kiev and declared, according to the Chronicle, that Kiev should be the "mother of Russian cities". In this way, one must assume, Kievan Russia began.

Kiev enjoyed a highly profitable position on the trade route between the Baltic and the Black Sea. The tenth century found pagan Kiev pursuing an aggressive policy against Byzantium, partly at least to safeguard trading outlets. Attacks were also made on the Eastern Slavs, who were between Kiev and the Volga trade route. More often than not, Kiev was successful.

But Vladimir, who reigned in Kiev from approximately 980 until 1015, both by converting Russia to Christianity (*circa* 988) and by marrying the sister of the Byzantine Emperor Basil II, forged political, religious and cultural links with Byzantium which were to give Kievan Russia a much enhanced international status, and to lend to the whole of early Russian cultural history a non-Roman, Byzantinist, Greco-Asian complexion. The conversion to Christianity marks a new stage in the evolution of Kievan Russia, introducing an era of about 100 years (1020 to 1125) when Kiev reached the zenith of its power, both in terms of international prestige and cultural attainment.

Vladimir's son, Yaroslav, managed to defeat the Pechenegs, to bring an end to the warfare with Byzantium, and to develop close family ties

13

with many of the leading royal houses of Europe. His greatest contributions were no doubt made in the internal affairs of the Kievan state,
especially with his code of laws known as the *Russkaya pravda* (*Russian
Justice*) and his patronage of the Orthodox Church. The first important
surviving work of early Russian literature—Metropolitan Ilarion's *Sermon on Law and Grace*—dates from Yaroslav's reign.

After his death, feuds among the princes dissipated the strength of
the Kievan lands. For a brief period under Vladimir Monomakh, who
ruled from 1113 to 1125, Kiev regained its former authority, though
throughout his reign he was engaged in wars against neighbouring tribes,
particularly the Polovtsians. Monuments to his reign include the founding of the town of Vladimir, and his *Poucheniye* or *Testament*, a work
offering many valuable insights for an understanding of the political and
cultural ethos of Kievan Russia.

When he died in 1125, the process of disintegration, already evident
in the second half of the eleventh century, quickly gained momentum.
It is hardly surprising that the greatest work of Kievan literature, *The
Lay of Igor's Raid*, which describes in richly imagistic language the
failure of a raid undertaken by a prince of Novgorod-Seversk against
the Polovtsians, should have laid great stress on the need for unity
among the princes of the Russian land. But such unity could not be
achieved. In 1237 no effective common front could be presented to the
invasion of the Mongols (or Tatars.). Under Khan Batu (or Baty), they
proceeded to pillage, raze and enslave one principality after another
until, in 1240, Kiev itself was destroyed. Simultaneously Novgorod was
attacked by the Swedes, and in 1242 by the Teutonic Knights. Under
attack from both east and west what had formerly been Kievan Russia
collapsed, being destined for almost 250 years to pay tribute to the
Mongol invaders.

Kievan Russia, consisting of fortified towns built chiefly of wood,
with their churches and market places, was a patchwork quilt of political
forms and allegiances, social contrasts, an economy divided between
trade and agriculture, and a culture in which the old pagan and the new
Christian were inextricably mixed. The princes of Kievan Russia were
both monarchs and merchants. As monarchs their powers were to some
extent curbed by their retinues. A retinue would form a council (duma)
of boyars whom the prince would consult; in a municipality such as
Novgorod, the prince's power would be curbed even further by an
assembly of townspeople. Even so, the prince as monarch was both a
warrior responsible for defending his town or principality from external
enemies, and judge or law-giver in the principality's internal affairs. The
boyars, often landowners in their own right, were free to serve which-

14

ever prince they wished, but with the gradual disintegration of Kiev's central authority, and the growth of agriculture, the boyars tended, like the princes and the peasants, to become attached to one locality. Originally, however, the princes of Kiev were merchants in the sense that they exacted tribute from subject tribes, and this tribute was then carried along the trade-route for sale in Constantinople. Yet trade seems to have been chiefly the concern of the princes and their retinues.

The peasants, whether free men or slaves, were concerned with agriculture, extensively cultivating the rich black earth of the steppe-land in the south, or using a more intensive two-field or three-field system of cultivation in the forest lands in the north.

Culturally, after the conversion to Christianity, the ancient pagan deities were merged with, rather than submerged by, new Christian beliefs. Kievan Christianity was fairly closely modelled on its Byzantine original. Despite the survival of paganism, Christianity quickly became part of the very essence of life in Kievan Russia, exerting a profound effect on political and social concepts, and bringing to all Russians the unity of a common language in the form of Church Slavonic. Christianity also brought Greek church architecture, modified (as was Church Slavonic by Old Russian) by a Russian taste for cupolas. Such stone churches as the St Sophia Cathedral in Kiev (1037) and the beautiful churches in Vladimir and Suzdal bear witness to the glory that was Kievan Russia. A still more vital and richer link with that early era is provided by the folk songs which tell of the great warriors of St Vladimir's court. What has survived, however, whether in the form of churches, icons, folk songs, or written literature, can give us no more than a glimpse, it seems, of that rich, noisy, saintly, embattled but glorious age at the beginning of Russian history.

There can be little doubt that the Mongol invasion not only laid waste much of the Russian land, and razed many of its fine towns, but the subsequent Mongol overlordship, by demanding the continuous payment of tribute, kept Russia in economic as well as political subjection. The Mongol invasion also divorced Russia from Byzantium, forcing the centre of Russian life to move from Kiev in a north-easterly direction and thus isolating Russia from European influences. In a cultural sense Russia became a backwater. On the credit side it may be argued that, in their concern for exacting tribute, the Mongols introduced such new organisational procedures as the taking of population censuses and *per capita* taxation, which may be regarded as the beginnings of a process of centralisation of government that achieved a final form in Moscovite Russia. In this sense the Mongols may be said to have put the iron of centralised autocratic power into the Russian political soul. But this contribution to Russia's future development, however far-reaching, does little to outweigh the loss; and it is a contribution, in any event, which can only be viewed with serious misgivings.

During the long period of subservience to the Mongol power, Moscow gained in influence and in strength. Its central situation between Ryazan in the south-east and Novgorod in the north-west, at the head-waters of four rivers and on three trade routes, enabled it to play a leading role among the Russian-speaking peoples. But its political power accrued chiefly as a result of a series of able, conservative and far-sighted rulers; and such stable political leadership led to economic stability, which in turn attracted both populations and trade from outside. One very important factor was the establishment at Moscow, in Ivan I's reign (the late 1320s to 1341), of the residence of the Metropolitan of the Orthodox Church, and thus the religious centre of the Russian people. The influence and guidance of the church helped considerably to enhance the prestige and authority of Moscow at a time when the Mongol overlordship, through internecine quarrels among the Mongol khans, had begun to show signs of weakening.

Moscow was able to withstand and repulse Lithuanian attacks, later in the fourteenth century, at the height of that country's power; and a Moscovite army even overcame a Mongol force at the battle of Kulikovo, in 1380. Although the Mongols subsequently returned to sack Moscow and re-impose their authority, they were no longer regarded as invincible. Moreover, the Mongol love of money had been one of the means by which Moscow had gained its pre-eminent position among the Russian principalities, and to this extent the Mongol overlordship proved to be to Moscow's advantage : rulers of Moscow had increased their domains and their authority by shrewdly acting as agents of the Mongols in exacting tribute. Vasily I (1389–1425) found it expedient to continue paying tribute to the Mongols while engaged for the greater part of his reign in a struggle against the Lithuanians.

By the time of his son's (Vasily II) death in 1462, three processes were at work which were to have a decisive effect upon the future character of Russia. Firstly, not only were Mongol raids on Moscovite territory repulsed, but the Mongols themselves were splitting into the separate khanates of the Crimea, Kazan and Astrakhan; secondly, towards the end of his reign Vasily II made determined efforts to overcome the opposition of Novgorod and Pskov to Moscovite hegemony; thirdly, in 1439, at the Council of Florence, agreement had been reached between the Greek Church and Rome to make common cause in face of the Turkish threat to Constantinople—an agreement which would

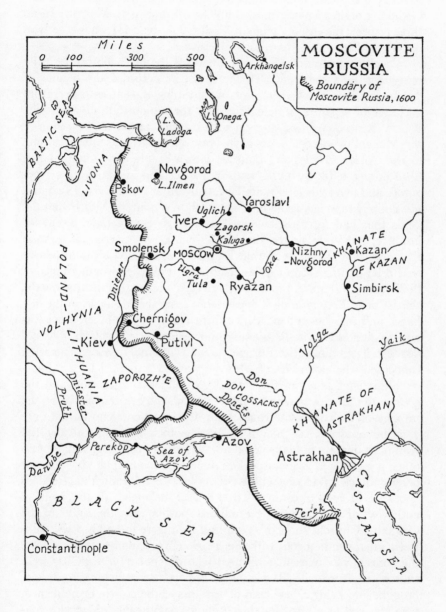

MOSCOVITE RUSSIA

Miles
0   100   300   500

Boundary of Moscovite Russia, 1600

Arkhangelsk

BALTIC SEA

LIVONIA

L. Ladoga
Neva

L. Onega

Novgorod
L. Ilmen

Pskov

Yaroslavl

Uglich

Tver

Zagorsk

Kaluga

Smolensk

Dnieper

MOSCOW

Nizhny
-Novgorod

Oka

KHANATE
OF KAZAN

Kazan

POLAND-

Ugra
Tula

Ryazan

Simbirsk

VOLHYNIA

Chernigov

Kiev

Putivl

LITHUANIA

ZAPOROZH'E

Volga

Yaik

Dniester

Pruth

DON COSSACKS

Don

Donets

KHANATE OF ASTRAKHAN

Perekop

Azov

Sea of Azov

Astrakhan

CASPIAN SEA

Danube

Terek

BLACK   SEA

Constantinople

seem to give the Pope the right to impose his authority on Russia—but in 1453 the Turks finally captured Constantinople, and the Eastern Orthodox heritage passed not so much to Rome as to Moscow. In all three respects the ensuing reign of Vasily's son, Ivan III, known as Ivan the Great of Moscow, was to prove decisive.

Of all the rulers of Moscow Ivan III is the first who can be truly recognised as a statesman. To him must be accorded the honour of "gathering Russia together"—of transforming it, that is to say, from a cluster of separate principalities into the nation-state of Moscovite Russia. A necessary first stage in such transformation was rejection of the Mongol overlordship. In 1476 Ivan refused to pay further tribute to the Golden Horde, and punitive measures taken by Khan Akmed were unsuccessful. By 1478, Ivan had succeeded in subjugating Novgorod, and five years later a similar fate overtook Tver. Even if Ivan did not entirely manage, as he had intended, to obtain for Moscow all the lands that had formerly belonged to Kievan Russia (Kiev itself, for instance, and Volhynia remained in Lithuania), his marriage in 1472 to the niece of the last Byzantine Emperor won for Moscow an extra-territorial heritage of much vaster import—the religious inheritance of the Byzantine Empire. From this there grew the concept of Moscow the third Rome. By obtaining independence from the Mongols on the one hand, and religious independence from Rome on the other, Ivan was able to give Moscovite Russia a significant degree of political independence in its relations with Europe. So far as internal developments were concerned, the expansion of Moscow was accompanied by a proportionate strengthening of the central governmental authority; and the greater the area over which Moscow ruled, the greater had to be the prestige of the Moscovite ruler. Ivan declared himself to be not only Tsar, but autocrat, sole ruler of all Russia, which implied politically that within his domain not only could no other prince challenge him, but no other prince could strictly speaking be autonomous. The very concept of autonomy—and along with it the very concept of individual freedom —ceased to have meaning. To the Tsar belonged all the political authority, all the land, all the military power, even the rights of the Orthodox Church. In Ivan's realm all men were to be his servile subjects. Thus, simultaneous with the creation of a nation-state there arose the concept of "treason" : all men who did not serve the Tsar were traitors to Moscovite Russia. The importance attaching to service brought into being a new class of servitors of the crown, or noblemen, who received as reward for their military or bureaucratic service conditional life tenure of certain lands or estates : these were the first "landowners", who were to play so important a part in nineteenth-century

Russian history. But there were also hereditary landowners, the aristo-cratic boyars, who found that the autocratic powers of the Tsar and the new class of noblemen-servitors were increasingly depriving them of their former authority. Consequently, as Moscovite Russia expanded territorially and the Tsar's central autocratic power increased, political tensions began to arise within the state between the Tsar and the boyars, and the boyars and the noblemen-servitors.

During the reign of Ivan's son, Vasily III (1505–1533), the expan-sion of Moscovite territory continued. At the same time the opposition of the boyars to the Tsar's authority was kept under control. But at Vasily's death, his son, the future Ivan IV, was only three years old, and the government of Russia passed into boyar hands. Their rule was arbitrary and selfish in the extreme. No one knew this better than the young heir to the throne, who, though duly honoured in public by the boyars, was privately derided and scorned by them.

Ivan IV, known as Ivan the Terrible as much for his terrible treat-ment of Russia's enemies as for the domestic excesses that occurred during his reign, is certainly the most enigmatic of all Russia's rulers. A predilection for cruelty, coupled with bouts of religious mania; states-manship, combined with unreasoning hatred of those he regarded as his enemies, were manifestations of an unbalanced personality. Many fea-tures of his reign suggest that he did not rule Russia so much as stage-manage Russian affairs, like a master of political *grand guignol*. He was careful to ensure, for instance, that his debut as Tsar in 1547 was a properly stage-managed ceremony. His marriage in the same year to Anastasya Romanov proved to be exceptionally happy, but the opening of his reign was marked by fires and rioting in Moscow, which almost cost him his life, and provided a foretaste of the turbulence that his rule was to bring to Russia. When the rioting had been quelled, he made public avowal that he would in future rule only with the support of the people. It seems that he had not only undergone the first serious psycho-logical crisis of his reign, but that he had also realised how dangerous was the power of the boyars.

His first political act after the disturbance was to set up a Chosen Council, the principal members of which were the Metropolitan Makary, an eloquent defender of the property-owning rights of the Church, and compiler of the *Lives of the Saints*; Sylvester, court chap-lain and famous principally as the supposed author of a manual of rules of conduct known as the *Domostroy*; and Adashev. Conducting the affairs of state in consultation with this Chosen Council, Ivan decided in 1550 to summon a *zemsky sobor* or conclave of the entire Russian people at which grievances could be aired, and Ivan's plans for judicial and local government reform could be publicly announced. Army reforms were also instigated, one of which was the creation of the first permanent regiment, the *streltsy*. A new code of laws, designed to supersede Ivan III's code of 1497, was also adopted. A church assembly of 1551 approved ecclesiastical reforms, couched in the form of a hundred chapters (*Stoglav*). Important taxation and central administrative reforms were also introduced during the first ten years of Ivan's reign.

In 1552, he made a successful campaign against Kazan, and four years later Astrakhan was also brought into subjection. In order to strengthen Russian military potential, rules were laid down governing the military service that every nobleman, whether boyar or servitor, had to offer to the state. Now every landowner was only entitled to his land on the condition that he served the Tsar by providing the correct number of armed and mounted fighting men proportionate to the size of his lands.

A further campaign, against the Crimean Tatars, yielded no decisive result. Important successes were gained in a thrust to the west, against the Livonian Order. Ivan's aim was to gain access to the Baltic, but his initial military successes could not be consolidated. The only lasting result of his attempt to create an outlet to the west was a trade agreement between Russia and England, which gave the English very favourable terms of trade, and allowed them to establish their own trading posts in Arkhangelsk and Moscow. Probably the greatest success—in terms of territorial aggrandisement—of Ivan's reign was the conquest of Western Siberia by the peasant-adventurer Yermak.

In 1553 Ivan fell seriously ill. Believing that he was dying, he called upon his boyars and personal counsellors to swear allegiance to his infant son. They responded by preferring to swear allegiance to his cousin, Prince Vladimir. Their unwillingness to acknowledge Ivan's son was apparently due to the relatively humble origins of his mother, Anastasya. Ivan recovered from his illness, but his distrust of the boyars, and especially his distrust of his two closest advisers, Sylvester and Adashev, had been so truly roused that from the late 1550s onwards his management of Russian affairs was directed almost entirely to eradicating this new "treason". The immediate occasion of this new policy was the sudden death, perhaps by poisoning, of Anastasya. Ivan's wrath was turned on Sylvester and Adashev, who were both summarily banished. Ivan then indulged in a curiously theatrical manoeuvre. In 1564 he suddenly departed from Moscow to Alexandrovskoye, about sixty miles from the capital. Two months later he announced that he wished to abdicate, though he stressed that he had no quarrel with the common people, only with the boyars and the clergy who were trying to usurp his authority. The Metropolitan and people of Moscow implored him to return as their Tsar. He agreed : on condition that he could establish a new system of government, and deal entirely as he wished with his enemies. Delegates came from Moscow to accept the Tsar's demands and, grown prematurely old as a result of a further psychological crisis, Ivan finally resumed his role as autocrat.

Russia, according to Ivan's plan, was to be split into two parts : one of them, including Moscow, became his personal domain, while the other was to be ruled over by a council of boyars and a Tsar, a Tatar prince called Simeon, to whom Ivan pretended to swear allegiance. The purpose of this split was to allow Ivan complete freedom to wage a war of terror against the aristocratic boyars and their supposed sympathisers within the borders of his own domain. This warfare was carried out by his private army, at first numbering 1,000, but later increasing to 6,000. They were clad in black and wore special insignia of a dog's head and a broom, symbolising their obedience to the Tsar and their willingness to sweep Russia clean of his enemies. By torture, massacre and pillage they spread unimaginable destruction. The most terrible of their assaults was on Novgorod, which was utterly devastated in 1570. The division of the realm into two parts continued until about 1576, during which time the country had become so weakened that in 1571 the Crimean Tatars were able to set fire to Moscow, carrying off enormous booty and thousands of prisoners. In addition, the war with Livonia proved disastrous for Russia. By 1582 Ivan was obliged to sue for peace and acknowledge that his attempt to reach the Baltic had ended in total failure.

Diseased, mentally unbalanced, married seven times since the death of Anastasya but never solaced, given to orgies of torture and drunkenness, Ivan was finally driven to howling despair when, in a fit of rage, he struck and mortally wounded Ivan, his son and heir. Dying, he was carried into his treasury, where he discoursed on the properties of the various jewels; but about noon on the day he was to die he called for a chess-board and set out the pieces, "all saving the king, which by no means he could not make stand in his place with the rest upon the plain board" — so reported Sir Jerome Horsey, agent of the Russian Company.

He had ruled by the divinest of rights, as the visible embodiment of the power of God on earth, and he had exacted from his subjects an obedience so complete and grotesque that they had even submitted to his tortures and praised God for their abominable sufferings. Ivan's reign broaches not so much the question of his madness, about which there can be little doubt, as the madness of his subjects, who in tolerating this tyranny set a precedent for their toleration of equally fiendish tyrannies

21

in later centuries. As one of the first English students of Russian history, W. R. S. Ralston, expressed it in 1874 :

> "Ivan the Terrible probably believed without a shadow of doubt that he had been invested with despotic power by direct celestial agency, and that all attempts to thwart his purpose or limit his will must be due, at least to infernal suggestion, if not to diabolical support. But even when every modifying influence is taken into consideration, and full attention has been paid to the peculiar features which the case presents, it must remain inconceivable to us, to whom freedom has come as naturally as the light of day or the air we breathe, how men could have witnessed the atrocities committed day after day by the terrible madman upon the throne, and not have made some attempt to stay his destroying hand."

From Moscovite to Petrine Russia

IVAN, as king, stood in his place on the plain board of Moscovite Russia through permitting no other person or class to challenge his authority. But though he suppressed, he could not eradicate the aristocratic boyars. As soon as he was dead they re-asserted that power which they had wielded with such wanton caprice during his minority. The years between Ivan's death in 1584 and the accession of the first of the Romanovs in 1613, the latter part of which has come to be known as "the time of troubles", brought to the boil the social, nationalistic and dynastic issues Ivan had managed to suppress through the sheer weight of his despotism. The ensuing history of Russia until the appearance of Peter the Great displays a three-fold development. In the first place, due not only to social pressure but also to a revival of national and religious feeling, boyar authority was finally replaced by a renewal of autocracy with the founding of the Romanov dynasty. At first tentatively, later more boldly, the autocracy began to assert its independence of all restraints until it became both imperialist and absolutist. But concomitant with this process, and the second important issue in the unfolding history of seventeenth-century Russia, was the growth of the service-nobility, upon whom the autocracy gradually placed exclusive reliance and whose exclusive interests it tended increasingly to represent. Thirdly, though, if both the autocracy and the nobility seemed to prosper, then the mass of the Russian people—the labouring peasantry—

fell into ever greater servitude to their noble lords and masters. The history of the Russian people during the evolution from the Moscovite to the Petrine era is a history of growing and deepening serfdom, of rebellion against such bondage, particularly by the runaway serfs known as cossacks, of increasing rural impoverishment and the degradation of peasants to the status of chattels.

Ivan was succeeded by his son Fyodor, a man of devout religious habits, who within four years had handed control of the country to his brother-in-law, Boris Godunov, a member of a Russified Mongol boyar family. When Fyodor died in 1598, Boris Godunov was elected his successor. The new Tsar soon discovered that he was being accused by rival boyars and the populace in general of having done to death Fyodor's younger brother, who would have been heir to the throne had he been alive. Such accusations must have been caused partly by the disastrous crop failures and ensuing famines which occurred during the first years of the seventeenth century. But they were also no doubt a consequence of the fact that with the death of Fyodor the previous ruling dynasty had come to an end. To this extent Boris Godunov was a "false" Tsar; and his "falseness" was to give rise to a succession of further "false" Tsars who claimed connection, usually extremely tenuous, with the previous dynasty. Out of this dynastic issue there grew "the time of the troubles".

The complications of this period are such that they can be described here only in the sketchiest of fashions. Within a space of ten years, three pretenders appeared in succession, two claiming to be Fyodor's dead brother Dmitry, and one claiming to be his son. Certain of the boyars were eager to establish a boyar dynasty, and one of them, Vasily Shuisky, was declared Tsar. A revolt of peasants and slaves developed under the leadership of Ivan Bolotnikov; and to make the period more complex, there were intrigues for Swedish and for Polish support, and there were divisions among the Poles themselves. When it seemed as if a Polish dynasty might be invested in Moscow, anti-Polish feeling was whipped up by the Orthodox Church. Eventually, a "council of the whole land" was formed, a kind of travelling provisional government, representing chiefly the interests of the townspeople and the lesser nobility. In alliance with a cossack force, this group emerged as the victors out of the long struggle, driving the Poles from Moscow, and ensuring that whoever became Tsar would not be a puppet of a foreign power.

The first act of the victors was to summon a huge *zemsky sobor*. All elements in the population, including the peasantry (the only instance, in fact, of a *sobor* containing peasantry), were to be represented. The *zemsky sobor* first met in 1613, and sixteen-year-old Mikhail Romanov was chosen to be the new Tsar. The Romanov dynasty was destined to rule Russia for exactly 304 years, until the abdication of Nicholas II on March 2nd 1917.

Tsar Mikhail, the new autocrat, ruled initially with the aid of a *zemsky sobor*, but neither this assembly nor the boyar council played more than a consultative role in the government of the country. The main problems facing the Tsar were to create a semblance of order out of the chaos of the previous years and to ensure a measure of stability in the nation's finances. The latter proved to be too difficult a task; but he was able to maintain his hold on the government, while for the most part avoiding any serious renewal of hostilities with foreign powers.

If the first Romanov's reign seems to be an oasis of tranquility after the stormy opening years of the century, then Tsar Aleksey Mikhailovich's reign, from 1645 to 1676, was a period of intermittent domestic unrest. Aleksey suffered from the besetting sin of all weak Romanovs : a proneness to choose as his favourites men of few scruples and even less ability. The most unscrupulous of his favourites, though also in this case the most able, was the boyar Boris Morozov, whose attempts to improve the financial situation of the state by levying a tax on salt sparked off serious riots in 1648 in Moscow and many other towns. In order to stabilise the nation's affairs, an extraordinary *zemsky sobor* was summoned, at which a new code of laws was drawn up, superseding that of 1550. This new code was known as the *Ulozheniye* of 1649.

Serfdom was now sanctioned as state policy. Though the nobles were called on to look after their peasants, they exercised both police and judicial powers over them (except in the case of a serious crime, such as murder), could mete out ferocious punishments at will, and, towards the end of the seventeenth century, were able to buy or sell them. But the serfs had their state counterparts—state peasants, that is to say, who paid dues, either in money or in produce, not to a nobleman-master, but to the state. In general the state peasants were situated on the poorer agricultural lands in the north of Russia or in Siberia.

The enactment of this new code of laws caused increasing discontent in the countryside. About the same time, a serious rift appeared in the Russian Orthodox Church. The new patriarch, Nikon, appointed in 1652, proceeded to introduce a series of long overdue revisions in holy writ which were followed by reforms in the ritual. There was immediately fierce opposition to this among a section of the Russian clergy, who branded Nikon a heretic and preferred to retain the old customs. In consequence they became known as the so-called Old Believers. This rift, or *Raskol*, in the Russian Church has never been healed. But Nikon went further than the Tsar would allow by asserting that the power of the church should be greater than the Tsar's power. He compared the power of the church with that of the sun, whereas the Tsar's power was only that of the moon. His reforms were recognised, but he was deposed from the patriarchate and banished. Probably the most significant and moving monument to this *Raskol* was archpriest Avvakum's autobiographical *Life*—a work which, in addition to demonstrating his faith as an Old Believer, can be regarded as the most important example of secular literature to emerge from seventeenth-century Russia.

In foreign affairs two very important events occurred during Aleksey's reign. Firstly, in 1653, after Bogdan Khmelnitsky had organised an uprising of Ukrainians against Polish rule, a *zemsky sobor* called for a union between Russia and the Ukraine, and in 1654 the Ukrainians swore allegiance to the Tsar. In addition to this, successes against the Poles led to the acquisition of Smolensk, Chernigov and Kiev—essential relics of the Kievan patrimony.

However, Aleksey's rule is to be remembered primarily for the rebellion organised by Stenka Razin among the Don cossacks. Razin was able to win widespread popular support by issuing proclamations against the nobility during his advance up the Volga in 1670, but he was captured in the spring of the following year and executed on the Red Square in Moscow.

The uneventful reign of Fyodor, Aleksey's son, from 1676 to 1682, ended with a problem over the succession. His young half-brother, Peter, was proclaimed Tsar, but intrigues left the future in doubt for about seven years. Thereafter, Russia was under a regency until 1696, when Peter finally became sole and undisputed ruler. From this moment can be dated the new, Petrine epoch in Russian history, an imperial phase that endured for more than two centuries.

Moscovite Russia, though revered by nineteenth-century Slavophils as a period when there existed a natural accord between the Tsar and his people, has neither the appeal of antiquity associated with Kievan Russia, nor the splendour that is called to mind by the imperial Russia of St Petersburg. It may well be that the unity of the Tsar and his people —a unity, let it be said, more apparent than real—gave Moscovite Russia a patriarchal cohesion, rigidity and cosiness which seemed, and may still seem to Russians at a later epoch, more "Russian" than the time preceding or following it. To the European visitor, as many memoirs attest, Moscovite Russia was as strange as is the Soviet Union to many Western visitors of the present day. Possibly that which seems most "Russian" in the Soviet Union—the holier-than-thou xenophobia, for instance, the concern with purity of doctrine, the supposed unity between ruler and ruled, the communalism and the militancy—has its source in Moscovite Russia and reflects in a modern form the ambiance of that pre-Petrine epoch.

Yet in Moscovite Russia of the seventeenth century all was not static. Just as the institute of the *zemsky sobor* was to die out, so did the boyar council. Neither of these was really democratic, and they played little more than a consultative role in the government of the country. Throughout Moscovite history the effectiveness of such bodies was limited by the ignorance and prejudice of the noblemen or boyars who were required to participate in them. Similarly, even though Ivan the Terrible had tried to introduce a form of local government, lack of personnel capable of performing such a function at provincial level obliged the central government to rely on military Governors. The central bureaucracy, composed of forty-odd ministerial offices, was a ramshackle mechanism of government run on traditional and formalistic lines by officials who occupied their posts largely for reasons of heredity. But despite ignorance, inefficiency and widespread corruption, Western influences were beginning to penetrate Russia, especially during the reign of Tsar Aleksey. Such were the innovations of the patriarch Nikon, the Latin and Polish influences accruing from the union with the Ukraine, the growth of the German "suburb" in Moscow, and the interest taken by the Tsar and his favourites in Western military science, metal manufacture, potash production and—not least—in the theatre. It is also noteworthy that one of the most profoundly traditional of Moscovite institutions, the order of precedence among the boyars, was abolished in 1682—a measure that permitted greater flexibility in appointments to senior posts in the state.

Moscovite Russia may be said to have left behind two legacies which, to the non-Russian imagination, may seem particularly characteristic. Firstly, from the mid-fifteenth century onwards, just as democratic principles within Moscovite territory were receding before the growing power of the autocracy, so below the Dnieper rapids, on the Don, Yaik and Terek rivers, there emerged new rough-and-ready democratic communities of runaway peasants or frontiersmen. These communities, exceptionally warlike and anarchic, were known as the cossacks. During the period of the persecution of the Orthodox Church in the Ukraine, the Dnieper cossacks became the chief defenders of the Orthodox faith, engaging in sporadic hostilities with both the Poles and the Turks. Nominally subjects of the Tsar after the union between Russia and the Ukraine, the Dnieper cossacks nonetheless tried to remain independent; but by the end of the eighteenth century they were finally subdued. The

Ulozheniye of 1649 drove many Russian peasants into the Don area, where conflicts between the established cossacks and the new arrivals provided fertile ground for Stenka Razin's propaganda.

The second legacy is artistic. On the one hand there is nothing more characteristic of Russian piety than the icon-painting attributed to Andrey Rublyov. On the other there is probably nothing more "Russian" to the Western imagination than the church architecture of the Moscovite period, despite the fact that most of the architects were Italian. The churches in the Kremlin, such as Fioravanti's Cathedral of the Assumption (1475–1479), are probably the best-known examples. The walls of the Kremlin, also the work of Italians, were constructed between 1485 and 1495; and the Gateway of the Redeemer was built by Marco Ruffo in 1491. But probably the most remarkable example of Moscovite architecture is the Cathedral of St Vasily the Blessed, at the eastern end of the Red Square, erected on Ivan the Terrible's orders between 1555 and 1560 to celebrate the capture of Kazan. In its combination of dazzling ornament and harmonious symmetry it aspires to heaven while at the same time suggesting the panoply of earthly power: in that, it typifies the Moscovite ideal.

The Eighteenth Century

"RUSSIA," wrote Pushkin, "entered Europe like a ship down a slip-way—to the clatter of axes and the thunder of cannon." The launching of Russia into Europe was the work of Peter I, known as Peter the Great. In physical proportions he was built for his age and his task, a giant among men, indefatigable in all his labours and his pleasures; to Pushkin, in his poem *The Bronze Horseman*, Peter resembled Falconet's equestrian statue, "the mighty sovereign of fate" who made Russia rear on her haunches above the abyss; in contrast to this grandiose interpretation of his historical destiny, all the evidence suggests that he was a man of eminently practical mind, with an insatiable appetite for every new item of scientific knowledge, and a genius for organisation. During the course of his reign (1696–1725) Peter the Great set the seal of his own character and his fascination for the West so firmly upon Russia that, whether in the shape of his fantastic city of St Petersburg or his many reforms modelled on Western lines, neither the country nor its people were ever again to be anything save part of Europe.

In Peter's case there can be little doubt that necessity was the mother of invention : the necessity of reaching the sea, the Baltic in the north and the Black Sea in the south, forced him into building a navy and organising a modern army. His playing at soldiers with his friends in the villages outside Moscow, which since gave their names to the Preobrazhensky and Semyonovsky guards regiments, laid the foundation for the army; his discovery in a barn of a broken-down English boat was the beginning of the navy. The war games of 1694 quickly became the land and sea attack on Azov of 1696 which captured the fortress. Having demonstrated that Russia could practise modern arts of warfare, he took an embassy to Europe in order to learn at first hand about European methods of ship-building, and to hire experts for the shipyards that he planned to build in Russia. The embassy visited Holland, and then went on to England, renting a house in Deptford and visiting Oxford, the Tower of London, the House of Lords, Portsmouth, Woolwich, the Royal Society. To Bishop Burnet, who met him, Peter seemed "designed by nature rather to be a ship-carpenter, than a great prince".

Having returned to the continent, Peter received news that there had been a revolt of the *streltsy* in Moscow. Abandoning his plan to visit Venice, he hurried back to his capital and there took decisive action against the insurgents. Not content with torture and decapitation of the *streltsy*—which were, after all, acceptable Moscovite methods of dealing with enemies—Peter ordered that his courtiers should shave off their beards and wear Western clothes. Moreover, at the beginning of the new century the Julian (Old Style) Calendar was introduced, which meant that the years of Russian history would henceforth be counted from the birth of Christ, not, as had been the previous practice, from the supposed beginning of the world (5508 B.C.). Though the Julian Calendar was still eleven days behind the Gregorian (New Style) Calendar which was being widely adopted throughout Europe, Russia was beginning to catch up.

The next ten years were to be decisive. By a peace treaty signed with Turkey in 1700 Azov was ceded to Russia. Peace in the south allowed Peter to devote all his energies to what has since become known as the Great Northern War against Sweden. In alliance with Poland and Denmark, Peter laid seige to the Swedish fortress of Narva, but Charles XII of Sweden, although only eighteen years old, proved quite equal to the new threat. Having forced Denmark to submit to peace terms, he at once attacked the Russians at Narva and inflicted on them a crushing defeat. Believing that the Polish threat was more serious than the Russian, Charles XII now directed all his efforts to defeating the Polish king, Augustus II, leaving the way open for the Russians to recoup their losses in the Gulf of Finland. Peter made the most of this opportunity. By

18th. CENTURY RUSSIA

Russian Western Border 1795

Areas acquired by Peter I, 1700–1721

0 50 100   200   300 Miles

FINLAND

Stockholm

BALTIC SEA

ST. PETERSBURG 1703

1795 (III)

Koenigsberg

PRUSSIA

1772 (I)

LESNAYA 1709

Pinsk

AUSTRIA

1793 (II)

Kiev

Moscow

Nizhny Novgorod

Kazan

Simbirsk

Penza

Tambov

POLTAVA 1709

1735

Jassy

Dniester

1791

Ochakov

Prut

Rymnik

Izmail

1783

1739

Donets

Don

Tsaritsyn

Volga

Danube

Sea of Azov

Azov

Kuchuk-kainardzhi

1783

Sevastopol

Taman

1783

BLACK SEA

TURKEY

Constantinople

Chesme

imposing heavy taxation, melting down church bells for cannon and forcibly levying new recruits, he was able to reconstruct his shattered army. Gradually Russia, with the aid of the newly-built naval vessels from the new shipyards, emerged into the Baltic. In 1702, where the Neva joins Lake Ladoga, Peter established the fortress of Schlüsselburg; in 1703 he founded his new capital, St Petersburg, on the Neva; the next year he constructed the fortress of Kronstadt on an island in the Neva's mouth. Soon much of Livonia and Estonia had fallen into Russian hands. Although there were successive rebellions against the new taxes and reforms, Russian military and naval strength continued to grow. It was therefore a very different Russia which, in 1707, had once again to face the threat of invasion by Charles XII, who had in the meantime succeeded in forcing Poland to come to terms.

At first the Swedish army advanced towards Moscow, but Charles soon decided to turn southwards into the Ukraine, where he hoped to exploit the help he had been offered by the *Hetman* Mazepa. The promised help turned out to be negligible, and Swedish reinforcements were intercepted at the village of Lesnaya. Isolated and short of supplies, the Swedes spent the winter of 1708–1709 on the open steppe. In the following spring Charles XII besieged Poltava, which however Peter succeeded in relieving in June. The subsequent Battle of Poltava ended in a decisive defeat for the Swedes, and forced Charles to flee to Turkey. With this one battle Russia emerged victorious from the Great Northern War and thereby ensured that practically the entire shoreline of the north-eastern Baltic became part of Russia. Despite the fact that Charles provoked Turkey into war with Russia, Peter's territorial expansion continued steadily. Even though peace terms with Turkey forced Peter to give up the fortress of Azov, in the Baltic area he had conquered Estonia and Livonia (1710), joined forces with Poland in a renewed anti-Swedish alliance which swept the Swedes from Pomerania (1712–1713), and invaded Finland in 1714. Hostilities with Sweden were renewed in 1719 and 1720, when Russian expeditionary armies were landed close to Stockholm, eventually forcing the Swedes to sue for peace. By the Treaty of Nystadt (1721), Russia acquired practically all the territory now occupied by the Estonian, Latvian and Lithuanian SSR's, and important strategic areas on the Gulf of Finland. Peter could now proclaim himself Emperor and Russia an empire. St Petersburg became in consequence an imperial capital as well as a "window into Europe". The victory over Sweden brought Russian expansion in the west to an end, but it was followed by a short victorious war against Persia, and the extension of diplomatic and trade feelers to the east, particularly towards China, with which commercial and diplomatic relations were established.

The many reforms instituted during his reign were in part determined by military needs, and in part by such factors as the need to improve the administration or to Westernise the state so that Russia should be not only imperial but modern in the European sense. The Petrine reforms involved a radical transformation of the country; there was hardly a single aspect of Russian life that did not feel the effect of Peter's vigorous and ruthless leadership. But it must not be assumed that Peter's reign represented a total break with Moscovite past. It involved both an acceleration of those Westernising processes which had already begun to be discernible in the latter part of the seventeenth century, and a deliberate crash programme of change and innovation. But as with all revolutions, whether imposed from above (as this one), or from below (as in 1917), whatever scars were inflicted on the nation's history at the moment of impact seemed less grievous with the passage of time.

The first changes initiated during Peter's reign were designed to increase state revenue to pay for the war against Sweden. The municipal reorganisations of 1699, and the later division of the country into large administrative units (or *gubernii*), were attempts at decentralisation which had the aim of facilitating the collection of revenue. In the absence of a properly organised central administration, these measures fell far short of what was desired; and in 1711 Peter created a central body known as the Senate, consisting originally of nine, later of ten councillors presided over by a Chief Procurator, which was given the task of supervising the work of the *gubernii* and acting as a supreme court. Intended initially to be a temporary body empowered to act in the Tsar's absence, the Senate became an important permanent institution of the imperial government; it remained in existence until after the Bolshevik *coup d'état* in 1917. In 1718 the old ministerial offices were replaced by new ministerial colleges, at first numbering nine—for war, the navy, foreign affairs, justice, state income, state expenditure, control of state income and expenditure, commerce, and manufactures —to which were later added three further colleges for mining and metallurgy, estates, and municipal administration. These colleges were run by committees headed by a president, a vice-president and other officials, numbering twelve in all. The gubernii were later reorganised into fifty provinces, each of which was headed by a Governor responsible to the colleges and the Senate. More far-reaching still was the introduction of a Table of Ranks, which created a hierarchy of fourteen grades in the army, navy and civil service. Promotion was by merit only, but service was for life. All officials who attained the eighth grade or rank became members of the nobility. By this means many former serfs were able to rise to positions of power in the state, but gradually the system led to the creation of a class of privileged hereditary bureaucrats, who suppressed all initiative in the lower ranks of the hierarchy. Perhaps even more damaging in the long run was Peter's hostility to the Orthodox Church, which made him curtail the patriarchate, and establish a Holy Synod, presided over by a Chief Procurator, which had control over church affairs. This was Peter's definitive act in secularising the state. He not only ensured that from henceforth the Orthodox Church would have to identify itself with the political interests of the autocracy, but he also made certain that all aspects of the state apparatus, including the armed forces, should become subject to his rule as absolute monarch.

Other measures enacted during Peter's reign were the introduction of life service for conscripts to the armed forces, the creation of special regiments of guards, and the establishment of a modern armaments industry for the production of flintlocks and cannon. The most remarkable of Peter's achievements was, of course, the creation of a Russian navy; by the time of his death it contained thirty-nine major ships of the line built in Russian shipyards on the Baltic. An inheritance law stipulated that the entire estate of a landowner should pass to one of his sons, preferably the eldest, not to all his sons as had previously been the practice; in this way many young members of the nobility were forced into government service. In 1718 a census of the population, conducted with the aim of levying a poll, or head, tax, increased the already heavy burden of taxation that the lower classes had to bear, and forced them into still greater dependence on their masters. Hardest hit were the servile workers in the new mines and factories. But all classes of the population had to contribute to state revenue through a proliferation of taxes on, among other things, such curious items as bath-houses, beards and oak coffins.

Though Peter the Great exacted both obedience and money from his subjects, he also saw to it that the Russian economy was not neglected. State funds were extensively deployed in encouraging mining and metallurgy in the Urals, a large textile industry and other consumer industries for the manufacture of glass, paper, paint, leather products and so on. By 1720, Russia had become a major exporter of iron and copper, particularly to Great Britain. Many factories built at government expense were transferred to private management at very attractive rates. The government also embarked on canal-building projects, promoted foreign and domestic trade, and through a protectionist tariff in 1724 encouraged a favourable trade balance. In the cultural sphere Peter paid special attention to technical education; he established an

Academy of Sciences, and fostered the translation and publication of technical literature. It was on his initiative that the first Russian newspaper was published. Among the many projects in which he took an active personal interest were prospecting for minerals, map-making and exploration, of which the most famous example is probably the Behring expedition, which he despatched shortly before his death to seek out the link between Russia and America.

If Peter made stupendous efforts to transform Russia, he could not so readily eradicate the conservatism and indolence in the Russian character. His son Aleksey, the child of his first marriage, though given an education designed to make him Peter's heir, steadfastly refused to abandon his conservative, Moscovite sympathies, and in 1718 was implicated in an alleged plot to overthrow the state. Imprisoned, tortured and forced to confess, he was sentenced to death but died in the Peter and Paul fortress before the sentence could be implemented. The indirect consequences were yet more tragic. There was now no obvious successor, since Peter left no male issue by his second wife, Catherine. In 1722 a law had been passed giving the sovereign the right to appoint his successor. But before he drew his last breath he was unable to name one, and this omission opened the way for an era of ridiculous misgovernment which contrasted strangely with the sublime achievement of Peter's own reign.

After his young grandson, Peter II, died in 1730, the Supreme Privy Council turned to Anna Ivanovna of Courland, daughter of Peter the Great's half-brother. In inviting her to ascend the throne the Council hoped to impose upon her certain conditions which would have reduced her role to that of a semi-constitutional monarch, subject in many respects to the Council's pro-boyar oligarchical dictates. Although Anna initially accepted these conditions, she quickly took advantage of the antagonism shown by an influential section of the nobility against the boyar oligarchy to overturn the Supreme Council; and, with the aid of the guards regiments, she was able to establish herself as autocratic Empress of Russia. During her ten years' reign, domestic affairs were almost wholly controlled by her German favourite, Ernst-Johann Biren, or Biron, who instituted a rule of terror, known as *Bironovshchina*, involving the execution or exile of many thousands of supposed opponents of Anna's power. The most important domestic measure during this period was the reduction in the nobility's obligatory service to the state from a lifetime commitment to a term of twenty-five years, and the exemption of one son from such service so that he might be enabled to look after the family estates. In foreign affairs, Russian troops achieved notable successes against the Turks in the war of 1735–1739, but most

of the gains were surrendered under the Treaty of Belgrade. This stipulated that the fortifications of Azov should be destroyed and that no
Russian naval vessels should be stationed in the Black Sea.

When Anna died in 1740, there was a struggle for power that culminated in a *coup d'état* organised by the Preobrazhensky guards, and
Peter the Great's daughter Elizabeth was proclaimed the new Empress.
Elizabeth represented a much stronger link with the Petrine era, but she
had none of the thrust or imagination of her father. Vain but kindly,
excessively extravagant and of a lazy, voluptuous disposition, she favoured a French influence at court, for it was largely due to French
support that she had succeeded in gaining the throne. Her love of display
and her fondness for dresses were private manifestations of an equally
strong public concern for stateliness rather than statecraft. The greatest
monument to her reign is the baroque magnificence of Rastrelli's Winter
Palace, in which regal stateliness unites with almost excessive feminine
adornment; but so far as statecraft was concerned, her rule was insipid.
She abolished Anna's cabinet and restored the powers of the Senate, but
her reign was not marked by any attempt to alleviate the lot of the
peasantry. On the contrary, she relied upon the nobility, and granted
them the exclusive right to own serfs.

Her reign opened with a war against Sweden, provoked by France,
which ended in 1743 with the Treaty of Abo giving Russia considerable
territory in southern Finland. Under Count Bestuzhev-Ryumin's guidance, Russia participated in the War of the Austrian Succession (1740–
1748) only in its final stages, but during the Seven Years' War (1756–
1763) despite Bestuzhev-Ryumin's hostility to a Franco-Russian alliance, Russia became allied with Austria and France against Prussia. In
1757 Russian troops invaded Prussian territory, and a successful campaign was pursued, largely at Elizabeth's personal insistence, and Koenigsberg was seized. Frederick II of Prussia attempted to stem the Russian
advance, but was defeated twice. In 1760 Russian troops temporarily
occupied Berlin, leaving memories of atrocities which were deliberately
revived by the Hitler government in 1944 in an effort to foster last-ditch
resistance to the advancing Soviet armies.

Immediately upon Elizabeth's death in 1761, her son Peter III made
peace with Frederick of Prussia, handed back all the hard-won gains and
drastically reversed the former anti-Prussian policy, to the bitter indignation of the army and the Russian families mourning their dead in the
Seven Years' War. The army was now obliged to wear Prussian-style
uniforms and to engage in Prussian drill practice. Rabid in his dislike
of Orthodoxy, the new Emperor deliberately offended the clergy by
demanding the removal of icons and aroused serious resentment among

broad sections of the population. But he also appeased the nobility by decreeing, in 1762, that all compulsory service to the state was abolished; the serfs, however, had to wait ninety-nine years, until 1861, for their own emancipation. The inequity of freeing the nobility from their obligations without giving an equivalent freedom to the peasants opened a running sore of bitterness in relations between the classes which, at this mid-point in the history of the Romanov dynasty, may be said to be the start of a process that led a little over a century and a half later to the blood-letting of revolution and civil war. The nobility became as a result of this decree a leisured class, to a very large extent independent of the state. But such leisure and independence were, in the course of time, to foster liberal hopes among sections of the nobility, to encourage the growth of a nobility-intelligentsia and, paradoxically, to provide a fertile ground in which the first seeds of Russian socialism could take root.

In 1745 Peter had made an arranged marriage with a German princess, Sophia of Anhalt-Zerbst, who, upon taking the vows of the Orthodox Church, had been renamed Catherine. In intelligence and ambition she entirely eclipsed her unstable and boorish husband. Their marriage was probably never consummated. Though Peter had several mistresses, he was by all accounts infertile. The incompatibility between Catherine and her husband soon led her to look elsewhere for love and affection. Of her many lovers—she is known to have had at least twenty during the course of her life—the first, Saltykov, was probably the father of her son Paul, born in 1754; and this probability has inspired the suggestion that there was no Romanov blood in any of the subsequent rulers of imperial Russia.

The general disgust felt at Peter III's pro-Prussian policies and his contempt for Orthodoxy—a contempt that Catherine, though a foreigner, did not share, for she had taken great trouble to ingratiate herself with the Russian people by devoutly observing their religion and customs—soon gave rise to plans for installing Catherine in her husband's place. In June 1762 she was proclaimed Empress after a *coup d'état* in which the guards regiments had again played a significant part. Peter was forced to abdicate, and within three days of the *coup* had been killed.

In this way, without fuss or hindrance, Catherine attained her ambition of becoming ruler of Russia. Her reign was to prove the most brilliant, in terms of territorial aggrandisement and international prestige, of any that had preceded it. She was a woman of considerable culture and learning, well versed in the work of the Encyclopaedists, an ardent admirer of Montesquieu's *L'Esprit des Lois* and Voltaire's *Essai sur les moeurs et l'esprit des Nations*. Beccaria's *Of Crime and Punish-*

35

ment and the *Annals* of Tacitus were also favourite handbooks of hers. From 1763 until 1777 she corresponded with Voltaire; this she did with several famous figures of the time, such as Diderot, D'Alembert, and Melchior Grimm. Though she patronised the arts, especially architecture and literature, her own attempts at literary creation had no more than ephemeral value. The whole cast of her character, her intellectual stamina, the persistence and regularity of her work fitted her to be an administrative, rather than a creative, genius. That she possessed such genius is undeniable; but in addition she had charm, strength of personality, and a talent for eliciting devoted service and lasting affection from those who were given the task of realising her ambitions for Russia. She has since come to be known to history as Catherine the Great—the last Russian ruler to be honoured with such a title.

At the outset of her reign Catherine's task was to consolidate her position as autocrat. She had both to gain the support of the nobility, upon whom she chiefly relied for her authority, and to forestall possible attempts to depose her in favour of her son, Paul—or even Ivan VI, who had been incarcerated in his infancy, when Elizabeth seized power. At the same time, the governmental apparatus of the country was badly in need of reform. One of Catherine's earliest acts was to reorganise the Senate into six departments and to divide up some of the ministerial colleges, thereby ensuring not only increased efficiency in these central organs of government but also their direct subjection to her autocratic will. She gave greatly increased powers to the governors in the provinces and, under pressure from the nobility, implemented a decree on the secularisation of church lands which had originally been introduced by her husband. Violent opposition to this measure came from the Metropolitan of Rostov, but Catherine had him brought to trial and imprisoned. So far as the serf problem was concerned, she attempted unsuccessfully to liberate the servile workers in industry. This failure, it seems, soon reconciled her to supporting the landowners' interests at the expense of aggravating the suffering of the great mass of the Russian people. In 1765, for instance, landowners acquired the right to send their peasants into penal servitude in Siberia; and soon afterwards the same punishment was extended to peasants who complained against their masters. To the modern mind it may seem that there was much hypocrisy in Catherine's professed concern for her subjects, whose lot worsened appreciably as a direct result of her temporising attitude towards their problems.

Initially, though, she had not intended to temporise. During 1765–1766 she devoted herself to framing an Instruction, which was designed to serve as the basis for a wholesale reform of Russian laws. By plagiarising for the most part from the works of Montesquieu and Beccaria, Catherine was able to prepare a remarkably enlightened document. But advisers to whom it was submitted for approval whittled away three-quarters of it. In its final form it represented both an *apologia* for benevolent despotism and, to some extent, an indictment of the burdensome taxation and legal impositions from which the peasants suffered. In its insistence that the use of torture in obtaining evidence during criminal proceedings should be abolished, it marked an important new departure in Russian attitudes to justice. But Catherine's Instruction is in fact irrelevant to history; it is relevant only to her own biography. Almost as irrelevant is the legislative commission which was first convened in Moscow in 1767 to set about re-codifying Russian laws, especially those enacted since 1649. Consisting of 565 deputies, it was an unwieldy body and far from representative of the mass of the Russian people, since there were no peasant deputies. It deliberated for a period of eighteen months, and was dispersed when war broke out with Turkey.

Though Catherine had renounced shortly after her accession Peter III's Russo-Prussian military alliance, in 1764 a defensive alliance was concluded between the two countries. This was to prove particularly valuable in ensuring the stability of Russia's borders during the war with Turkey. In 1769 Russian troops invaded Moldavia where, under the generalship of Rumyantsev, they won a series of remarkable victories over the more numerous Turkish forces. Victory on land was accompanied by victory at sea : two Russian squadrons sailed from Kronstadt to the Aegean, and in 1770 defeated a much superior Turkish fleet in Chesme Bay. In 1771 the Crimea was invaded and all the most important Turkish outposts were captured. Alarmed by these Russian successes, the Austrian government decided to come to Turkey's aid. However, at this point Russian attentions were diverted to Poland, where religious strife had given rise to a civil war in which France, Austria and Turkey gave their support to a confederacy of Polish feudal landlords, in their struggle against the King of Poland. This was Stanislas Poniatowski, who had been appointed to the throne by Catherine, and was one of her former lovers. As head of a multi-religious and multi-national state, where the constitution virtually ruled out effective legislation, he had only nominal control. In 1772 Catherine, tired of attempting to suppress the revolt of the confederates, agreed to Frederick of Prussia's plan for partitioning Poland in collaboration with Austria. As a result of this first partitioning of Poland, Russia acquired a large area of Belorussia, including such towns as Vitebsk and Mogilyov, and all the territory up to the Dvina and the Dnieper.

Despite this extraordinary diplomatic victory, the position of Catherine's Russia was by no means secure. Catherine's own position as Empress was never so seriously threatened as at this moment. Though she might derive entertainment from her philosophical and political discussions, the oppressive régime of serfdom which she had done so little to alleviate was an invitation to the masses to revolt against her rule. In 1773 a Don cossack, Emelyan Pugachyov, gathered round him a horde of 30,000 Yaik cossacks, many of whom were Old Believers, and laid siege to the fortress of Orenburg. Pugachyov proclaimed himself Peter III, established his own court, and issued decrees against landowners and government officials. Governmental authority soon collapsed along the entire length of the Yaik River; landowners were either murdered or fled in panic to Moscow. But the rebellion lacked proper leadership and organisation, and successive defeats were inflicted on the rebels, frustrating several attempts to re-group and push westwards.

This internal threat made the government keen to end the war with Turkey. The Turks similarly, having suffered overwhelming defeats at the hands of the Russian commanders, Rumyantsev and Suvorov, were glad to sue for peace and in 1774 agreed to the Treaty of Kuchuk-Kainardzhi; this gave Russia territory between the Bug and the Dnieper, an outlet from the Azov Sea, and the right to free passage for Russian merchantmen through the Bosphorus and the Dardanelles. The Crimean Tatars were declared to be independent, but this in fact opened the way for the subsequent Russian annexation of the Crimea. This treaty meant that Russian troops were free to crush the Pugachyov rebellion, which they accomplished towards the end of 1774.

This revolt provoked Catherine into initiating certain reforms in local government, which aimed at strengthening the local administration. In 1775 legislation was introduced dividing Russia into fifty new provinces (as Peter the Great had done), but sub-dividing each of them into approximately ten counties, of about 30,000 inhabitants. Though the governors of the provinces were appointed by the Senate, the local administration was left to the nobility; and the dominance of the nobility gave the management of affairs at local level, especially in the appointment of officials and in the administration of justice, a distinct class bias. Simultaneously, the cossacks of the Dnieper were stripped of their independence and large numbers were later transferred to the Kuban; the autonomy of the Don cossacks was also abolished.

The first war with Turkey had not ended to Catherine's satisfaction, but her prestige among the ruling monarchs of Europe had been so enhanced by her diplomatic victory in the first partition of Poland and her suppression of Pugachyov, that she was called upon to mediate between Austria and Prussia over the Bavarian succession, a direct result of which was the Treaty of Teschen of 1779. Catherine further enhanced Russia's international prestige by uniting practically all the nations of Europe in an Armed Neutrality against Great Britain during the American War of Independence. But a clarification of the Treaty of Kuchuk-Kainardzhi had obliged her to withdraw her troops from the Crimea. To further her ambitions in the south, the Prussian alliance was abandoned, and an alliance was concluded with Austria in 1781. Shortly afterwards Potyomkin, the most famous of Catherine's many favourites, began to implement her decision to annexe the Crimea by embarking upon an ambitious programme of naval shipbuilding and the creation of a naval base at Sevastopol.

The most important of the measures that Catherine introduced in Russia's internal affairs was enacted in 1785. This was a charter for the nobility, which significantly increased their power and prestige by giving them the right to elect their own marshals of nobility in their own localities, endorsed the voluntary character of their service to the state, exempted them from corporal punishment and personal taxation, ensured that they could only lose their noble status by court order, and guaranteed them the exclusive right to ownership of their serfs and their estates. A similar though largely ineffective charter was granted to the towns, which established six grades of towndwellers according to property qualifications, and empowered them to elect mayors and municipal councils. But the effect of this charter was simply to give a disproportionate say in municipal affairs to the richest merchants.

If Catherine did little more than accept the *status quo* in Russia's internal affairs, then so far as Russia's relations with Turkey were concerned she displayed a lively determination to get everything changed. The most remarkable manifestation of her ambitions in this respect was her triumphal progress to the Crimea in the company of the Austrian Emperor and the King of Poland in 1787. This ostentatious visit to her southern possessions was deliberately calculated to provoke Turkish hostility; and it succeeded. That same year Turkey demanded back the Crimea, and landed troops at the mouth of the Dnieper; these were, however, soon repulsed by Suvorov. After a long siege, Potyomkin took the Turkish fortress at Ochakov. Meanwhile, urged on by Great Britain and Prussia, Sweden had declared war on Russia, and Swedish guns were even heard on the Neva. But King Gustavus of Sweden, faced with revolts in his own capital and the threat of a Danish invasion, made peace with Russia in the summer of 1790. Then Suvorov's victories in the south, and a successful sea battle fought by Admiral Ushakov, forced the Turks to accept the Treaty of Jassy (1791), which recognised the

Russian annexation of the Crimea, and transferred the border between Russia and Turkey from the Bug to the Dniester.

Catherine had succeeded in realising Peter the Great's dream of extending the Russian Empire to the Black Sea, though Potyomkin's more ambitious vision of a Kingdom of Dacia extending to Constantinople remained no more than a chimera which was to excite Russian messianic hopes throughout the coming century, until the revolution of 1917. This was to be one of the mainsprings of what was later called the Eastern Question. But the French revolution of 1789 cast a shadow over Catherine's triumphs. As the revolution became gradually less liberal in character, culminating in the execution of Louis XVI and Marie Antoinette, so Catherine's hatred of Jacobinism became correspondingly more marked. Fearing that the unsettled conditions in Poland might be a threat to her own rule, she proceeded, once again in collaboration with Prussia, to a second partition of Poland. This gave Russia the remaining parts of Belorussia, most of Lithuania, and all of the Ukraine west of the Dnieper, including a population of 3,000,000. Polish attempts to preserve independence were ruthlessly crushed by Suvorov, in the course of 1794. Afterwards, Poland was partitioned for a third time, now, as in the case of the first partition, between Russia, Prussia and Austria. Russia received Courland, the rest of Lithuania and the Ukraine; Prussia seized the area between the Nieman and the Vistula, including Warsaw; and Austria took Galicia, including Cracow. Poland disappeared from the map of Europe, a circumstance for which Catherine the Great was largely responsible, though she had the justification that the Polish territory annexed to the Russian Empire had at one time been part of Kievan Russia.

When Catherine died in 1796, she was succeeded by her son, the Emperor Paul. A martinet, fond of Prussian-style uniforms and drill procedures, Paul was determined, so far as his limited intelligence and vision would permit, to reverse his mother's policies and to undo as much as possible of her work. This attitude no doubt resulted from the fact that, during his mother's lifetime, he had never been permitted to have any part in the government of the country. Catherine had been justified in treating her son with little respect. He was subject to uncontrollable rages and caprices, and when he finally acquired autocratic power he proceeded to use it with an arbitrariness and an attention to petty detail which verged on madness.

The most significant of his innovations in domestic affairs was his curtailment of the nobility's right to retire voluntarily from state service. He also endeavoured to ensure that peasants should not work more than three days in each week on their masters' lands or on holidays, especially

Sundays. He attempted to reduce some of the privileges of the nobility with the aim of preventing palace revolutions and of subjecting the nobility to the rule of the bureaucracy. Though he tried to encourage education and trade, he also extended serfdom to the southern Ukraine, the Azov and other newly acquired areas of the Russian Empire and handed over many thousands of state peasants to the nobility for re-settlement. Primogeniture in the male line was the new rule of succession introduced by Paul, and the prestige of the church was also greatly improved during his reign. But members of the nobility were forbidden to travel abroad, the censorship was increased, private educational establishments were closed down, the importation of foreign, especially French, books and music was forbidden. The attempts to suppress French revolutionary influences reached such lengths that the wearing of French fashions and the use of such words as "citizen" or "father-land" were strictly prohibited.

Hatred of the French also governed Paul's actions in foreign affairs. In 1798 Russia became a leading member of the second anti-French coalition in company with Great Britain, Austria, Turkey, Naples and Portugal. In support of this new coalition Admiral Ushakov took a Russian fleet through the Straits, captured the Ionian islands from the French and operated along the Italian coast, helping to drive the French from Naples. Suvorov, although in disfavour after Paul's acces-sion, was appointed to command combined operations with Austria : in a brilliant campaign, he succeeded in driving the French from Lom-bardy.

Paul's allies in the second anti-French coalition were almost as alarmed by the Russian successes as they were by the power of Napo-leon. Fear of Russian naval vessels in the Mediterranean induced a wave of Russophobia in Great Britain; Austria, though glad of Russian assistance in clearing the French from Italy, deliberately forced Suvorov to retreat across the Alps, thus enabling Austrian authority to fill the vacuum left by the French defeat. Disillusioned, Paul switched his allegiance to Napoleon, whom he now regarded as a guarantor of stability in Europe. By breaking with Great Britain, Paul seriously jeopardised Russia's foreign trade; and the only tangible outcome of the new alliance with Napoleon was a fantastic plan to send an ill-equipped army of Don cossacks to invade India. Before the alliance had had time to develop further, Paul was strangled to death in March 1801 during a palace revolution organised by his favourite, Count Pahlen, and condoned by his liberal-minded son, the future Alexander I.

During the eighteenth century, through the statesmanship of Peter and Catherine, the prowess of Russian armies and the assimilation of

European ideas and techniques, the groundwork was laid for the emergence of Russia as a major power. But economically, socially and culturally, Russia remained, to a great extent, a backward nation. Though the population of the Russian Empire increased between the middle and the end of the century—due, in part, to the annexation of new territories—from approximately 16,000,000 to 36,000,000, about 53 per cent were serfs working on the estates of a nobility who comprised barely more than 1 per cent of the population. In addition, about 39 per cent were state peasants, and 6 per cent were house serfs, deprived of land and entirely dependent upon employment in the manorial houses of the nobility. Mention should also be made of the small though growing numbers of factory workers, whether hired or attached to factories as "possessional workers" or simply as serfs.

Economically the most rapid advances were made in foreign trade, which increased fivefold, in terms of the rouble value of imports and exports, between 1760 and the end of the century, due chiefly to the development of the ports on the Baltic which Peter had gained during the war with Sweden, and to Catherine the Great's need for foreign revenue. Trade also began to develop through the Black Sea ports and in Asia. But Catherine's lavish expenditure, whether in maintaining the finest court in Europe, in her generosity to favourites or in pursuing her wars against Turkey, led to the creation of a national debt, which in turn involved raising loans, particularly in Holland, and the issue of large quantities of paper currency. The result was a fall in the value of the rouble and increasing inflation. The taxation burden on the peasantry became correspondingly more oppressive. Practically nothing was done, however, to modernise agricultural production, even though Catherine established a Free Economic Society in 1765 for the discussion of agricultural questions. When the question of the abolition of serfdom was raised, the matter was quietly shelved.

The Petrine reforms, the nobility's acquisition of their freedom in 1762, and the high standards set by Catherine tended to increase the already sharp cleavage between the nobility and their serfs. The wealthier members of the nobility, in attempting to emulate or outshine the splendour of Catherine's court, maintained their own huge palaces, orchestras, theatres and ballet companies, mainly staffed by serfs, some of whom were sent abroad to learn their particular arts. Such social pretence permeated the Russian attitude towards education and culture. Though Catherine might have established the Smolny Institute for educating daughters of the nobility, and a medical school, by the end of the century there were secondary schools in only half the provincial towns of Russia. Education was for the most part limited to an acquisition of the social graces. Efforts were made to develop popular education (there were over 300 such elementary schools in existence at the end of the century), but it was church schools that helped to foster educational standards, though chiefly of course for religious purposes; the ordinary clergy, nevertheless, became increasingly impoverished as a result of the secularisation of church lands. The most outstanding event in the sphere of education during the eighteenth century was the creation of Moscow University (1755), destined to become, and to remain, the greatest centre of learning in Russia.

Moscow University is now named after Lomonosov (1711–1765) who was instrumental in bringing the university into being. The son of a fisherman in the Arkhangelsk region, Lomonosov managed to spend four years at Marburg University, after which, on his return to Russia, he applied himself to exploring every known branch of the sciences, making several important discoveries in physics, astronomy (the discovery of atmosphere on Venus, for instance), meteorology, mineralogy, optics and other subjects. His encyclopaedic interests included the writing of the first scientific grammar of the Russian language; he also defined three styles in Russian, the high, middle and low, which proved to be a very influential step in modernising the language; and in his lifetime he acquired a justifiably high reputation for his literary work, his odes, the most famous of which were in honour of Peter the Great, his plays, his treatises on such subjects as the making of glass, and his researches into Russian history. Apart from Lomonosov, other figures who contributed during the eighteenth century to the beginnings of Russian literature were the satirist Kantemir (1709–1744) and the poet Derzhavin (1743–1816), the greatest exponent of Russian Classicism, who composed eulogies to Catherine but was a great deal more than a court poet, as his *Ode to God* and his famous lyric poem, *The Waterfall*, magnificently attest. The beginnings of an indigenous Russian drama also belong to Catherine's reign: the stilted tragedies of Sumarokov (1718–1777) were popular at the time, though the satirical comedies of Fonvizin (1745–1792), *The Brigadier* and *The Minor*, the latter satirising Russian attempts to ape French tastes, have permanent literary value. Catherine's interest in literature encouraged the growth not only of private publishing, but also gave rise to the appearance of numerous periodicals. Much of the more serious social criticism which appeared in these periodicals was the work of the Freemasons, notably Novikov (1744–1818). His outspoken criticism, especially of serfdom, led to his arrest in 1792 and imprisonment in the Schlüsselburg fortress.

Catherine's love of satire was never more than skin deep. After the French revolution she became extremely sensitive, and repressive, towards any sign of disapproval of her rule. The first open indictment both of serfdom and of Catherine's despotism appeared in 1790 when A. N. Radishchev (1749–1802) issued from his own printing-press 650 copies of his remarkable book, *A Journey from St Petersburg to Moscow*. Radishchev, influenced by the ideas of the French Enlightenment, particularly by Rousseau and Mably, offered a documentary picture of the evils of serfdom—of peasants sold like chattels, forced to work a six-day week on their masters' lands, driven into forced marriages, flogged and fettered at their masters' whims—which were to be witnessed on a journey between the two Russian capitals. The book had an avowedly revolutionary purpose. Radishchev was arrested, sentenced to death, but sent finally into ten-year exile; from which, however, he was released after Catherine's death—only to commit suicide in 1802, when threats of further persecution were made against him by the authorities. His book and his personal fate were to set the tone both for the literature of the future—seemingly documentary in form, revolutionary in intent—and for the future fates of those who, like Radishchev, were bold enough to speak the truth in the artificial and oppressive atmosphere of imperial Russia.

Chapter I

1801 – 1825

The Napoleonic Invasion

Upon his accession in 1801 Alexander I attempted to remain neutral in the general European war against Napoleon. Napoleon's power increased so rapidly, however, that the young Emperor had by 1805 brought Russia into a third anti-French coalition which included Great Britain, Austria and Sweden. Moving his armies eastwards in the autumn of 1805, Napoleon soon achieved a series of swift and devastating victories against the new allies and entered Vienna in triumph in November. A combined Austrian and Russian army, commanded by Kutuzov, at first pursued a policy of retreat which so incensed Alexander that he countermanded it. The result of this decision was the Battle of Austerlitz, fought early in December 1805. The combined Austrian and Russian forces were decisively defeated, the Austrians sued for peace and the Russians retreated quickly across the border into their homeland.

As the first military confrontation between Russia and France in the nineteenth century, Austerlitz could hardly have been less auspicious. Despite this defeat, Alexander did not abandon his anti-French policy. When Prussia, though temporarily in alliance with France, turned to Russia for help in throwing off the French yoke, Alexander concluded a secret military agreement with the Prussian monarch. In September 1806, after Prussia had broken with France, Alexander came to the aid of his new ally, only to find that the Prussian armies were to succumb to Napoleon at Jena and Auerstädt within three weeks of the outbreak of hostilities. Russian armies continued to offer strong resistance throughout the winter of 1806–1807—a notable example of Russian military fortitude was the exceptionally bloody battle of Preussisch Eylau (February 1807)—but all attempts by Alexander to keep the Prussian–Russian alliance alive were ended by the defeat of the Russians at Friedland in June. A week after the battle Alexander and Napoleon met at Tilsit on the River Nieman and signed a treaty which provided, among other things, for the creation of a new Grand Duchy of Warsaw.

The Tilsit peace was little more than a *détente*. Neither Napoleon nor Alexander was keen to continue the war, but the extreme likelihood of future war was nonetheless inherent in the provisions of the Tilsit Treaty. To Napoleon Tilsit meant that he was now free to deal as he wished with Europe and yet could still, if necessary, turn upon Russia

47

again, for he had acquired the right to station troops in the Grand Duchy of Warsaw—an admirable jumping-off ground for an invasion of Russia. To Alexander the treaty gave him an opportunity to pursue the war with Persia over the annexation of Georgia, though Russian participation in the Continental Blockade against British shipping seriously damaged Russian foreign trade and caused murmurings of political dissatisfaction in St Petersburg. Despite the disadvantages, Alexander at first adhered to the new alliance with enthusiasm. Encouraged by Napoleon, he proceeded to take military action against Sweden, Britain's sole remaining ally, and after a protracted campaign succeeded in annexing Finland and the Aland Islands (September 1809). War then flared up with Turkey in the south. In the spring of 1809 Russian troops under Kutuzov forced the Danube and advanced into Bulgaria, but decisive results were not attained until 1811. A year later the Turks were forced to agree to a treaty by which Bessarabia, between the Dniester and the Pruth, was ceded to Russia. In the meantime relations between Alexander and Napoleon, particularly after their meeting at Erfurt (1808), had seriously deteriorated. Alexander began to make friendly overtures to Austria, but Austria, in attempting to assert her independence, was defeated at Wagram in July 1809 and obliged to submit to extremely harsh peace terms. By 1811 the Tilsit peace had exploded : both Napoleon and Alexander were actively engaged in military preparations.

Napoleon's pretexts for invading Russia seem absurdly flimsy by comparison with the grandeur and horror of the event itself. His aim was, as it had been ever since 1803, to subdue Great Britain. To this end he hoped, by invading Russia, to open a route to India. In addition, he hoped to force Alexander to accept the Continental Blockade and to acknowledge his, Napoleon's, supremacy on the continent of Europe. In preparation for war with France Alexander concluded agreements with Sweden and Turkey which ensured their neutrality. This meant that Russia was free to devote the most efficient and experienced of her troops to the defence of her western frontiers. Elaborate defence plans were drawn up by the Prussian General Phull, in whom Alexander placed great confidence, and about 210,000 troops, distributed in three armies, were made available for active service. Although the troops were mostly young men, they were led by officers who had had experience of fighting Napoleon in the campaigns of 1805–1807. Their equipment, including artillery, was of Russian manufacture, but in no sense inferior to the best that Napoleon's armouries could oppose to it. Indeed, it is probable that the Russians were better armed than their opponents, for the Russian ratio of cannon to soldiers was approximately 7 : 1,000 whereas the French ratio was only 4 : 1,000. Napoleon, on the other hand, assembled a Grand Army of at least 600,000 men for the expedition against Moscow. The nucleus consisted of picked French troops, veterans of many previous French victories; but the majority consisted of troops from the many nations under Napoleon's rule. To the Russians it could hardly fail to seem as if the whole of continental Europe, from Spain to Poland, had taken up arms against their country.

On the night of June 12th (OS) 1812, without any formal declaration of war, Napoleon despatched his Grand Army, consisting initially of about 420,000 men, across the Nieman in three columns. The Russian defence plan depended upon a fortified encampment in the region of Drissa. The numerical superiority of the French forces, however, made it obvious to the Russians that any attempt at this stage in the campaign to fight it out toe to toe with Napoleon would be to court disaster. A policy of retreat was initiated. Alexander left his headquarters at Vilna and returned to St Petersburg; the Russian first and second armies, under Barclay de Tolly and Bagration, undertook a series of rearguard engagements while retreating eastwards to Vitebsk and Smolensk. The war quickly became a struggle for national survival, especially when the French armies entered predominantly Russian territory. The paradox of Napoleon's policy which dictated that he should invade Russia in order to make Alexander into his ally prevented him from exploiting the serf problem to his advantage. Although there were some peasant revolts in the wake of the retreating Russian armies, Napoleon was keen to preserve the social *status quo* and the repressive measures enforced in the conquered territories served to unite all sections of the Russian population against the invaders. There can be little doubt that the deliberate destruction of crops and provisions by the local population and the growing partisan activity obliged Napoleon to deploy in garrisoning and the protection of supply lines troops which could have been better used in pressing home the military advantage which he enjoyed in the initial stages of the campaign. Napoleon's primary aim was to inflict a decisive defeat on the Russian first army and the need for such a success drew him, like a mirage, ever deeper into the emptiness of Russia.

By August the Russian first and second armies had joined forces before Smolensk. A significant reduction in the numerical disparity between the two sides had now been achieved. The Russian forces, numbering about 120,000 men, remained intact, whereas Napoleon's active troops numbered less than 200,000 and were widely dispersed. Smolensk was captured in early August after a fierce Russian rearguard action and considerable French losses. The Russian armies retreated towards Moscow, repelling and evading repeated French attempts to force a pitched battle on French terms. At this stage disagreement between Barclay de Tolly and Bagration forced Alexander to agree reluctantly to the appointment of Kutuzov as the Russian commander-in-chief. Kutuzov, by this time a man of sixty-seven, took stock of the situation and decided, under the pressure of circumstances and demands from the court in St Petersburg, that Moscow would have to be defended. Borodino, a village twelve kilometres west of Mozhaysk on the Smolensk–Moscow highway, appeared to offer a good position for a defensive engagement.

By August 24th French troops had advanced to Borodino. Napoleon realised that the Russian right flank was not readily approachable and proceeded to attack the Russian left wing at Shevardino. Bitter fighting continued for a whole day, but by evening the defenders had been forced to retire to newly prepared positions further back. The scene was now set for the Battle of Borodino, which was fought on August 26th between a Russian force consisting of 120,000 men and 640 artillery pieces and 135,000 French troops aided by 587 cannon. Napoleon attempted to turn the Russian left flank, but when this failed he concentrated his attacks on the left and centre of the Russian defensive positions. The main brunt of these attacks, lasting more than six hours, was borne by the Russian second army under Bagration, who was mortally wounded during the battle. Napoleon was pressed by his Marshals to release his guard, so that the Russian centre might be broken conclusively. The appearance, however, of Russian cavalry on the French left made Napoleon call a temporary halt to the attacks in the centre. Though the attacks were later renewed, by the evening of the battle both sides occupied approximately the same positions as they had occupied at the start. The losses on both sides have been variously estimated. It is probable that the French lost about 58,000 men, the Russians about 40,000; whatever the exact figures, they were enormous losses sustained in one of the least conclusive battles in history.

Kutuzov had only one aim in mind : to keep his forces intact. He retreated through Moscow without offering further resistance. When, a week after Borodino, Napoleon and his staff looked down on Moscow, it was generally believed that the campaign in Russia had ended. Peace overtures were at once made to St Petersburg, but Alexander had sworn at the outset that he would not make peace until the last Frenchman had left Russian soil. Moscow was meanwhile literally turning to ashes in Napoleon's hands. A fire which is supposed to have started after the French entry into the city destroyed three-quarters of it. At the height of the conflagration the flames were so bright that it seemed to Napoleon, watching through the windows of his room in the Kremlin, that night had been turned into day. It became obvious that Moscow could not serve as winter quarters for the Grand Army and on October 7th the first columns moved out on the long return march to Europe.

The retreat of the Grand Army falls into two stages. Initially, in moving in a south-westerly direction towards Maloyaroslavets, Napoleon gave the impression of wishing to continue military action against Kutuzov. Maloyaroslavets was stormed by the French and captured on October 12th, but at this point Napoleon directed his troops northwards, towards Mozhaysk and the route taken by the advance in the summer. In a military sense, therefore, the retreat can be said to have begun at Maloyaroslavets when Napoleon turned his back on Kutuzov, choosing retreat rather than his former policy of pursuit. Politically a failure, the invasion of Russia was now about to become a military disaster. Encumbered with loot, starving, inadequately clothed, the Grand Army set off on the march to Smolensk, traversing on its way the battlefield of Borodino with its grisly remains and leaving behind it a far more terrible trail of dead and prisoners. Until Smolensk, the first stage of the retreat, hunger, leading in some cases to cannibalism, seems to have been the worst scourge of the French ranks, already harassed as they were by the attacks of Russian partisans and army units. When Smolensk was reached and discovered to be empty of supplies, the retreat entered its second stage. Now, added to the torments of hunger and the Russian attacks, was the torment of the climate. It had been a relatively warm autumn by Russian standards; until early November there had been no severe frosts; the temperature only began to fall after November 5th, when the French moved westwards from Smolensk. From mid-November onwards there were 20-23 degrees of frost (Reamur) by day, 30 degrees by night. This second stage of the retreat was to be the death agony of the Grand Army. Although it was a stroke of genius on Napoleon's part which prevented the Russian Generals Wittgenstein and Chichagov from encircling him on the River Berezina, no amount of genius could save the greater part of his army. Of the 600,000 men under Napoleon's command who had taken part in the invasion of Russia hardly more than 30,000 recrossed the Nieman on December 2nd, seven months after the invasion had begun.

The myth of Napoleon's invincibility ended in the horrific disaster of the retreat from Moscow. It is a great turning-point in history. On the one hand, it signalled the end of Napoleon's rule in Europe; on the other, it was the point at which Russia emerged into full nationhood, assumed to the full the imperial heritage bequeathed by the eighteenth century and entered Europe as the mightiest nation on the continent. Of the many reasons advanced for the failure of the Napoleonic invasion none is more important than the fact that the Russians were not decisively defeated at Borodino. Thereafter Kutuzov's ability to maintain and exploit the fighting efficiency of his troops was to redeem the surrender of Moscow, whereas for Napoleon the capture of Moscow represented a cul-de-sac, both politically and militarily, from which the only escape was retreat; but it was a retreat made militarily hazardous by the fact that the enemy was not defeated.

The true victor of the campaign against Napoleon was the Russian people, but it fell to Alexander I to wear the laurels. After his return in triumph to Vilna on December 11th he ordered an army of over 100,000 men to cross the Nieman in January 1813. The Russian–Prussian alliance was renewed, which eventually became a coalition of Russia, Prussia, Austria and Great Britain. After the defeat of Napoleon at Leipzig in October 1813, on Alexander's insistence the war was carried on to French soil and in March 1814 the French capital surrendered. Russian troops marched into Paris on March 31st. An eye-witness account gives us a glimpse of that spring morning :

"At nine o'clock in the morning we approached the suburbs of Paris; in front marched a division of light horse-guards with the cossacks at their head; a short distance behind rode the Emperor (Alexander) surrounded by a brilliant suite, and behind followed, first grenadiers, then guards on foot, courassiers, and several battalions of Austrians, Prussians and Baden troops. It was a beautiful morning and hourly the air became clearer and more congenial. Enormous crowds of people filled the streets, roofs and windows; at first the inhabitants seemed apprehensive and exclamations of joy were not as yet the rule; their astonishment continued a short while, as they asked unceasingly : 'Where's the Emperor?' 'There he is! There's Alexander!' They shouted. 'How graciously he bows to us, how gently he speaks to us!' Having imagined that they would find the Russians to be a half-savage people, worn out by their campaigns, speaking an incomprehensible language and dressed in outlandish clothes, they scarcely believed their eyes when they saw how handsome were the Russian uniforms, the gleam of their weapons, the gay appearance of the soldiers, the healthy colour of their faces, the politeness with which the officers addressed them and the ready wit with which they answered them in French. 'You're not Russian,' they told us, 'you must be emigrés.' They soon discovered their mistake, and the news about the unusual qualities of their conquerors flew from mouth to mouth, thunderous praise greeted the Russians everywhere, women fluttered white handkerchiefs from windows and balconies, greeted us with waving arms, and instantly one end

of Paris to the other rang with shouts of 'Long live Alexander!'
'Long live the Russians!' uttered by a million voices."

It is a picture which has the ingenuous exuberance of a patriotic
print of the time. The triumphant entry of the Russians into Paris in
1814 was the glorious postscript to the Russian victory over Napoleon's
Grand Army in 1812. Alexander quickly became the idol of Paris and
he repaid French flattery by being the soul of leniency and magnani-
mity in his edicts. Napoleon was permitted to become monarch of Elba
after his abdication as French Emperor and by the first Peace of Paris
(May 1814) the Bourbons were restored, as constitutional rather than
absolute monarchs, to the French throne. Under Alexander's aegis it
seemed that the Napoleonic era in Europe had been brought to a satis-
factory conclusion.

A less glorious postscript was to follow. The Congress of Vienna,
which was intended to re-arrange the map of Europe after Napoleon
had re-drawn it so many times, opened in September 1814. Here
Alexander again played a leading role, but his plans for incorporating
the Grand Duchy of Warsaw into the Russian Empire caused a rift
between Russia and Prussia, on the one hand, and Great Britain,
France and Austria on the other. Eventual agreement was reached over
the Polish question, most of the Grand Duchy of Warsaw being ceded
to Russia as a constitutional kingdom within the frontiers of the Russian
Empire. Then, in the spring of 1815, Napoleon escaped from Elba.
Alexander's authority, already tarnished by the squabbles over Poland,
was further diminished by the fact that Russia took no part in the
Battle of Waterloo (June 1815). Great Britain, in the person of Welling-
ton, had the last word in formulating the second, and much harsher,
Peace of Paris of November 1815 and in banishing Napoleon, this
time as a prisoner-of-war not as a monarch, to the island of St Helena.

Alexander's plan for Europe took the form of a Treaty of Holy
Alliance between Russia, Prussia and Austria of September 1815 which
obligated the rulers of the great continental Powers to observe Christian
principles in their relations with their peoples and with each other.
Alexander's aims in conceiving this Holy Alliance were no doubt noble,
if a trifle idealistic; in practice the Alliance was to lead to an ever-
widening division between ruler and ruled in the name of the *status quo*,
legitimism and the divine right. The Holy Alliance was to become the
symbol of reactionary, absolutist government, hostile to all kinds of
constitutionalism and democracy. Amplified into the Quadruple
Alliance of Russia, Prussia, Austria and Great Britain in November
1815, and later into a Quintuple Alliance, which included France, it

was to exert a baleful influence upon European affairs for at least a decade. Yet it did not prevent the gradual worsening of relations between Great Britain and Russia. As the imperial Powers on the western and eastern borders of continental Europe, Great Britain and Russia were to be mutually distrustful of each other's expansionist aims and interests for the next hundred years. The British policy of non-intervention in European politics and Russia's role as self-styled gendarme of Europe were the result of differing traditions of government, differing stages of economic and social development and differing—insular as compared with continental—attitudes towards their neighbours. Both Powers endeavoured to expand their colonial territories and spheres of influence without upsetting the delicate power-balance in Europe. In the end it became inevitable that the two empires should come into conflict at the point where Britain's maritime interests conflicted with Russia's attempts to break out of her land-locked isolation : the Eastern Mediterranean, the Straits and Turkey.

Russia under Alexander I

ALEXANDER I was a man of strange paradoxes and his reign (1801–1825) has an equally paradoxical character. Brought up under the supervision of his grandmother, Catherine the Great, he was tutored by La Harpe in the ideas of the Enlightenment; but he was also on friendly terms with the ultra-reactionary Arakcheyev, into whose hands he was later to put so much of the responsibility for governing Russia. Thus, beneath his handsome, courteous, rather distant façade Alexander I tended to combine the extreme contrasts of absolutist liberal and idealistic martinet. Similarly paradoxical, though probably more easily explicable, is the way in which his early predilection for liberal ideas gradually deteriorated—the change probably occurred at the time of Napoleon's capture of Moscow, the central episode in Alexander's reign —into a fondness for religiosity and mysticism. The final impression is of a reign which went sour : Alexander's liberal ideas of government soured into the scheme for military settlements, high-minded mysticism soured into reactionary Orthodoxy, the liberator of Europe became the king-pin of the Holy Alliance. It is no wonder that he has been called "the enigmatic Tsar" and a still unresolved aspect of his enigma is the legend that he did not die in 1825 but adopted the guise of a wandering holy man, Fyodor Kuzmich, who reputedly died in Siberia in 1864.

During his reign the Russian Empire continued to expand. Military conquest led to the annexation of Finland and Bessarabia, a large area of Poland and much territory in the Caucasus. By 1815 this meant that the population of the Russian Empire had increased to an approximate total of forty-five million. Over half the adult population consisted of serfs, to which should be added approximately sixteen million state peasants and a further two million crown peasants. Since less than 4 per cent of the population lived in towns, Russian life was overwhelmingly rural in character. As it had done for at least a previous century and a half, the greater part of rural Russia under Alexander I presented a picture of estates, varying greatly in size and profitability, whose lands were divided up between the landowners and their peasant serfs. The land ostensibly in the possession of the peasants was allotted by the peasant "commune" to the various peasant households and these allotments usually took the from of strips of land held either on permanent tenure or on a repartitional basis and frequently divided and subdivided between various members of the household. The landowner of an estate exercised, through his feudal rights, total jurisdiction over his peasants, except in such cases as murder and robbery; and under the serf system the peasant worked for his master either according to the system of *barshchina* or the system of *obrok* or, as happened in many areas, a combination of these systems. *Barshchina* denoted the work which a peasant had to do on his master's land, as a feudal obligation to which the landowner had every right. In 1797, as has already been mentioned, Paul attempted to enforce a three-day *barshchina* or three-day stint of work by the peasants on their masters' lands, but such three-day *barshchina* frequently became a four- or five-day working stint, sometimes indeed occupying the whole week, so that at the height of the harvesting the peasant might be forced to harvest his own crops at night. *Barshchina* was regarded as the harsher of the two systems. *Obrok* was a form of quit-rent payable by the peasant to his master either in natural produce or in money. In the most favourable cases this meant that the landowner permitted his land to be worked by his peasants as if it were their own land, for which they paid an annual rent. The advantage to the peasants of the *obrok* system was that it allowed a proportion of each peasant household to find employment elsewhere : in seasonal work, local industry or trade. The landowner also benefited from this, because the amount of *obrok* payable to him was assessed not on the basis of the profitability of his own land but on the basis of the total likely income of his peasants. *Obrok* was the system more frequently used on the larger estates. It did not require the presence of the landowner, since the collection of the rent could be left to a bailiff or estate manager, and it was an easy way of providing the nobility with the income that they needed for living in the big urban centres or abroad. If the *obrok* system was commoner in the northern areas of Russia, then *barshchina* predominated in the richer agricultural areas, in the black-earth belt and in the Volga region.

The Russian economy was dominated by grain crops, primarily wheat; and this concentration on grain crops had the effect of discouraging the kind of diversification needed to give Russia a balanced rural economy. Animal husbandry was in general neglected. Though sugarbeet, potatoes, hemp and flax were also cultivated on a large scale, there were few attempts to apply modern techniques in any branch of Russian agriculture. By comparison with agriculture, industry played only a small part in the economy. It has been calculated that in 1804 the manufacturing and mining industries employed about 225,000 workers, a figure which had risen by 1825 to about 340,000. The manufacturing industries, particularly cotton, wool and linen, agglomerated about the main towns in central Russia: Moscow, Kostroma, Kaluga, Ryazan, Tver and, of course, about St Petersburg in the north. Industry tended to grow at the fastest rate where labour was hired, especially in the cotton industry. Serf or semi-servile labour was employed chiefly in the cloth- and paper-making factories on the estates of the nobility and in the mines and iron foundries of the Urals. Production of cast-iron in 1800 has been estimated at approximately the equivalent of British production at the time; but it is worth noting, as an indication of Russian industrial backwardness, that sixty years later British cast-iron production was twenty-four times greater.

During Alexander's reign Russian foreign trade and tariff policy underwent considerable fluctuations. His accession initiated a period of expansion in foreign trade, especially with Great Britain, to which were exported hemp and flax and considerable quantities of animal fats, iron, wheat and sail canvas. After Tilsit, and with Russian participation in the Continental Blockade, trade with Great Britain stopped. A tariff law of 1810 permitted the import of certain British goods in neutral ships, and this evasion by Russia of the Continental Blockade was one of the reasons which prompted Napoleon to invade. Between 1816 and 1822 there was some liberalisation in tariff policy, but after that a more restrictive policy was adopted which persisted until the mid-century. Internal trade, of course, far exceeded foreign trade in volume, though it cannot be said to have increased significantly during Alexander's reign. In general, the industrial north and centre of Russia supplied the primarily agricultural and cattle-raising south with manufactured goods. Such goods were often carried by itinerant traders from one end of Russia to the other, though the most important means of distributing goods were the famous fairs, such as the Nizhny-Novgorod fair which provided an inlet for goods from Asia and China. Cotton goods manufactured in Ivanovo-Voznesensk, for instance, would be sold in Moscow and at fairs throughout Russia and Siberia, in the Ukraine, Georgia, Central Asia and Persia. In exchange wheat, cattle, horses, sheep, butter, wool, dried fruits, etc., would find their way northwards. A serious drawback to internal trade was the poor condition of roads and transport in general. So chaotic were transport arrangements that grain from the lower Volga region sometimes might not reach St Petersburg until two years after it was harvested. Fearing that railways might be a danger to public morals, the government was for a long time reluctant to sanction railway-building. It was not until 1838, in the reign of Nicholas I, that the first railway was completed between St Petersburg and the Tsar's private residence of Tsarskoye Selo.

Russian finances during Alexander's reign were in a state of chaos. The campaigns prior to Tilsit could only be financed by the issue of paper money, and by 1812 the government had no reserves for the waging of a prolonged war. Such budgeting as there was revealed a deficit of one hundred and twenty million roubles at the start of the war, while the cost to the Russian treasury of the campaigns of 1812–1814 amounted probably to the enormous sum of nine hundred million roubles. On the credit side, British subsidies assisted the Russian war effort; yet the bulk of treasury income came from taxes levied on the peasantry. Such a heavy taxation burden led, naturally, to frequent defaultings. In an effort to cover these and other deficits four domestic loans were floated in the last ten years of Alexander's reign. The nobility, in endeavouring to increase the income from their estates, resorted to the practice of enlarging their own lands at the expense of the peasants' allotments. The peasantry suffered great hardship from this process of land-deprivation. It was becoming more than ever obvious that the deficiencies of serfdom far outweighed its advantages.

Alexander did little to alleviate the condition of the peasantry. The right to own agricultural land was extended to merchants, state peasants and certain classes of town-dweller in 1801. Serfdom remained untouched save for a law of 1803 which gave landowners the right on their own initiative to free their peasants with land against some kind of redemption payment. Such peasants were given the status of "free tillers". The nobility, not unnaturally, adopted a very unfavourable attitude to this law and it had little effect on the mass of the peasantry; less than $\frac{1}{2}$ per cent of the total serf population acquired their freedom in this way during Alexander's reign.

57

His failure to do anything for the peasantry coincided with his failure to introduce constitutional reforms, though his reign had opened with the promise that far-reaching changes would be made. Soon after his accession he instituted an "unofficial committee", consisting of four of his closest friends, who were given the task of formulating plans for a grandiose reform of the government and its institutions. Though they were keen admirers of the British style of constitutional monarchy, they felt that Russia was not ready for such a system and in the final reckoning very little came of their deliberations. In 1802 the Petrine colleges were reorganised into eight ministries : war, navy, foreign affairs, interior, justice, finance, education and commerce, but in 1810–1811 the ministry of commerce was abolished and a ministry of police created, in addition to administrative centres for religions, transport and financial control. Despite an attempt by the "unofficial committee" to increase the administrative and judicial power of the Senate, nothing came of this beyond a reaffirmation of the Senate's role as supreme court. Certain steps toward reform, however, were taken in the sphere of education, at least in the sense that plans were drawn up for introducing universities in each of the six educational regions into which Russia was divided by an enactment of 1803. At that time, apart from the famous Lyceum at Tsarskoye Selo, three universities already existed : Moscow University, the Polish university at Vilna and the German university at Dorpat. Three new universities were created—in St Petersburg (1819) and in Kazan and Kharkov, but the last two remained for many years little more than training colleges for entrants to the civil service. Similarly, schools were to be set up in the provincial centres in each county, and there was to be at least one parish school in every two parishes. But lack of financial support by the government and indifference towards such education on the part of the nobility left even such modest plans largely unfulfilled. The figures for university students in the predominantly Russian universities—405 in 1809, 1,700 in 1825—show that progress in the development of higher education was far from adequate.

In 1808 Speransky (1772–1839), the son of a village priest who rose to a position of great eminence under Alexander I, was commissioned by the Tsar to draft new plans for reforms. His proposals, though conservative and aiming at no more than a realistic compromise between the monarchical principle and the principle of government by law, proved to be too realistic for Alexander. Adapting Speransky's scheme, the Tsar established a State Council, which was a body for making laws appointed by the Tsar and subject in every aspect of its constitution and activity to the Tsar's dictates. Alexander also adopted the principle that appointment to senior positions in the civil service should be conditional upon the passing of a qualifying examination. This provision excited strong resentment among the nobility and led eventually to Speransky's fall from favour, but not before he had made a comprehensive survey of Russia's finances and proposed reforms which were later to help in safeguarding Russia's financial viability. A measure of autonomy was granted to the Finns after the annexation of Finland in 1809, but the one area of the Russian Empire, Poland, where Alexander's liberalism actually bore fruit in the form of constitutional government, suffered the contradictory fate of enjoying a constitution whose liberal spirit proved to be insufficiently liberal for the patriotic aspirations of the Poles and quite incompatible with the essentially illiberal attitude of the Tsar's appointees in Warsaw.

After 1815, in the "era of congresses" when the major European Powers held periodic meetings to discuss their affairs, Alexander tended to devote an increasing amount of his time to international matters. The government of Russia passed virtually into the hands of Arakcheyev. The most notorious of Arakcheyev's undertakings was his organisation of the "military settlements", which were intended by Alexander to reduce the cost of maintaining a standing army. Whole regions were designated as such "military settlements". The peasants in these regions were forcibly drafted into the army and became soldier-farmers, all their activities being regulated by strict military etiquette. Any infringement of the inhuman regulations was mercilessly punished. The "military settlements", however, proved to be a costly enterprise and were poor evidence of the Tsar's solicitude for his subjects. So bitter was the peasants' resentment that there were serious uprisings, especially in 1818 and 1819. Arakcheyev suppressed them with sadistic ruthlessness, but the seriousness of the general unrest in Russia was brought home still more forcefully by the mutiny of the Semyonovsky guards regiment in St Petersburg in 1820. The regiment in fact mutinied against the Prussian-style discipline which Alexander had introduced into the army, but it was not difficult for the inhabitants of St Petersburg to deduce that both the soldiers of the Semyonovsky regiment and the peasants in the "military settlements" were living under approximately the same harsh conditions of military servitude.

The influence of Arakcheyev was felt very strongly in the universities and in general in the cultural life of the country. All teaching had to be justified by reference to the Bible. It was thought irreligious, for instance, for students to learn anatomy by dissecting corpses. Ignorance was sanctioned in the name of the political and social stability of the country by such prominent figures as Prince Golitsyn, the Procurator of the Holy Synod, who was appointed Minister of Education in 1816, and Archimandrite Photius, who gained favour at court by his loud defence of Orthodoxy. But the prevailing reaction was dictated chiefly by Alexander's need to uphold the sentiments of obedience and legitimism upon which he had based the Holy Alliance.

If there may seem to have been little outward social or political change in the Russia of Alexander I, then in the sphere of literature, particularly in poetry, changes were abundant. Romanticism, and all that it implied, replaced the Classicism and Sentimentalism which had dominated Russian literature in the second half of the eighteenth century. The Romantic movement was led by Zhukovsky (1783–1852), whose original work and translations from German and English Romantic poetry—his translation of Gray's *Elegy* is a fine example—introduced into Russian literature a new awareness of feeling, new melodiousness and purity of diction. At the same time Krylov (1769–1844), though of an older generation and essentially conservative in outlook, was writing his fables which mocked ignorant pomposity and commended simple good sense. Similarly, Karamzin (1766–1826), despite the fact that he was the leading exponent of Sentimentalism, brought to Russian literature a sensibility which drew attention to contemporary social problems (*Poor Liza*, 1792; *A Knight of Our Time*, 1804). His most important contribution, if not directly to the literature then to the national consciousness which the literature was beginning to create, was his *History of the Russian State,* which began to appear in 1816. As a piece of historical interpretation, its thesis was conservative; as a revelation of Russia's past, it opened the doors to an understanding of the need for change.

Zhukovsky may have emphasised feeling for its own sake, but the influence of Byron, prominent during the 1820s, laid emphasis specifically on the individual's feeling; and Romanticism in its Byronic phase became synonymous with the protest of the individual against society. Although the famous satirical comedy *Woe from Wit* (1823) by Griboyedov (1795–1829) cannot be called Byronic, the play's hero, Chatsky, epitomised such protest by an individual against social norms and conventions. Chatsky's criticism was implicitly directed, in a Decembrist spirit, against the whole social and political structure of Russia; and not the least significant feature of such criticism was the fact that the brilliant and eloquent Chatsky found himself "superfluous" in the Moscow society to which he had returned. Finally, branded as mad, he was expelled from Moscow because he had too much "wit" or mind of his own.

The effect of Byronism is probably to be seen most clearly in the work of Alexander Pushkin (1799–1837), recognised to be Russia's greatest poet and certainly the greatest literary figure in this period. Byronism is to be seen so clearly in Pushkin because he was by inclination and inheritance a man of Classical temper. The neo-Classical world of the Lyceum at Tsarskoye Selo (now Pushkino) where he was educated, and the eighteenth-century inheritance of Classicism which he absorbed in his youth, imbued all his work, despite its range and variety, with a lucid simplicity, balance, harmony and restraint. He first fell under the influence of Byron during his exile in Odessa and Kishinyov (1820–1823). Before that time he had only written one major poem, his colourful, imitation folk-tale *Ruslan and Lyudmila* (1820); after it, he was to write *The Prisoner of the Caucasus* and *The Fountain of Bakhchisaray*, narrative poems which were obviously Byronic in inspiration if not wholly Byronic in manner. In 1823 the problem of the individual's relationship to society began to emerge clearly for the first time in his work when he embarked on his famous "novel in verse" *Eugene Onegin*. Based, at least initially, on Byron's *Don Juan*, it was to tell the story of a St Petersburg dandy who left the Russian capital ostensibly out of dissatisfaction with the artificiality of that society, in order to find "freedom" on an estate bequeathed to him by an uncle. But such freedom was not to be found.

The autocracy, in fact, feared nothing so much as the idea of freedom. Pushkin was exiled from St Petersburg in 1819 for writing, among other things, an *Ode to Freedom*. Griboyedov's *Woe from Wit* was suppressed by the censorship. However, censorship of the printed word, the increasing use of police spies, the prohibition of all secret societies, including Masonic lodges, could not prevent the spread of liberal ideas. In such circumstances literature began to play the role of the nation's conscience. For Ryleyev, the Decembrist poet, the civic duty of the poet as citizen was paramount. This idea was to find many echoes in later Russian literature. And for Pushkin, when all talk of political freedom was ended by the failure of the Decembrist revolt, the poet's role became that of a prophet who would "with his words set light to the hearts of men".

The Decembrist Revolt

THE revolt of December 14th 1825 was a consequence of the disillusionment experienced by certain members of the younger nobility when they realised that the Tsar's professed liberalism might express itself in the granting of constitutions to Poland and Finland, but in their own homeland, Russia, it was not to be allowed to interfere with the absolute authority of the autocracy. Though there were parallel revolutionary movements in other parts of Europe, the revolutionary movement in Russia grew out of specific Russian conditions and owed little to European models. Economically stagnant, with a peasantry oppressed by the twin burdens of serfdom and excessively heavy taxation, corrupt in its judiciary and its governing bureaucracy, Russia in the last decade of Alexander's reign presented a sorry contrast not only to other European nations, but to that image of Russia, the liberator of Europe, which had been born in 1812. The disillusionment and dissatisfaction of the revolutionaries sprang chiefly from the feeling that the spirit of 1812 had been betrayed. Tolstoy acknowledged this more than thirty years later when, in contemplating a novel on the Decembrists, he realised that he would have to turn back to the events of the campaign against Napoleon, and particularly to 1812, in order to discover where Decembrism began. His epic novel *War and Peace* was the result of this process; it is probably the greatest monument to those members of the Russian nobility who eventually became known as "the Decembrists".

The first Decembrist revolutionary society was formed in 1816. It was called the Union of Salvation, later renamed the Society of True and Faithful Sons of the Fatherland, containing between twenty and thirty members, of whom the most prominent were Alexander Muravyov, his second cousin Nikita Muravyov, the brothers Sergey and Matvey Muravyov-Apostol, Prince Trubetskoy and Pavel Pestel. They were army officers whose main aims were the abolition of serfdom and the replacement of the autocracy by some form of constitutional monarchy. In 1818 this first organisation was voluntarily dissolved and its place taken by a larger body, embracing about 200 members, called the Union of Welfare. The aim of this enlarged secret society was to create, by active good works in the educational and social sphere, a climate of public opinion in which revolutionary ideas could flourish. It was organisationally more elaborate than its predecessor, with a central directorate and various semi-autonomous local bodies, but it lacked real political direction and cohesion. The most radical elements, led by Pestel, were strongly in favour of replacing the autocracy with a republic and the Union's directorate was won over to this view at a meeting in St Petersburg in 1820. At the beginning of 1821, however, a conference of the Union's representatives in Moscow decided that the Union of Welfare should be abolished. Its place was quickly taken by a Southern Society, under the active leadership of Pestel, and shortly afterwards by a

Northern Society headed by Nikita Muravyov, Prince Trubetskoy, Nikolay Turgenev, Prince Obolensky and the poet Ryleyev.

Communication between the Southern Society, which had its centre in the second army, then quartered in the Ukraine, and the Northern Society, centred in St Petersburg, was extremely difficult. Lack of communication between these two revolutionary centres contributed to the failure of the revolt. Yet the geographical distance separating them was symbolic of an equally important divergence of views on the methods and aims of the revolution.

The most important surviving document of the Decembrist movement is Pavel Pestel's *Russian Truth* which was discussed and approved by the Southern Society. Pestel was a man of great erudition and powerful, if cold, intellect. His plan, as expressed in *Russian Truth*, envisaged the abolition of both serfdom and the class structure of Russian society. The new republic would be based on egalitarian principles. All land, having been recognised as the common property of society, would be divided into two equal parts, one half for social use, the other for private management. There can be little doubt that such a plan, if properly applied, would have had the effect of seriously diminishing the power of the landowning nobility, and it would also no doubt have paved the way for capitalist developments in the Russian countryside. Less appealing was the extreme nationalist sentiment which pervaded Pestel's work. He favoured the Russification of all the territories within the confines of the Russian empire and displayed an arbitrary disregard for the autonomy of subject nationalities. Moreover, in effecting these plans, he was not averse to regicide, and he anticipated that the provisional government to be established after the overthrow of Tsarism would exercise dictatorial powers for a period of eight or ten years.

The Northern Society's proposals were less radical. Nikita Muravyov's projected constitution foresaw a constitutional monarchy and a federated state system. The serfs were to be freed with land allotments, but the property rights of the landowners were to be maintained. Although at one time Prince Trubetskoy believed that the Tsar himself could be persuaded to implement these reforms, others in the Northern Society, notably Ryleyev, became convinced that the monarchy would have to be deposed in favour of a republic. There was also a general feeling that their aims could only be achieved through a *coup*. Such questions as the precise powers of the ensuing provisional government, the duration of its rule and whether or not a Constituent Assembly should be summoned seem never to have been satisfactorily decided.

In general, therefore, it can be said that both Societies were agreed on the need for some kind of representative government in place of the autocracy and the need to abolish serfdom. The differences between them were dictated, firstly, by the fact that the Southern Society, because it was so far removed from the centre of power in St Petersburg, could afford to be more radical, outspoken and Utopian (and with the affiliation to the Southern Society of a body known as the Society of United Slavs in the summer of 1825, it even acquired a pan-slav complexion), whereas the Northern Society in St Petersburg had to be more cautious in its plans. But the differences were also due, secondly, to the social composition of the two societies, the Southern Society being composed chiefly of members of the lesser nobility, men of only moderate wealth and status, the Northern being composed of wealthy aristocrats. Attempts to iron out these differences were made in 1824 and 1825 by Pestel and Prince Trubetskoy, but there was no real agreement on means and purposes, least of all on the extent to which the support of the mass of the population would be needed in order to make the revolt a successful *coup d'état* in the name of the Russian people.

Although the revolt was provisionally fixed for the spring of 1826, the sudden death of Alexander I at Taganrog in November 1825 brought the matter unexpectedly to a head. The succession, since Alexander died childless, passed automatically to Grand Duke Constantine, but he had already renounced his right to the throne as a condition of his morganatic marriage to Countess Grudzinska. By a secret agreement of 1823 the succession had passed to his younger brother, Grand Duke Nicholas. Because this agreement had been kept secret, it was publicly assumed that Grand Duke Constantine was to be the new Tsar. For a period of nearly three weeks there was a state of interregnum during which Constantine, then in Warsaw, reiterated his unwillingness to accept the crown and Nicholas in St Petersburg hesitated to announce his own succession until Constantine's abdication had been made public. To the members of the Northern Society this confusion over the succession appeared to make the time opportune for revolt. But during this unsettled period news of the conspiracy had reached the ears of Nicholas through a young associate of the Decembrists, Rostovtsev, who was later to play a prominent part in the Emancipation of the serfs. The conspirators now had two equally distressing choices to make : they could either take the oath of allegiance to Nicholas and await the inevitable retribution, or they could come out into the open, unprepared though they were, and attempt to force the issue. Entertaining no great hopes of success, they took the latter course.

On the morning of December 14th 1825, when the garrison of St Petersburg was to take the oath of allegiance to Nicholas I, as the new Tsar, between three and four thousand troops and thirty officers assembled on the Senate Square demanding Constantine and *konstitutsiya* (i.e. "constitution", but this latter demand, thought by the rank and file of the soldiery to be a reference to Constantine's wife, may be more part of legend than history). The Governor-General of St Petersburg, Miloradovich, who had been sent by Nicholas to parley with the insurgents, was shot from his horse by Kakhovsky, one of the insurgent officers, and mortally wounded. Apart from this incident, there was no attempt to use force. Indeed, the tragic paradox of the Decembrist revolt was laid bare at this crucial moment. The indecisiveness of the insurgents on the Senate Square was due in very large part to their fear of arousing the populace of the capital, for there was no guarantee that a popular uprising against Tsarism would be able to discriminate between the Decembrists and other members of the nobility. In the event, though there was some popular support for the insurgent troops, the affair soon became pointless. Shortly before the early northern dusk, at about three o'clock in the afternoon, loyal troops under Nicholas were brought up, the insurgents surrounded, and after three cannon volleys the revolt ended. Attempts by the Southern Society to support the northern insurrection were foiled by the arrest of Pestel and other southern leaders. However, two officers of the southern army, Sergey Muravyov-Apostol and Bestuzhev-Ryumin, made determined efforts to arouse sympathy for their cause. The Chernigov regiment, quartered near Kiev, was the only section of the army to respond and, under the leadership of Muravyov-Apostol, it came out in revolt at the end of December, though within a week it had surrendered to government troops. This concluded what has since come to be known as the "Decembrist" revolt, named after the December of 1825 when it occurred.

The subsequent investigations, conducted under the personal supervision of Nicholas I, involved 579 persons, of whom 121 were later tried by a special criminal court. Five of the ring-leaders—Pestel, Sergey Muravyov-Apostol, Bestuzhev-Ryumin, Kakhovsky and Ryleyev —were hanged and more than 200 were sent into exile in Siberia.

The Decembrist revolt is important for three main reasons: it marked the beginning of the Russian revolutionary movement against the autocracy, with which much of the history of nineteenth-century Russia will be concerned; it was to serve as an inspiration and a model for the future intelligentsia, engendering a spirit of service and self-sacrifice among the educated classes which was to endow the struggle against the autocracy with a quasi-religious, missionary fervour; it was also, in the tragi-comic grandeur of its failure, to put the autocracy on its guard against the nobility upon whom it relied chiefly for support, to make reform look like treason and any concession to liberal feeling a betrayal of sovereignty. But the harsh punishment meted out to the Decembrists was to have the effect of depriving Russia of practically a whole generation of its most intelligent and cultured citizens. For this reason, in the ensuing period of reaction, Decembrism was to acquire a perhaps not wholly merited glamour in the eyes of the younger generation, as can be seen from Herzen's eloquent tribute :

"The Decembrists were a phalanx of heroes nurtured, like Romulus and Remus, on the milk of a white beast. . . . They were like legendary warriors, clad in pure steel from head to foot, warrior-champions who went out knowingly to face certain death, in order to arouse the younger generation to new life and to purify the hearts of children born into an atmosphere of executions and servility."

Chapter II
1825 – 1855

Reaction under Nicholas I

SERVILITY was to be the watchword of the new Tsar. Born in 1796, Nicholas was given a wide-ranging, if superficial, education which concluded with military service and extensive foreign travels. In 1817 he married Princess Charlotte of Prussia, by whom he had four sons and three daughters. His marital connection with Prussia helped to increase his admiration for the Prussian style of monarchical government. Nicholas believed in autocracy as a divinely sanctioned principle. The Tsar was to be, in his view, the source of law and the summit of the hierarchical pyramid of government. Ideally, such a government would be monolithic, exacting and receiving obedience at all levels in dutiful reverence for a Tsar who was at once both servant and master of his subjects. Such a well-drilled world made no allowances for human fallibility. With his military bearing and handsome face he looked every inch the autocrat, but as Queen Victoria acutely observed when he visited London in 1844 "he seldom smiles, and when he does, the expression is *not* a happy one"; and the Marquis de Custine, who met him a decade earlier, noted that "he cannot smile with his eyes and his mouth at the same time". For all his love of military display, Nicholas was subject to phobias: he abhorred officers, fireworks and cannons and after the disastrous fire at the Winter Palace in 1837 he developed an obsessional fear of flames and smoke. Such was the man who governed Russia for thirty years as absolute monarch and virtual military dictator. Yet Russia during his reign stagnated in corruption, maladministration and grievous economic sloth, and in the end military dictatorship proved to be wholly inadequate both to preserve Russia from invasion from without and to maintain the rigid system within its borders.

Nevertheless, at the beginning of his reign Nicholas was fairly successful in pursuing and implementing the foreign policy of Alexander I. Although Alexander I, governed by considerations of legitimism, had failed to support Ipsilanti and the Greek rebellion against Turkish rule in 1822, the policy of both Alexander and Nicholas towards Turkey was expansionist. But any expansion of Russia to the south naturally brought her into conflict with Great Britain, who saw in any such move a threat to British spheres of influence in the Middle East and British dominion in India. Partly, it seems, as a result of British encouragement, the

Shah of Persia revoked the Treaty of Gulistan (of 1813), which had given Russia a strong position in the Caucasus, and invaded Russian territory in June 1826. A Russian force was soon able to turn the tide of the Persian advance and to march on Teheran. The Persians capitulated and under the Treaty of Turkmanchay (1828) agreed to Russia's right to naval bases on the Caspian Sea. Coincidental with the final stages of the Russian campaign against Persia the Turkish fleet was destroyed by a combined force of British, French and Russian naval vessels at the Battle of Navarino in October 1827. The ensuing Turkish declaration of war against the Christian powers was the opportunity that Nicholas needed. Although unsupported by Britain and France, Nicholas could now declare "legitimate" war against Turkey. In June 1828 Russian troops occupied Moldavia and Wallachia, but further military gains were delayed until the spring of 1829 when the Russians succeeded in capturing Silistria and Adrianople and advancing to within a short distance of Constantinople. In September 1829 the Turkish sultan came to terms with Russia by signing the Treaty of Adrianople which guaranteed Russia access to the mouth of the Danube, considerable territories in the Caucasus and the free passage of Russian merchant vessels through the Bosphorus. The circumstances were such that Nicholas found it more in Russia's interests to maintain the *status quo* in the area of the Bosphorus than to kill off Turkey, Europe's "sick man". For who knows what popular uprisings there might have been had the Ottoman Empire been destroyed?

In 1830 Nicholas had evidence enough of the disorders fermenting within the borders of Russia. The Paris revolution of July 1830 paved the way for a rising in Warsaw. Like so many insurrections in history this rising soon lost its momentum due to inadequate and divided leadership. Although the Polish diet, meeting in Warsaw in December 1830, boldly proclaimed that the insurrection was a movement for national liberation, many of the insurrection's leaders were as fearful of a popular uprising as they were of Russian countermeasures. The consequent war between the Poles and the Russians was costly and tragic. After a series of bitter engagements a Russian army advanced to the gates of Warsaw and finally stormed it at the end of August 1831. Throughout 1831 the peasant population had played only a minor and reluctant part in the defence of Polish interests. This was a revolt of upper-class, intellectual and officer cadet elements against Russian domination, and it failed chiefly for the reasons that the Decembrist revolt had failed—lack of unified leadership and lack of popular support. To Nicholas the Polish uprising of 1830–1831 was unmistakable proof that liberalism was unworkable. The Polish constitution was revoked and Poland was incorporated into the Russian Empire. A gradual but very thorough process of Russification was initiated which penetrated every aspect of Polish life, including religion. As Nicholas somewhat obtusely expressed it, speaking of his Polish subjects : "They must be made *happy* in spite of themselves".

No sooner had the Polish revolt been suppressed in the west than more trouble once again arose on Russia's southern borders. In November 1831 Egypt rebelled against Turkey. The Turkish sultan appealed for help to Britain and France, but with little success; for Russia, on the other hand, this seemed to be a perfect opportunity to strengthen her hold over Turkey. After much deliberation of how the situation could be best exploited, Nicholas sent some 10,000 men through the Bosphorus in April 1833 and landed them on Turkish soil, ostensibly with the aim of aiding the sultan in his struggle against Mehemet Ali of Egypt. The sight of Russian troops on the Bosphorus precipitated the arrival of British and French naval squadrons. The Crimean War might have occurred twenty years earlier had there not been some skilful diplomatic manoeuvring by General Orlov, the Tsar's special envoy to Constantinople. A result of his activities was the Treaty of Unkiar Skelessi of July 1833 — a kind of mutual assistance pact between the Ottoman and Russian Empires which contained, to the distress of the Western Powers, a secret clause appearing to give Russian naval vessels a right of free passage through the Dardanelles. Though a Straits Convention annulling the Treaty of Unkiar Skelessi and declaring the Straits neutral was signed between Britain, Russia, France, Austria and Prussia in 1841, suspicion of Russian motives in the Middle East became the guiding *motif* of British diplomatic policy for twenty years after 1833. British support for the Caucasian hill tribes in their struggle against the Russians; the capture by the Russians on the shores of the Caucasus of the British vessel *Vixen* in 1836 with an alleged cargo of arms on board; British instigation of attacks by tribesmen on Russian forts along the Caucasian shore (in 1840); and the activities of British agents in Afghanistan and the khanates of Khiva and Kokand served to exacerbate, sometimes to extreme crisis point, the relations between the two countries. On the surface, relations appeared to improve after Nicholas's visit to London in 1844, but the threat of war nonetheless remained.

Outwardly, at least until the Crimean War, the Russia of Nicholas I may have seemed to be a great imperial Power; inwardly, the trappings of autocracy were a thin cover for a corrupt body politic and a socio-economic order undermined by serfdom. Nicholas was not only shocked by the Decembrist revolt which had inaugurated his reign; he was genuinely aggrieved that members of the nobility should turn against their Tsar. Partly in order to obtain information about the state of the nation and partly for the purpose of drafting reforms, Nicholas placed his reliance on secret committees; but their activities were usually so secret and their findings so hedged about by compromise and a desire to preserve the existing form of the state that the reformative effect of laws promulgated as a result of these committees was negligible. The ineffectual legislation introduced during Nicholas's reign tended for the most part to aggravate the backwardness of a country already labouring under severe handicaps.

The first such secret committee, under the chairmanship of Count (later Prince) Kochubey, was set up in December 1826 to examine all the documents found in the chancery of the former Tsar, to assess their value and suggest revisions. This committee met frequently from 1826 to 1830 and thereafter infrequently until its dissolution in 1832. As many as eight committees were appointed, until 1848, to investigate serfdom. But the most important of the new agencies created by Nicholas were the Second and Third Sections of His Majesty's Own Chancery. The Second Section was established in January 1826 under Speransky to codify all existing legislation. The first stage in its work, probably the most important contribution to government undertaken during the reign of Nicholas I, was completed in 1830, when a complete collection of the laws of the Russian Empire from 1649 to 1825 was published in forty-five volumes; in 1832 a systematic collection of those laws still operative was published in fifteen volumes. In July 1826 the notorious Third Section was established under General Benckendorff. Originally intended as a means of collecting information about political activities in the state and the equally suspect behaviour of sects, dissenters, counterfeiters, foreigners and so on, the Third Section in fact became a secret police and a most important instrument of government. Benckendorff himself, though a die-hard reactionary, has been branded by history as a sinister Chief Gendarme. It would be more correct to regard him as a man of rather amiable disposition whose sinister attributes were the result of his being the loyal servant of a suspicious Tsar. Upon his death in 1844 he was succeeded by Count (later Prince) Orlov, the architect of Unkiar Skelessi, who remained head of the Third Section until the death of Nicholas in 1855.

The gravest domestic problem which faced Nicholas during his reign was the problem of serfdom—"a powder magazine in the foundations of the state", as Benckendorff described it. Frequent peasant uprisings, many of which had to be suppressed by military force, were the real barometer of social discontent. Nicholas regarded serfdom as an evil, but as he declared in 1840 "to tamper with it now would be, of course, an evil still more perilous". The resultant legislation was half-hearted, temporising and tragically inadequate, as befitted the Micaw-berish spirit which informed Nicholas's domestic policies even at the best of times. In 1827, for instance, a law was passed prohibiting land-owners from depriving their peasants of land by selling the land without the serfs. The committee of December 1826 also prohibited the trans-ference of peasants to the mines, while the collection of laws published in 1832 obliged landowners to look after their peasants in time of famine, for which purpose the government was even willing to provide subsidies; but the distribution of such subsidies could not be enforced because the local authorities were in the hands of officials elected by the nobility. In 1835 a secret committee appointed to examine the possi-bility of abolishing serfdom produced no results and a new committee appointed in its place in 1839 succeeded only in formulating a statute about "obligatory peasants" (in 1842) which allowed landowners to free their peasants from serfdom and place them in a category of peas-ants who "obliged" themselves to perform certain services (*barshchina*) or pay certain *obrok* in return for land placed by mutual agreement at their disposal. As was pointed out at the time, it was the landowners who should have been "obliged" to free their serfs in this way; it is note-worthy that out of ten million male serfs only 24,000 received their free-dom under this statute. For political reasons, since the majority of land-owners were Polish, fairly strict "inventory regulations" were imposed in the western Russian provinces in the 1840s which defined the amount of land to be allotted to the peasants and the amount of their dues. In 1847 such regulations were introduced in the provinces of Kiev, Vol-hynia and Podolia and later in Lithuania and White Russia. A law of 1847 also permitted peasants in Russia to buy themselves out with land by whole villages if the landowners' estates were sold to repay debts, but this law fell into abeyance after 1848. Throughout this period the in-debtedness of the landowners was on the increase. In 1843 more than 54 per cent of all estates were mortgaged, and in some areas of Russia landowners were even willing to free their serfs with land provided they were willing to cover part of their masters' indebtedness.

State peasants fared a little better than their counterparts on the landowners' estates. In 1837 a Ministry of State Domains was estab-lished under the relatively liberal administration of Count Kiselyov. Some of the poorer state peasants had their allotments increased; *barsh-china* was abolished on rented estates; wealthier peasants received some economic encouragement (which served in fact to increase the disparity between rich and poor state peasants) and the peasants were given greater autonomy in their communes, but were placed under government administrators who had unlimited right to interfere in agricultural and domestic matters. Such reforms were conservative, the positive benefits to the peasantry being offset by the bureaucratic procedures which accompanied them. Ironically enough it was only in Siberia, with its Russian population of two million by the mid-century, that peasants were able to achieve freedom : there were only thirty-six landowners in the whole of Siberia and less than 1 per cent of the peasants were serfs.

In the financial field, the major event of the reign was the currency reform of 1839–1843 initiated by Kankrin, the economical but unimaginative Minister of Finances (until 1844). This reform made the silver rouble the basic currency and had the beneficial effect of reducing the volume of paper money. Kankrin also reintroduced tax-farming in liquor, which had been a state monopoly since 1817; but corrupt bureaucrats were merely replaced by corrupt tax-farmers and the system was officially abandoned in 1854. Kankrin's conservatism manifested itself most obviously in his opposition to the building of railways. It was not until 1851 that the first major railway on Russian territory, the Moscow–St Petersburg line, was opened and by the time of the Crimean War Russia had less than 1,000 versts* of railway, none, moreover, between Moscow and the south. During the reign Russian foreign trade expanded slowly, the value of exports rising in terms of gold roubles from 85,000 at the beginning of the reign to 225,000 at the end; this represented about 3·6 per cent of world trade during the thirty-year period. In industry, the most rapid expansion occurred in textile, especially cotton, manufacturing, but a considerable proportion of this increase was due to *kustarnoye proiszvodstvo*, i.e. the practice adopted by manufacturers of handing out work for peasants to be done in their own homes. Sugar production increased spectacularly and there was a marked increase in the production of metal goods. By 1860, if workers in mining and metallurgy are included, the total figure for workers employed in industry (as distinct from agriculture) could be estimated at 800,000 or slightly more than 1 per cent of the total population at the time; about one-third of these workers were servile, the remainder hired, and a considerable proportion of the labour force consisted of women and children.

Reaction under Nicholas I took many forms, but it expressed itself most clearly in four major respects : in the Tsar's personal attitude towards the nobility, in education, in the theory of "official nationalism" and, finally, in the repressive measures taken against all kinds of ideological and cultural innovation. The Decembrist revolt persuaded

* One *verst* = 1,166 yards, or 0·66 mile.

74

Nicholas that political independence had to be denied to the nobility. Although the government made efforts to raise the social status of the nobility, noblemen were not expected to display any more political enterprise than was required of loyal servants of the Tsar. In the sphere of education, a significant attempt was made to reduce the nobility's reliance upon private tutors and private schools, since it was thought, not without some justification, that such private education had been an important factor in fostering liberal ideas among the Decembrists and others of their generation. Such considerations prompted the educational changes of 1828, whereby the provincial schools introduced under the 1803 educational reform gradually evolved into Gymnasiums with the division of the curriculum into separate courses for the classics, on the one hand, and the sciences, including mathematics (along the lines of the German *Realschule*), on the other, both courses lasting seven years. The science course was intended to be an end in itself, whereas the course in the classics was intended for those students who wished subsequently to enter a university. The introduction of formalities governing entrance to these Gymnasiums and an increase in fees tended to prevent the poorer classes from sending their children to these schools while encouraging the nobility to do so. University autonomy was also curtailed by giving the Minister of Education greater control over the activities of professors and by the appointment of inspectors who were responsible for investigating the conduct of students.

The theory of "official nationalism", first propounded by Count Uvarov, the Minister of Education, in 1833, was probably the most absurd manifestation of reaction during the reign of Nicholas. Uvarov, who was said never to have read a Russian book and wrote only in French or German, declared, to the Tsar's obvious gratification, that the Russia of Nicholas I was based on the trinity of Orthodoxy, Autocracy and Nationalism. This theory served to enforce the complacent view that autocratic Russia, the leading member of the Holy Alliance, was a bulwark of faith and solid feudal virtue against a mutinous, democratic West. Nationalism was defined as unswerving devotion to the autocracy; and the broad masses of the Russian people, it was argued, were essentially conservative and anti-revolutionary. A by-product of Romanticism, the phraseology of "official nationalism" was loose and emotional, but it tended, if only in an oblique fashion, to meet the need for some specifically Russian theory of nationality. For a time during the 1830s it found adherents amongst both future Westernists and Slavophils. The "official", repressive aspect of the doctrine was not at first readily apparent; yet its "official" supporters, like the devoted Stalinists of a later epoch, executed masterpieces of adulation for the Tsar-

75

autocrat, such, for instance, as the fanciful idea of Bulgarin, editor of the quasi-official daily paper *Northern Bee*, that in honour of the Tsarist family "the empire should be renamed Romanovia, and we—Romanovites". In fact, Uvarov's "official nationalism" was a makeshift *apologia* for the repressive mechanism wielded by the state against writers, thinkers, publicists, academics and anyone who dared to express his own opinion, especially on anything remotely connected with political matters. Its weapons were censorship and, where censorship failed, imprisonment, exile or execution.

The stifling atmosphere induced by the reaction at the end of Alexander I's reign and the deepening of the reaction under Nicholas found expression in literature in the type of the "superfluous man". The first such literary type was Griboyedov's Chatsky, who has already been mentioned; the second, and more important, was Pushkin's Eugene Onegin who ostensibly left St Petersburg society in order to find "freedom" but instead was to discover, in his meeting with Tatyana, the heroine of the novel-in-verse, *Eugene Onegin*, the extent of his own superfluity, his moral, as well as his social, worthlessness. At the same time as he was engaged on writing *Eugene Onegin* (1823–1831), Pushkin also wrote his historical drama *Boris Godunov* (1825) which, though it dealt with the "time of troubles" immediately preceding the accession of the Romanov dynasty in 1613, underlined the problem of kingship and the question as to whether a Tsar had the right to rule without popular consent—a matter of great contemporary significance in view of the Decembrist revolt. Reproved by Nicholas personally, Pushkin was nonetheless permitted to return from his provincial exile on condition that all his work was subjected to the Tsar's personal censorship. Towards the end of the 1820s and the beginning of the 1830s Pushkin turned to prose, writing in sparse, economical narrative form such works as *The Tales of Belkin* (chiefly at Boldino in the autumn of 1830), *The Captain's Daughter* (1836) and *The Queen of Spades* (1834), his prose masterpiece of phantasy and realism. Yet, in such narrative poems as *Poltava* (1828), his "little tragedies" *Mozart and Salieri*, *The Covetous Knight* and *The Stone Guest* (all composed during the 1830s) or in the most brilliant of his poetic works, *The Bronze Horseman* (1833), Pushkin remained supremely the poet whose lucidity of expression, gaiety, occasional pessimism, musicality, wit, sensibility and discipline, expressed in so many different forms, were to provide the example and inspiration for much subsequent Russian literature. "Genius is good", said Zhukovsky on the occasion of Pushkin's death in a duel in 1837; a goodness of honesty, simplicity with art, intelligence with love, informed

Pushkin's genius, lending truth and objectivity to the otherwise hypo-critical age in which he lived.

Already during Pushkin's lifetime poetry was being superseded by prose. Nikolay Gogol, ten years younger than Pushkin, first came into prominence at the beginning of the 1830s with the publication of his *Evenings on a Farm near Dikanka*, humorous and macabre tales of life in his native Ukraine. These were followed in 1835 and 1836 by his four stories in the collection *Mirgorod* and the first of his *St Petersburg Stories* which were to mark the change in his work from humour and Romanticism to a grotesque comic realism. In 1836 his comedy *Revizor*, a satire on the bureaucracy, received its first production in St Petersburg and was enthusiastically applauded by the Tsar himself. Despite the apparent freshness of his humour and satire, Gogol, the man, was as involuted and complex as is his prose style. His attitude to the world was uniquely his own, owing little or nothing to foreign influences. Another kind of literary subjectivity is to be encountered during the 1830s in the work of the young poet Lermontov (1814–1841), but his is a Romantic subjectivity, deeply pervaded by the spirit of Byronism. His poems have a richer visual imagery and a greater emotional expressiveness than are to be found in the lyrics of Pushkin; yet his poetry falls short of Push-kin's in its lack of breadth, its preoccupation with the poet's ego and in its Byronic posturing. Lermontov's is the story of a poet's career cut short before full maturity had been reached. His career falls into two parts: 1828–1832, when he composed much *juvenilia* and a handful of very striking lyrics, and 1837–1841, when he wrote such fine works as *Death of a Poet* (1837), a bitter indictment of the Tsarist authorities for their intrigues which led to Pushkin's death, *Duma* (1838) in which he in-dicted his own generation for its passivity (though in fact this was an unfair judgment) and his magnificent long poems, *Mtsyri* (1840) and *Demon* (1841). Yet his greatest work is probably his only completed prose work *A Hero of Our Time* (1840) which offered, in a complex narrative form, a further portrait of a hero, Pechorin, who found him-self "superfluous" in Russian society. Pushkin's Eugene Onegin may have been presented objectively, as a social type; Lermontov added a new dimension of psychological portraiture to his characterisation of Pechorin. Both writers in their respective ways were to lay the founda-tion for what has since come to be known as the "social-psychological" novel, the greatest achievement of the realistic tradition in Russian literature.

The Forties

THE "forties", as a period of intense intellectual and cultural ferment, may be said to begin in 1836 with the publication of Chaadayev's *Philosophical Letter* in the journal *Telescope* and to conclude with Belinsky's death and the Paris revolution in 1848. During this short period of barely more than ten years, despite the reactionary régime of Nicholas—indeed, very largely because of it—Russia acquired an oppositional intelligentsia versed in the latest social and political ideas of Europe; it was also a period which witnessed a fierce polemic between the Westernists and Slavophils; from this period there also emerged a new humanism, which gave a new, realistic, humanitarian complexion to Russian literature and art.

Chaadayev's first *Philosophical Letter* was, as Herzen described it, "a pistol shot at dead of night" in the complacent, reactionary atmosphere of Nicholas's Russia. Though not intended as such, it came to be regarded as the first overt attack upon "official nationalism" and the first sign of political protest after the failure of Decembrism. Yet Chaadayev (1793–1856), a guards officer and mystic, was not antimonarchist, nor was he a man of great political perspicacity. His criticism of contemporary Russia was based on a teleological interpretation of history and the notion of Christianity as a unifying social force. Russia had never, in Chaadayev's view, progressed hand in hand with other nations. "We belong," he wrote, "neither to the West nor to the East. Standing as it were outside time, we have not been affected by the universal education of the human race." The historical experience of unified Christian development, which had given the social precepts of duty, justice, law and order to the Roman Catholic countries of Western Europe, had remained merely theory and speculation in Russia. Russians were not conditioned to the civilised virtues, Chaadayev claimed; Russia was static. Russia had not experienced the intense cultural and physical activity which corresponds to a nation's youth. "We grow," he wrote significantly, "but we do not mature." Why, then, was Russia so backward and how was she to catch up with Europe?

Chaadayev answered that Russia was backward because she had received Christianity from the "corrupt source" of Byzantium and not from the unified Christian cultures of Europe. But Christianity for

Chaadayev was not only a moral system; it was also an eternal divine force which acts universally throughout the spiritual world. "We must," he declared, "first of all enliven our own faith by every possible means and give ourselves a genuinely Christian impulse, because everything in the West has been created by Christianity." The only way for Russia to achieve this was by learning for herself all that had already been learned by the nations of Europe during fifteen centuries of unified Christian experience.

Chaadayev's *Philosophical Letter* so shocked the authorities that he was officially declared insane and subjected for a year to a series of compulsory medical inspections. He subsequently offered a partial recantation of his views in another work ironically entitled *The Apology of a Madman*. In this work he claimed that he loved his country, but he could not learn to love it blindly. "I love my country," he wrote, "as Peter the Great taught me to love it." Official patriotism still remained abhorrent to him, but he could now see more hope for Russia because lack of a past also meant lack of prejudice. Russia could therefore be more receptive to new ideas and could be great in the future by initiating her past from the present moment forward.

It is possible to discern in Chaadayev's thinking elements of both Westernism and Slavophilism, though the former clearly predominates. What does one mean by these terms? Briefly, Westernism was the standpoint adopted by those members of the intelligentsia during the "forties" who believed that Russia's future lay in adopting, and adapting to Russian circumstances, European concepts of government and social organisation; for this reason, Westernists admired Peter the Great for having orientated Russia towards Europe. The Slavophils, on the other hand, abhorred Peter the Great as anathema and concentrated their attention, in a somewhat Romantic and uncritical spirit, upon Russia's indigenous heritage of Orthodoxy, the unity of the Tsar and his people and an idealisation of the peasant commune.

Slavophilism was really a criticism and rejection of Europe in an attempt to justify the greater "purity" of Russia. Its major exponents during the "forties" were Ivan Kireyevsky (1806–1856) and Khomyakov (1804–1860). Kireyevsky advanced the view that true Christian faith had been undermined in Europe by excessive rationalism, while Western thought itself had reached the point where it could go no further along its abstract, rational path. What the Russian seeks, in Kireyevsky's interpretation, is an inner wholeness of the reason, a concentration of intellectual powers whereby all the separate activities of the spirit can fuse into one living, higher unity. European rationalism led to separatism and disunity, whereas the concept of wholeness had pervaded the whole of Russian history, making the Tsar and his people one, causing no distinction between classes, no separation between the individual and society. Kireyevsky called upon his contemporaries to reconsider the teachings of the holy fathers of the Orthodox Church and thus escape from the onesidedness of European civilisation. Khomyakov also believed that the individual, if he is to realise himself fully, must become part of the Church. Torn as man is by the conflicting principles of freedom and necessity, he can only achieve freedom in a kind of "togetherness with the Church". Truth is thus freely revealed to man through the Church (i.e. Orthodoxy), not imposed upon him, as it is under Roman Catholicism. Khomyakov, a man of great erudition, meditated deeply upon these questions and saw in the peasant commune, in the form of the Russian state and in the relationship between the Tsar and his people the same "organic wholeness", freely entered into and freely attained, which he stressed in speaking of the individual's relationship to the Church.

These ideas—very largely due to their strong patriotic bias and mystical highmindedness—had a profound and lasting influence, particularly as they were transmuted through the work of Gogol and, later, of Dostoyevsky. But the reality of Russian life, especially when it was compared with the changes occurring in Europe, encouraged a more radical, political re-thinking of the course that Russia should take in the future. Necessarily, owing to the censorship and the power of the autocracy, such re-thinking was conducted in a vacuum by young men who saw little likelihood of their ideas being put into practice. Under the repression of the autocracy the ideas espoused and fostered by the young intelligentsia became excessively radical, fiercely humanitarian and, in many ways, as unrealistically Utopian as were the Christian ideals of the Slavophils.

The activities of these young intellectuals, predominantly Westernist in outlook, began in the Moscow university circles of the early 1830s. Interest in Hegel and Feuerbach, a passionate devotion to the ideals of the French Revolution and to the Utopian Socialism of Saint-Simon and Fourier, an abhorrence of serfdom and all forms of arbitrary government were characteristic of the most important of these university circles —the circle of Alexander Herzen (1812–1870) and of his close friend Nikolay Ogaryov (1813–1877). More exclusively philosophical in its interests was the circle of Stankevich (1813–1840), which promoted an interest in Idealism and was supported by such future Slavophils as Ivan and Pyotr Kireyevsky and Konstantin Aksakov. The most literary of the circles was organised by Vissarion Belinsky (1811–1848), but it was also the most short-lived. News reached the university authorities that Belinsky had written a play, *Dmitry Kalinin*, which attacked serfdom, and he was forthwith expelled from the university in 1832. In 1834 Herzen and Ogaryov were arrested. The persecution of the new, educated stratum of Russian society which came to be known as the intelligentsia had begun.

Herzen, the child of an illegitimate union between a wealthy Russian nobleman, Ivan Yakovlev, and a young German girl, Louisa Haag, was born on the eve of the Napoleonic invasion of Russia. During his boyhood he was strongly influenced by Voltaire; at Moscow University he acquitted himself brilliantly, but after his arrest in 1834 was exiled until early 1840 when he was permitted to return to St Petersburg, only to be exiled to Novgorod a year later. In 1842 he was allowed to take up residence in Moscow and in 1847 left Russia for voluntary exile in the West. Thereafter, though disillusioned by Western Europe even before leaving Russia and more deeply disillusioned by the events of 1848, he lived for the greater part of his active life in London where he made his reputation as a publicist, editor of the "free" Russian journal *The Bell* and author of *My Past and Thoughts*, a vivid but not wholly reliable series of reminiscences.

Inevitably it was his socialism which was to exert the greatest influence on his generation, because after leaving Russia he was to advocate with ever-increasing frequency the idea that Russia could become socialist through the peasant communes—an idea that was to be the mainstay of the Populism of the sixties and seventies. Freedom, however, especially the freedom of the individual in ethical and political terms, was Herzen's ideal. He was an eminently civilised man and all his work provides evidence of the intelligent, civilised scrutiny to which he subjected the casuistry, hypocrisy and philistinism of his time. Yet Herzen had his limitations : he was not so much a leader of men as a goad to their consciences, not really a revolutionary so much as a nobleman in revolt against his heritage, less a practical politician than an orator who hoped that opinions alone would change the world.

Belinsky, unlike Herzen and the majority of "the men of the forties", was a *raznochinets*—that is to say he was neither of peasant nor of noble extraction. He came from that stratum of Russian society composed of those who occupied minor places in the lower ranks of the bureaucratic hierarchy. In the course of time the term *raznochinets* (pl. *raznochintsy*) was used to define those men of modest birth who, having acquired some form of education, were enabled by this means to become "classless". The *raznochintsy* were subsequently to form a considerable proportion of the intelligentsia. Belinsky was the first of such men to achieve prominence outside government service. The hard circumstances of his upbringing and the fact that he had to fend for himself very largely in matters of education lent a toughness and fieriness to his publicistic activity that was to bring him many followers. He was to exert a powerful influence upon the intellectual life of Russia during the "forties" and succeeded in moulding a whole generation of writers to his views.

After his expulsion from Moscow University, he turned to literary journalism. His first major work was his *Literary Reflections* (1834) which argued that a specifically Russian literature did not as yet exist. Literature for Belinsky was a passion. He made it his life's task to "discover" Russian literature and to guide it along the path to realism. Inseparable from this process of "discovering" literature was the more personal process of discovering for himself a realistic attitude to life in theory as well as in fact. Theory, it may be remarked, was of paramount importance to the Russian intelligentsia, and to no one more so than to Belinsky.

In 1840 he discovered socialism, and from that moment forward all his publicistic activity became a vehement crusade in the name of socialist ideals. Literature was now given the aim of criticising the reality of Russian life. Though Belinsky never used the term "realism", he spoke during the 1840s of the emergence of a "natural school" in Russian literature which had brought literature "closer to reality"; for this reason, it is now common to speak of Belinsky as the advocate of "critical realism" in literature, meaning a literature which, though depicting life in realistic terms, was at the same time to be critical of that reality. Belinsky's socialism was part and parcel of his attitude as the leading spokesman of Westernism, but it was also accompanied by a deep love for Russia and the Russian people, for "the insulted and injured" in Russian society. He also held sacred the idea of individuality and was, above all, despite his theorising, a brilliant, fastidious and perceptive literary critic who judged writing always in terms of the writer as an individual, always searching for and encouraging new talent.

In an atmosphere of polemic between Westernists and Slavophils, with continuous discussion in the press and in private of such questions as the meaning of nationality, the purpose of literature, the significance of the natural sciences, the relationship between Russia and Europe, Russia during the "forties" began to educate herself, as Chaadayev had advised. The resultant education was unbalanced and hurried. The emphasis placed by Belinsky on "reality" in literature and the absence under Tsarism of any open forum for the discussion of everyday topics encouraged the growth of a type of committed literature which combined journalism and *belles lettres*.

With the publication in 1842 of the first part of *Dead Souls*, Gogol established himself as the leading writer of the period. This half-novel, half-poem depicted, in terms at once both grotesquely real and comically extravagant, the exploits of the acquisitive hero, Chichikov, who attempted to buy dead serfs or "souls" in order to provide himself with the means of becoming a landowner. It was immediately apparent that this book, apart from being a remarkable example of prose literature, could be interpreted as an indictment of serfdom. More or less simultaneously with *Dead Souls* Gogol also published his tragi-comic portrait of a St Petersburg clerk, Akaky Akakiyevich, in *The Greatcoat*. These two works had the effect, firstly, of initiating a tradition of prose as the dominant form in Russian literature, secondly, of introducing both rural and urban themes and, thirdly, of concentrating attention upon the "little man", the peasant or the poor clerk, who had not hitherto figured prominently in major literary works. The total effect of Gogol's work, and Belinsky's criticism, was to make literature socially conscious, humanistic, truthful and concerned to arouse pity and indignation at the plight of the downtrodden and oppressed.

The work of all the new writers who emerged during the 1840s illustrated this new committed attitude. Dostoyevsky (1821–1881) with his *Poor Folk* (1846), entered Russian literature as one of Belinsky's disciples, though his subsequent investigation of pathological states of mind was to arouse Belinsky's disapproval. Turgenev (1818–1883), the writer of the "forties" to be influenced most powerfully by Belinsky's teaching, first made a name for himself with his studies of peasant life in *A Sportsman's Sketches* which began to appear in 1847 in the journal *The Contemporary*, to which Belinsky contributed some of his most important articles at the end of his life. Nekrasov (1821–1878), editor of *The Contemporary*, was strongly influenced in his poetic work of the 1840s by Belinsky; indeed, throughout his life he was to be under the spell of Belinsky's example. Herzen's literary work, especially his portrait of the "superfluous man", Beltov, in his novel *Who is Guilty?* (1847) and Goncharov's contrast between provincial romanticism and bourgeois realism in his *An Ordinary Story* (1847) were facets of this new trend in literature; the same civic attitude is discernible in the work during the "forties" of such lesser writers as Grigorovich, Pisemsky and Saltykov-Shchedrin. In the theatre also, both in the plays of Turgenev and Ostrovsky and in the activities of the actor-manager Shchepkin in the Moscow Maly (i.e. Little) Theatre, realistic, social themes began to dominate the repertoire. In music, Glinka introduced folk-song *motifs* into his famous operas *Ivan Susanin* (1836) and *Ruslan and Lyudmila* (1842), and in the sphere of painting the depiction of scenes from Russian life became the major concern of such artists as Venetsianov and Fedotov. The most famous painter of the period, A. A. Ivanov (1806–1858), who devoted the greater part of his life to the painting of one work, *The Appearance of Christ to the People* (now in the Tretyakov Gallery in Moscow), can be said to have couched his religious subject in "popular", realistic terms.

Literature, however, was the dominant form of artistic expression during this period. When, after having been acknowledged as the leader of the "natural school" with his work of the early 1840s, Gogol in 1847 published his *Selected Passages from a Correspondence with Friends*, a sententious work coloured by his own peculiar reactionary Slavophilism, Belinsky regarded it as a betrayal. His answer took the form of a *Letter to Gogol*, written in Salzbrunn in July 1847, which was to become Belinsky's testament and the single most influential political document of the "forties". Apart from branding Gogol, in his famous phrase, as "a preacher of the knout and an apostle of ignorance", he denounced him for being so far removed from Russian reality that he failed to see that Russia had no need of salvation in mysticism, but only in civilisation, enlightenment and humanitarianism. Russia, Belinsky emphasised, was a land where men were traded like beasts, where a man did not even have the self-respect of a proper name, where there were no guarantees of personal liberty, of honour or property, where there was not even law and order "but only vast corporations of various bureaucratic thieves and plunderers". The most vital contemporary questions facing Russia were, quite simply, the abolition of serfdom and corporal punishment and the strictest possible implementation of what laws already existed. Gogol's Christianity was diabolic and his support of the Orthodox Church an insult to Russia, for true Christian feeling cannot countenance that one man should be another man's slave and Russians were, in any event, a profoundly atheistic people : "Voltaire," declared Belinsky in a graphic passage, "who extinguished with the weapon of his satire the bonfires of fanaticism and ignorance in Europe, is more a son of Christ . . . than all your priests, bishops, metropolitans and patriarchs". Belinsky's *Letter to Gogol*, though only known in Russsia in an illegal form, was to lay the foundation for an "intelligentsia Christianity" or "secular religiosity" which denounced Orthodox Christianity as an instrument of Tsarist repression and substituted for it the ideal of socialism as the true expression of Christian feeling.

The high promise offered by the "forties" ended with the Paris revolution in 1848. One of the first victims of the ensuing intensification of reaction, which made the Russian government literally appear to be, as the Marquis de Custine had described it, "the discipline of the camp substituted for the civil order", was the young Dostoyevsky, arrested for reading aloud Belinsky's *Letter to Gogol* at a meeting of the Petrashevsky group. Petrashevsky himself, the author of a *Pocket Dictionary of Foreign Words*, published in 1846, had organised a group for the discussion of political and social questions, at which much attention was devoted to the Utopian Socialism of Fourier and to the possibility of organising revolution in Russia. In April 1849, thirty-nine members of the group were arrested and, on the Tsar's orders, were subjected to a gruesome charade of execution by firing squad which was commuted at the last moment to penal servitude. Dostoyevsky's brush with death on this occasion and subsequent ten-year exile were to transform him, paradoxically, from a vague socialist into a confirmed Christian.

The Crimean War

THE Paris revolution of February 1848 ended the reign of Louis Philippe. Constitutional governments were established in Austria and Prussia and a wave of national liberation movements swept through Europe. Faced with such an alarming situation, Nicholas I broke off diplomatic relations with France and planned to invade, but in 1848 Russian troops did no more than occupy Moldavia and Wallachia, from which they withdrew in 1851. The situation in Austria, especially with the resignation of Metternich, the central figure in the Holy Alliance, caused more immediate alarm in St Petersburg than did events in Paris. Nicholas made strenuous efforts to bolster the failing Habsburg régime of Emperor Ferdinand I; upon his abdication and the accession of his nephew Franz Josef relations between Austria and Russia improved. Russian attention was now turned to Hungary where a revolt under the national leader, Louis Kossuth, had broken out in March 1848. Partly in order to support the Habsburgs and partly to safeguard Russia's borders from the infection of revolution, Nicholas undertook, in collaboration with Austria, to suppress the Hungarian revolt. After a surprisingly prolonged and costly campaign Kossuth submitted to the far more numerous Austrian and Russian forces. The Hungarians laid down their arms in August 1849, hoping for clemency from Nicholas, who, however, handed the remaining leaders of the revolt over to the Austrian authorities. The severe sentences imposed on the insurgents caused shock throughout Europe, particularly in France and Great Britain.

Kossuth with other Hungarian leaders had meanwhile fled to Turkey. Demands for extradition were made by Austria and Russia and when the Turks refused to comply diplomatic relations were severed. At this point British public opinion demanded a show of strength in favour of the Hungarian refugees. British ships entered the Dardanelles in direct violation, it seemed, of the Straits Convention of 1841. The ships were withdrawn after a fortnight, but this action seems to have had the effect of averting armed conflict between Russia and Turkey. The problem of the Hungarian refugees was then settled by negotiations between the interested parties. However, for the first time a clear anti-Russian alignment of the major Western Powers, France and Britain, in support of Turkey, had come into being, which was to foreshadow the military alignment in the Crimean War five years later.

Franco–Russian relations seemed for a while to improve after the accession of Napoleon III. The same can also be said of relations between Russia and Great Britain. On the surface, an appearance of agreeable understanding was maintained, but latent hostility towards Russia was steadily growing. Blame for the coming conflict attaches to both sides. British suspicions were aroused by Nicholas's proposals of 1853 that Turkey should be partitioned between Russia, Britain and Austria, as a result of which Russian troops might, if only on a temporary basis, be stationed in Constantinople. Such a suggestion met with an instantly hostile response in London. Moreover, Nicholas's proposals displayed a lordly indifference to French interests. Initially France and Russia clashed over the Holy Places. Since the beginning of the 1840s Roman Catholicism had been demanding recognition of its rights in Jerusalem, then part of the Ottoman Empire. In 1850, aided by Napoleon III's interest in the Catholic claims, the French asked for the key to the Church of Bethlehem and the right to replace a silver star in the birthplace of Christ. This encroachment upon rights which had for long been the sole prerogative of the Greek Orthodox Church caused bitter resentment in St Petersburg. The Turks were slow in reaching a decision, but by the end of 1852 the French requests were met. Nicholas now invoked the sacred rights of the Orthodox Church, made a show of military force in the south and despatched a special envoy to Constantinople to demand the return of the Orthodox rights and to propose a secret Russo–Turkish alliance by which all Orthodox believers in the Ottoman Empire would be guaranteed Russian protection. This proposal, like the proposals for the dismemberment of Turkey (both proposals were made simultaneously in February 1853), appeared in the eyes of the Western Powers not only to violate Turkish sovereignty but to signal the end of the Ottoman Empire.

Events soon overtook all diplomatic attempts to prevent war. Russian troops entered the Danubian principalities in July 1853 as a result of the Turkish refusal to accept Russian demands. Turkey declared war against Russia in October and at the end of November suffered a crushing defeat at the Battle of Sinope, when Russian ships under Admiral Nakhimov destroyed a portion of the Turkish fleet. Such indignation was aroused in the West by this alleged "massacre" that a combined Franco–British naval force was sent through the Bosphorus into the Black Sea in January 1854. Diplomatic relations between St Petersburg, Paris and London were broken off; an anti-Russian alliance was formed between Britain, France and Turkey; the withdrawal of Russian troops from the Danube was demanded by ultimatum.

Nicholas was faced by a situation which he had long attempted to avoid. He had always been keen to have the support of one or another European Power in any military action that he might contemplate against Turkey. Now, however, Austria and Prussia, his two closest allies in the ostensible Holy Alliance upon which Nicholas, like his predecessor, had placed such hopes, refrained from taking sides. The Russia of Nicholas found itself at war with a coalition of Western Powers aiding Turkey, whose purpose was to force Russia to withdraw from the Danube, to enforce freedom of navigation on the Danube, to revise the 1841 Straits Convention and to make Russia abandon the claim to protect Orthodox Christians in Turkey.

At the outset of war with Russia British opinion favoured naval operations in the Baltic and the White Sea. But it soon became clear that the centre of operations was to be the Black Sea area. In September 1854 an allied expeditionary force of some 60,000 men landed at Eupatoria in the Crimea with the aim of capturing the Russian naval base of Sevastopol. The landings were made without incident. At the battle of Alma, the first land engagement between Russian and allied forces, the Russians were defeated after inflicting heavy casualties upon the expeditionary troops. The Russians then retreated to Sevastopol. The greater part of the Russian Black Sea fleet was sunk at the entrance to Sevastopol harbour and the siege of the fortress began. The delay occasioned by the need for the expeditionary forces to bring up their heavy artillery gave the Russians the chance to throw up defence works to the south. Russian attempts to raise the siege by attacking the British at Balaklava and, ten days later, at Inkerman led to the repulse of the Russian forces. But inept and indecisive generalship at the allied headquarters, appalling muddle in supply arrangements, wholly inadequate medical facilities and the consequent losses through sickness, disease, malnutrition and the bitter Crimean winter, for which the allied troops were singularly ill prepared, turned the campaign into a hideous and protracted test of endurance. Throughout 1855, from February until September, when Sevastopol finally capitulated, ferocious attacks were made upon the fortress. Russia then submitted and in the Treaty of Paris, signed in March 1856, surrendered her territories at the mouth of the Danube and in southern Bessarabia, abrogated her right to maintain naval bases in the Black Sea, to safeguard the interests of Christians in the Ottoman Empire and to exercise a protectorate over the Danubian principalities.

What conclusions can be drawn from the Crimean War? In general terms, it can be said to have been a struggle between capitalism and semi-feudalism, between bourgeois Europe and reactionary Russia. It brought an end to Nicholas I's policies, both foreign and domestic. Imperial Russia was never again to enjoy the power or prestige in foreign affairs that it enjoyed before 1855; and Nicholas's death in February of that year was also to signify the demise of the quasi-military dictatorship that he had personally wielded in domestic affairs. In military terms, the war was to provide evidence of great but futile heroism—the charge of the Light Brigade at Balaklava, for instance, or the defence of Sevastopol by its courageous Russian garrison. Yet, despite the heroism, the Crimean War was to teach the unmistakable lesson that modern war was not heroic, and no one was to learn this lesson better than the young artillery officer, Count Lev Tolstoy, whose experiences at Sevastopol were to provide the material for his *Sevastopol Stories* and for his deliberately unheroic treatment of war in *War and Peace*. The Crimean War also initiated a new style of warfare: trench warfare, and it was thus to anticipate the methods of the First World War. Finally, as a trial of strength, it revealed the weaknesses in both sides; but—most important of all—it obliged even the most conservative elements in Russia to recognise the need for reforms.

IMPERIAL RUSSIA
1815–1914

⫿⫿⫿⫿ Black-earth Belt
—·—·— Russian Border

0 50 100 200 300 Miles

FINLAND

Åland Is.
Helsinki
Stockholm
Kronstadt
ST. PETERSBURG
Dorpat · Tsarskoye Selo
Pskov
Vologda
Riga
Kostroma
Tilsit
Tver
Ivanovo-Voznesensk
Drissa · Vitebsk · Borodino
Kazan
Tannenberg
Vilna
Vyazma · Maloyaroslavets
Nizhny-Novgorod
Minsk
Smolensk
Moscow
Warsaw
Mogilyov
Kaluga · Ryazan
Simbirsk
Lodz
Tula
Brest-Litovsk
Penza
BALTIC SEA
Niemen

Tambov

Chernigov
VOLHYNIA
GALICIA
Kiev
AUSTRO-HUNGARY
Kharkov
Don
Dnieper
Donets
Volga
Dniester
BESSARABIA
Krivoy Rog
DONBASS
Pruth
Kishinyov
Taganrog
Rostov-on-Don
Odessa
ROUMANIA
Bukharest
Eupatoria
Azov Sea
Danube
Sevastopol
Inkerman
CASPIAN SEA
Constanta
Balaklava

AUSTRO-HUNGARY
Danube
MOLDAVIA
RUSSIA
BOSNIA
HERZE-GOVINA
SERBIA
ROUMANIA
WALLACHIA
BLACK SEA
BULGARIA
Plevna
EASTERN RUMELIA
CONSTANTINOPLE
Bosphorus
TURKEY
Adrianople
San Stefano
Dardanelles
AEGEAN SEA
GREECE

RUSSIA AND TURKEY
1877–78
0 100 200 300 Miles

Irkutsk
L. Baykal
RUSSIA
Chita
Trans-Siberian Rly.
Nikolayevsk
SAKHALIN
MANCHURIA
Amur
MONGOLIA
Chinese Eastern Railway
Kharbin
Khabar-ovsk
Peking
Mukden
Vladivostok
Liaotung Peninsula
Yalu
Port Arthur
KOREA
CHINA
Straits of Tsushima
JAPAN
Shanghai

RUSSIA AND JAPAN
1904–5
0 100 200 400 Miles

CHAPTER III

1855–1881

The Epoch of Great Reforms

ALEXANDER II, who ascended the throne upon the death of his father in February 1855, was born in 1818, and one of his earliest recollections was the artillery fire which dispersed the Decembrists on the Senate Square; it is to his credit that upon his accession he granted an amnesty to the surviving Decembrists in exile in Siberia. Educated by the poet Zhukovsky in humanitarian sentiments, he nonetheless retained an admiration throughout his life for the principles, if not for the style, of his father's rule. He rejected any idea of representative government and believed in maintaining the policies of the Holy Alliance. His reputation as the "Tsar-Liberator" was due less to any deep-rooted conviction of the need for such reformative measures as the Emancipation of the serfs than to a vague, humanitarian solicitude for his subjects which, though good in itself, was politically both naïve and short-sighted. His choice of advisers was more fortuitous, it seems, than deliberate and he was prone to have favourites of doubtful integrity. History would judge him more favourably if his reforms had been more wholehearted and his administration more efficient. As it is, the most scathing judgment probably does him the most justice—that he was, in the words of Queen Victoria's representative at his coronation, "well-intentioned, but weak as water".

The opening years of the new Tsar's reign, once the manifesto announcing the end of the Crimean War and intimating forthcoming changes was made public in March 1856, saw a revival, on an ever-greater scale, of the publicistic activity which characterised the "forties". The intensification of the censorship and other repressive measures enforced during the last seven years of Nicholas I's reign damped down, but certainly did not extinguish, the intellectual life of Russia; as soon as conditions permitted, both Herzen in his London exile and the most radical of the journals in Russia, *The Contemporary*, began to revive interest in social and political matters. Upon learning that Nicholas was dead, Herzen threw coins to the London urchins outside his house who ran about the streets giving "Hurrahs!" and shouting, "Impernickel is dead! Impernickel is dead!"; to Russia, on the other hand, in the first number of his "free" journal, *Polar Star*, which began publication in 1855, Herzen offered a threefold programme of reform : the Emanci-

pation of the serfs with land, freedom of the printed word and the abolition of corporal punishment. In 1857, with his fortnightly journal, *The
Bell*, which was smuggled regularly into Russia, Herzen's publicism became even more topical and trenchant. But *The Contemporary* had also
begun to speak with a new voice, that of Chernyshevsky (1828–1889)
who from 1855 until his arrest in 1862 was the journal's leading con-
tributor and who, along with his young colleague Dobrolyubov (1836–
1861), became the guide and mentor of the younger, predominantly
raznochinets, intelligentsia. In addition, there were those among the
nobility who professed liberal views, notably Kavelin, Milyutin, Unkovsky and Turgenev (the novelist), and they, either through their literary,
journalistic or official activity, energetically promoted the reformist work
of the period.

Yet the initiative for the greatest of the reforms, the Emancipation
of the serfs, belongs to the Tsar himself. Addressing the Moscow nobility
in the spring of 1856, Alexander mentioned the need to abolish serfdom
"from above", but he did not wish to embark on any such reform without learning of the nobility's feelings and proposals in the matter.
Alexander hoped that, if he trusted the nobility as his father had demonstrably failed to do, the process of reform would be made easier and his
own role less authoritarian. The nobility's response was in general cool.
Meanwhile, the Minister of Internal Affairs, Lanskoy, along with his
assistant, Levshin, began to collect information about the serf problem.
He reached the conclusion that the problem was open to three solutions:
the peasants could either be freed by decree without land; or serfdom
could be abolished, but the peasants would have to pay for such land
as they retained; or the peasants could be "obliged" to perform certain
services for their masters either on a temporary basis or indefinitely.
Although these proposals were to form the basis of later discussions,
Alexander was still hopeful that some concrete initiative would come
from the nobility. When this failed to materialise, he appointed a secret
committee in January 1857 to collate such information as was available
and to frame proposals. The committee soon became bogged down in
absurd trivialities and deliberated for eight months without result. In an
effort to overcome this procrastination, Alexander appointed his brother,
Grand Duke Constantine, to the chairmanship of the committee in
August 1857. A more effective spur to reform, however, came from the
Lithuanian nobles who petitioned the Tsar that they should be allowed
to give personal freedom to their peasants but retain the land for themselves. Alexander would have none of this. In November 1857 he issued
a rescript, based on Lanskoy's proposals, which stipulated that the land
should be considered the property of the landowners but that the

peasants must have the right to purchase their allotments over a given period and should be allowed to use sufficient land to ensure their subsistence and to pay taxes, for which they would pay either in *barshchina* or *obrok* according to a fixed scale. This rescript, accompanied by instructions that committees of the nobility were to be formed to discuss the proposals and to prepare reports within six months, was sent not only to the Lithuanian nobles but to all provincial governors and marshals of nobility throughout the Russian Empire.

The abolition of serfdom could now be openly discussed in the press. The secret committee became a Main Committee for Peasant Affairs, designed to work out the details of the reform, and during 1858 committees of the nobility were formed in all the provinces. It soon transpired that economic self-interest, not altruistic concern for the welfare of the nation, guided the nobles in their deliberations. Landowners in the black-earth areas, for instance, who derived their incomes exclusively from agriculture, wished to liberate their serfs without land or with as little land as possible, whereas in the non-black-earth areas of northern Russia, where commerce and industry predominated, the landowners were quite willing to free their serfs with land provided they did not lose the income from the peasants' *obrok* payments. Fear of the Emancipation laid bare all the greed and cruelty of the landowners towards their serfs. Many landowners forcibly moved their serfs to poor lands, exiled them or gave them over for recruitment to the army—inhuman measures which so appalled the Tsar during his travels through Russia in the summer of 1858 that he immediately prohibited such practices by decree. In March 1859 the actual drafting of the reform was set in motion by the establishment of Drafting Commissions under the liberal and former associate of the Decembrists, General Rostovtsev, aided by other pro-reform liberals such as Nicholas Milyutin, recently appointed Deputy Minister of Internal Affairs, and the Slavophil, Yury Samarin. Against them were ranged many bitter opponents of the reform, but by dint of hard work—work so hard and exhausting that it drove Rostovtsev to his death in February 1860—the liberals managed to push through the reform, although they were forced to compromise with the conservative elements on many issues. Moreover, although the Tver marshal of nobility, Unkovsky, had prepared a liberal plan for obligatory redemption by the peasants of both their own allotments and additional lands, the majority of the proposals from the provincial committees of the nobility demanded reductions in the peasants' allotments and stringent redemption payments, with tragic consequences for the liberal spirit of the reform and for the future of Russia. By October 1860 the work of the Drafting Commissions, under the chairmanship of the reactionary Count Panin, was completed. The draft reform was then passed to the Main Committee for consideration and afterwards to the State Council for endorsement. At each stage the reform was bitterly contested, but the only serious emendation was made by Prince Gagarin, who proposed that the landowner might give his peasants a quarter of the land allotment due to them under the law whereupon, if they agreed, all their obligations would cease. These, the so-called "beggars' allotments", were approved by the State Council and confirmed by the Tsar, who finally signed the Emancipation Act on February 19th 1861. It came into force on March 5th.

The Emancipation Act, comprising seventeen major statutes and a host of lesser provisions, was a complicated and bulky document of over 300 pages. On the face of it, it gave the serfs their freedom. Among the personal rights which they now enjoyed were the freedom to marry without the consent of their masters, the freedom to enter into contracts or obligations with other private persons, to engage in trade and industry, and to go to law. The property rights granted to the "free village dwellers", as they were now called, entitled them to acquire property, to make free use of any land purchased by them and to inherit property in accordance with local customs.

Yet such freedom was conditional upon the signing of agreements with the landowners about the purchase of land rights and the fulfilment of financial and other obligations to the peasant commune, of which each "free village dweller" was to be a member. Until such agreements were made the peasants remained "temporarily obligated" to the landowner. Moreover, no peasant had the right to give up the allotment of land received under an agreement with the landowner and to leave the commune until nine years after the publication of the Emancipation Act. The stipulations governing the size and value of the land allotments were detailed and strict. If the area of land worked by a peasant before the reform was greater than the maximum average size laid down in the Emancipation statutes, then the surplus land was handed back to the landowner (these portions subsequently became known as the "cut-off parts", otrezki); if it was less than the minimum average size, the landowner had to make up the deficit by surrendering some of his own land or reducing the peasant's obligations. In the overwhelming majority of cases this meant that the land available for the peasant's personal use was reduced : it has been reckoned that the peasants had to surrender between 18 per cent and 40 per cent of the land worked by them before the reform. Even so, in most provinces the landowners had the right to retain at least one-third, sometimes as much as a half, of the good agricultural land, leaving only the poorer land for peasant allotments. As for the peasants' obligations, these were assessed on the basis of inventories defining the land actually possessed by the peasants and the redemption payments, whether in money or in services, required of them. Such inventories had to be completed within two years of the Emancipation Act and confirmed by an arbitrator. What the peasants had finally to pay for their land was computed by capitalising at 6 per cent the annual charges on each allotment. These charges ranged from twelve to eight roubles for the maximum average size of allotments — charges which did not reflect the market value of the land, its productivity or the actual size of the allotments. The smaller the allotment, the greater was the average charge. Since very few peasants were able to buy their allotments outright, the government advanced to the landowners up to 80 per cent of the total due to them for surrendering their land to the peasants, the balance being found by the peasants themselves. These advances, plus interest, were then to be repaid by the peasants over a period of forty-nine years. Such an arrangement served to compensate the landowners not just for the loss of their land, but, more significantly, for the loss of their feudal rights. The inevitable result was a breakdown in redemption payments by the peasants, the accumulation of arrears, reassessment of the redemption rates (by a law of 1896 the redemption process was to continue until the 1950s) and the enforced impoverishment of large numbers of peasant households. In addition, despite the personal rights acquired by them, the peasants remained subject to recruitment for military service and to corporal punishment.

In retrospect it may seem that the greatest weakness of the Emancipation Act was its failure to treat the peasant as an individual. Bismarck is reputed to have said that Alexander II had done a great thing in emancipating the serfs but "that Emperor would do even more for Russia who should free the peasants from communal proprietorship". The Emancipation Act, like most laws framed by bureaucrats for implementation by a bureaucracy, referred to the peasants in terms of communal groupings. For instance, they were not taxed according to their incomes but on a *per capita* basis and the taxes were to be paid, not individually, but through the peasant communes on a system of mutual agreement between the members of the commune. These communes, though they elected "elders" with both organisational and disciplinary powers, such as the right to impose fines, to make arrests, or to order enforced labour (the assemblies of the communes enjoyed still greater powers), were placed under direct government control by the police and the local administration, and above them were established administrative regions with their own elders and assemblies and a regional court for trying minor civil and criminal cases. Above both the communal and regional administrations was placed an arbitrator of the peace elected from among the local landowners. Even if this were not a sufficient curtailment of the peasants' freedom, serious economic barriers to advancement were created by allotting the land to the communes, not directly to individual peasant households. The land once allotted would be reallocated by the commune to the peasant households either on hereditary tenure or on a repartitional basis, meaning that it could be redistributed among the households if the communal assembly so decided. This latter procedure gave the peasant little incentive to improve his own land, even if he could afford to, since it might well be redistributed at some later stage to someone else. More serious still, however, was the fact that, whether held on hereditary or repartitional tenure, the total amount of land received by the peasants under the Emancipation was not, even in the most favourable instances, equal to more than half the amount of land which they had worked as serfs, when they would spend approximately three days in each working week on their masters' land. Thus it may be said that their allotments under the Emancipation were equal to approximately half their earning capacity and they were obliged, as a consequence, to rent more land from the landowner, offer themselves as hired labour or find other work in order to be able to subsist, let alone to pay their taxes or fulfil their obligations. The effect was to increase land hunger, raise rents and cause greater peasant impoverishment, though, on the credit side, it must be stressed that the Emancipation had the effect of accelerating the change-over from a barter or natural system of economy to a money economy, with a consequent growth of capitalist forces.

Those most severely affected by the Emancipation Act were the house serfs. Entirely deprived of land, many of them gradually drifted to the towns to seek employment. The emancipated servile workers in the factories on the estates of the nobility and in "possessional" enterprises abandoned their employment in large numbers—a process which led to a serious drop in production in woollen manufactures, for instance, and in mining. The crown peasants (i.e. chiefly those employed on the Tsar's estates or in the royal households) were emancipated on relatively favourable terms in 1858, as were the state peasants in 1866. They received, on average, larger allotments and more lenient redemption terms.

As might have been, and was, expected, the Emancipation Act quickly caused bitter disillusionment both among the peasantry and the intelligentsia. There were peasant revolts in Penza and Kazan provinces, the most serious occurring in the village of Bezdna where, in April 1861, the peasants rose under the leadership of a certain Anton Petrov. The revolt was suppressed by military force at a cost of almost 500 lives. Although the government was able to bring the situation in the country-side under control by the summer of 1861, the Tsar's half-hearted liberalism had been overstrained. Soon after the publication of the Emancipation Act he dismissed its two chief architects, Lanskoy and Nicholas Milyutin, and appointed the nondescript Valuyev as Minister of Internal Affairs. This apparent return to reaction did not prevent the enactment during Alexander's reign of a series of important reforms in local and municipal government, the judiciary, finances, education and the armed forces.

The local government reform of 1864 brought into being the *zemstvo* (pl. *zemstva*)—elective bodies at both provincial and county levels, comprising an assembly and an executive elected for three-year terms. There were three categories of electors and three electoral procedures for the election of *zemstvo* representatives. The first two categories of electors were composed, on the one hand, of landowners and owners of trading or industrial undertakings, and, on the other, of urban dwellers, in both cases the right to vote being governed by property or income qualifications. The third category comprised the peasantry, whose delegates were chosen by the regional assemblies. The *zemstvo* assemblies elected the members of the provincial assemblies, a procedure which gave a dominant role to the nobility, more especially since regional and provincial marshals of nobility were to be the chairmen of the respective *zemstvo* assemblies. Nevertheless, the creation of such *zemstva*, ultimately in a majority of Russian provinces, introduced a semblance of democratic government into Russian life which was naturally to lead to demands for further democratic concessions. These were not to be granted, even in mild form, until the revolution of 1905. Despite this, the *zemstva* succeeded in becoming centres of liberal thought and activity. Under their auspices schools and hospitals were built, roads were kept in repair, prisons were maintained, agriculture, industry and trade were encouraged to the extent permitted by the *zemstva* revenues, which were derived from local rates. To staff and run the institutions set up by the *zemstva* a large professional and technical personnel was recruited, which was eventually known as "the third element" in the state and gradually began to exert an important radical influence in politics. Less striking was the municipal reform of 1870, which, though it made provision for the establishment of municipal dumas or councils, executive boards and mayors to be elected for four-year terms, ensured disproportionately high representation to those who paid the highest taxes.

The 1864 reform of the judiciary was, in essence and intention, the most enlightened piece of legislation to be introduced by the Russian autocracy; yet it had the boomerang effect of revealing how unenlightened and unjust, in a political sense, was the autocracy itself. In essence, the reform led to a simplification of the judiciary. At local level, minor civil and criminal cases were tried by justices of the peace elected by the *zemstva* or by municipal dumas; above these were the regional session courts. Major civil and criminal cases, the latter with a jury, were tried in district courts above which were chambers of justice. The highest court of appeal was the Senate. In intention, the reform was designed to make all equal before the law, to separate the judiciary from the administration, to ensure the incorruptibility of judges by making their appointments permanent and well remunerated, to lay court proceedings open to publicity, to enable defendants to have the protection of qualified lawyers and to allow preliminary investigation by an examining magistrate, instead of by the police, in criminal cases. In general, these intentions of the reform were successfully realised largely due to the calibre of the personnel attracted into the legal profession. But the competence of the courts was diminished in 1866 by the transfer of censorship cases to the chambers of justice; in 1867 by Count Pahlen's decision, as Minister of Justice, to make examining magistrates temporary appointments; in 1871 by entrusting to the security police the preliminary investigation of crimes against the state, which could be settled by administrative processes without trial; and in 1872 by transferring imporant political cases to a special court of the Senate. Similarly, though corporal punishment was officially abolished in 1863, it was retained in the army, among convicts and exiles, and could be administered to peasants on the orders of the regional courts.

The reforms in local and municipal government and the judiciary were natural consequences of the fact that the Emancipation Act had deprived the nobility of their former power. They were also attempts to modernise Russia, to make the institutions in the country at large less feudal and antiquated. But the liberalising effect of such reforms was compromised at the outset by the hostility of the intelligentsia towards the Emancipation Act and by the subsequent attempts of the government to whittle down the autonomous power of both the *zemstva* and the courts. This process of giving with one hand and taking with the other was evidence enough of the nervousness and faint-heartedness of an autocracy engaged in pursuing the contradictory course of attempting to modernise Russia without modernising itself. In the sphere of finances and education the effects of this nervous wavering were also evident.

In 1860 the State Bank was founded for the issue of short-term loans in place of the former official credit agencies which had been almost bankrupted by the Crimean War and the economic crisis of 1857–1859. Shortly thereafter a law was passed abolishing the former system of tax-farming in liquor and imposing an excise tax on the sale of spirits. The most important innovation, however, was the centralising of finances and budgeting under the Ministry of Finances. Budgeting procedure and taxation were also reformed, the budget was made public (from 1862) and several important measures were introduced by the very capable bureaucrat, Tatarinov, to ensure control of spending. Reitern, the Minister of Finances from 1862 until 1878, made serious though ultimately unsuccessful attempts to raise the value of the paper rouble by floating foreign loans (£15,000,000 was raised in Great Britain in 1862), and by encouraging private banks and foreign investment, especially in the building of railways. But foreign control of railway building had disastrous results and Russian credit abroad was damaged by the uneasiness in Russian internal affairs. Russian railway contractors proved to be more successful. Yet, despite Reitern's efforts, there were continuing budget deficits and the Russo–Turkish War of 1877–1878 dealt a final blow to the value of the rouble, reducing the paper rouble to sixty-three copecks and enormously increasing the national debt.

The reforms in the universities and schools were at first remarkably liberal. By a university charter drawn up by the liberal Professor Kavelin, and introduced by the equally liberal Minister of Education, Golovnin, the universities were, in 1863, permitted to elect their own councils, rectors and deans, though the Minister retained the power to approve the nominees for these posts. The universities were also opened to all who wished to attend, regardless of social background, with the exception of women, for whom special courses were started at St Petersburg University in 1869. In 1864 a charter for secondary education led to the creation of classical and science Gymnasiums, each with seven-year courses, and pro-Gymnasiums with four-year courses. Primary schools could also be opened by local bodies, such as the *zemstva*, or by private persons, and secondary education now became available to women in special "Empress Mary" schools. But the shock caused by Karakozov's attempt to assassinate Alexander II in 1866 led to the dismissal of Golovnin and the appointment of the reactionary Count Dmitry Tolstoy in his place. Tolstoy altered the 1864 charter by a law of 1871 which extended the course in the classical Gymnasiums from seven to eight years, laying great emphasis on such "harmless" studies as mathematics and the classics (forty-nine hours a week for Latin, thirty-nine hours for Greek) and very largely eliminating such "harmful" studies as history, geography, modern languages and the sciences. The science Gymnasiums were abolished and their place taken by scientific technical schools. University entrance was limited to those who had passed through the classical Gymnasiums. Control over primary schools was placed in the hands of inspectors. One of the first of these, by an odd piece of historical irony, was Ilya Nikolayevich Ulyanov, the father of Vladimir Ilyich Lenin, who took up his post in Simbirsk in 1869.

The final important reform of Alexander II's reign was the reform of the armed forces. Notable reformist work had been done by the Tsar's brother, Grand Duke Constantine, not only as chairman of the Main Committee on Peasant Affairs, but also as Minister of Marine. Naval reform, though, was less important after the limitations placed upon the Russian navy by the Treaty of Paris than was reform in the army. This was undertaken by General Dmitry Milyutin, an able administrator of enlightened views. He reorganised the central military administration and set up fifteen military regions. A large-scale programme of re-equipment and modernisation was begun, but the most significant change was the introduction in 1874 of universal conscription in place of the previous practice of peasant recruitment for a twenty-five year period. All males over twenty years of age were liable to conscription—for six years' active service in the army and seven years' in the navy, though the possession of educational qualifications could reduce the period of service to as little as three months. The main result of this reform was to create a large body of reservists and to reduce the cost of maintaining a large standing army. Officers' training was greatly improved and serious attempts were made to stamp out illiteracy among the rank and file. Although these were major reforms, in the final reckoning they failed to provide Tsarist Russia with armed forces capable of withstanding the modernised armies of either East or West, as 1904–1905 and 1914–1917 were to show.

Such, in brief, were the main reforms of the "epoch of great reforms". They were great only in the sense that they constituted major leaps forward by an administration that had previously been exceptionally backward. They were attempts to catch up with, rather than to overtake or improve on, similar practices in modern European countries. Though liberal in character, such reforms were concessions to liberalism rather than deliberate attempts to introduce liberalism "from above". They were probably successful in postponing revolution against Tsarism, but they were not sufficiently revolutionary to make revolution any less inevitable.

The Sixties

THE period known as the "sixties"—approximately from 1856 to 1866—witnessed the emergence in Russian intellectual life of a new kind of intelligentsia, predominantly *raznochinets* in character, with new social and political aspirations. These were called the "new men" or the "men of the sixties" or, as their detractors were inclined to call them, the "nihilists". Under the influence of Chernyshevsky's publicism in *The Contemporary*, they learned a total obedience to the natural sciences, to the anthropological principle that man was not body and soul but solely body, to Materialism, to the idea that art was no more than "a textbook on life" and life no more than a series of socio-economic problems which could be rationalised under socialism, to "rational egoism" as the guiding principle of human conduct and, finally, to revolution as the only means of overcoming Russia's backwardness. These ideas were more cogent, systematic and purposeful than the highminded liberalism of Herzen's *The Bell*. Also, they had a pseudo-scientific appeal for *raznochintsy* who tended to equate liberalism with the nobility and wished above all to eschew all authority, whether of the family, the church or the state, in favour of scientific progress.

Before the Emancipation Act of 1861 these ideas were fiercely debated in the press and in intellectual circles generally, but there was no open opposition to the government until the Act had been promulgated. As soon as the Emancipation statutes had been studied, both Herzen and Chernyshevsky attacked them as frauds. Herzen, for instance, welcomed the peasant disturbances of 1861 and called upon the youth of Russia, chiefly the students, to "go to the people"—a call which may be said to mark the beginning of the Populist movement. Chernyshevsky also came to the conclusion that the peasantry were now ripe for revolution. During 1861 a series of inflammatory pamphlets appeared, written by Chernyshevsky and his associates or sympathisers. Such were the three issues of the broadsheet *Velikoruss* which demanded a democratic constitution, or Shelgunov's revolutionary proclamation "To the Younger Generation". The appearance of such illegal literature particularly affected student opinion, giving rise to student revolts in the universities of St Petersburg and Moscow. Equally disillusioned by the Emancipation, the nobility of Tver, under their marshal of nobility, Unkovsky, petitioned the Tsar to summon a representative assembly (in 1862). The government removed Unkovsky from his post as marshal and the Tver nobility at once retaliated by creating twelve Unkovsky scholarships at Moscow University. But this was no more than an isolated example of liberal militancy. The majority of liberals amongst the nobility were content to support the government in its reformist activity. Real militancy manifested itself in two ways: in the proclamation "Young Russia" of May 1862 and in the organisation of the first "Land and Freedom" movement.

"Young Russia" was the work of a nineteen-year-old student, Zaichnevsky, who had organised a student group at Moscow University. Arrested for professing revolutionary views, he composed his proclamation while in prison, from which it was smuggled and then secretly printed in Ryazan before being distributed in St Petersburg. The demands which the proclamation made for the establishment of a federal-republican system in Russia based on socialist principles, and the call for an uprising of peasants against the Tsar, had the twofold effect of causing considerable alarm in government circles and introducing a Jacobinist note into the younger generation's approach to the peasantry. The appearance of this proclamation in St Petersburg coincided with several large-scale fires, which, it was rumoured, had been started by the nihilists.

Ogaryov, Herzen's collaborator on *The Bell*, had declared in 1861 that what the peasants really needed was "land and freedom" and that this could only be achieved by combining the anti-government activities of the intelligentsia with the peasant disturbances. Under the slogan "Land and Freedom" the first organisation of this name was formed in St Petersburg in the autumn of 1861 by Nicholas Serno-Solovyevich, with the active connivance of Chernyshevsky. It is difficult to ascertain the precise activities, or the extent, of this clandestine organisation. It was, however, supported by Herzen in London and it had connections with a revolutionary group founded by a Russian officer, Potebnya, among Russian troops quartered in Poland. The interception, in July 1862, of letters from Herzen, Bakunin and Ogaryov to various persons in Russia led the Third Section to make thirty-two arrests (in the so-called "affair of the thirty-two") which included Serno-Solovyevich and Chernyshevsky. The "Land and Freedom" organisation continued to exist, but its hopes of inflaming revolutionary sentiment in Russia in collaboration with the Polish revolutionary movement were dashed by the failure of the Polish revolt of 1863. Herzen miscalculated the reaction of Russian public opinion over the Polish question. It was all very well to talk about the Poles as "brothers", but when the "brothers" were murdering Russian soldiers, patriotic feelings amongst the Russians became more important than considerations of fraternal socialism. The influence of *The Bell* declined markedly after 1863. Similarly, with the arrest of Chernyshevsky and the eight-month suppression of *The Contemporary* in 1862, revolutionary activity amongst the younger intelligentsia was temporarily suspended.

Although no concrete evidence of Chernyshevsky's revolutionary work was produced at his trial, he was convicted and sentenced to exile in Siberia. His public humiliation on Mytnin Square in May 1864 prior to being exiled—his so-called "civil execution"—evoked bitter resentment among the intelligentsia and occasioned a withering attack upon the government by Herzen. But the intelligentsia was already being invited to adopt an apolitical course in their struggle to overcome Russia's backwardness. This course was advocated by Dmitry Pisarev (1840–1868), whose articles in *The Russian Word* urged the young "thinking realists" to concentrate their attentions wholly upon the natural sciences so that, through an abrogation of all aestheticism and all that was socially or morally worthless, they might devote themselves to improving economic conditions. Pisarev was also arrested in 1862 and wrote many of his articles in prison; the puritanical ruthlessness of his thinking was to influence many subsequent revolutionaries by encouraging them to regard themselves as dedicated to a sacred vocation. Meanwhile, a conflict over revolutionary methods was occurring in a small group of students which had been organised by Ishutin. He conceived the idea of forming a revolutionary body known as *Organisation*, within which would be a smaller and highly secret guiding body known as *Hell*. Within these revolutionary bodies there were those who favoured propaganda as the most practical means of inciting revolution, while others favoured terrorism. In 1866 this controversy was temporarily ended by a member of the Ishutin group, Dmitry Karakozov, a young man of noble birth, who fired at the Tsar while the latter was about to enter his carriage after a walk in the Summer Garden in St Petersburg. He missed his target, was arrested and, when asked to explain his action, declared that he had tried to kill the Tsar in order to bring freedom to the Russian peasantry. He was hanged. Public opinion was shocked by Karakozov's "nihilistic" act; *The Contemporary*, as the journal which had fostered nihilism, was finally banned and all the members of Ishutin's group were arrested. A period known as the White Terror ensued which, though in itself it did not last long, was to initiate a period of reaction in Russian domestic policies lasting almost forty years.

The activities of the nihilistic revolutionaries during the "sixties" were so limited in scope and achievement that they would hardly be worth recording were it not for the fact that the history of Russia in the nineteenth century inevitably points to the revolution of 1917. Yet it is important to remember that Russian public opinion, including peasant opinion (in so far as it is possible to gauge it), remained generally loyal to the Tsar during the decade 1860–1870. Revolutionary feeling had yet to take root in Russia at large; it remained the passionate concern of a handful—a growing handful, admittedly—of the radical intelligentsia. The first concrete evidence of a broadening of the revolutionary movement is to be discerned only after 1866, by which time two generations of the intelligentsia had either passed from the scene or were on the point of disappearing. Herzen, for instance, was to die in 1870, but his voice had already ceased to exert an important influence; Chernyshevsky's voice, and many other voices belonging to the "men of the sixties", still echoed loudly, but they were echoes only, not the exhortations of men still active in intellectual life.

The new voices which were heard in the latter half of the 1860s belonged to exiled writers such as Bakunin, Lavrov and Tkachyov. Bakunin, though of Herzen's generation, was unlike Herzen in believing exclusively in the need for peasant revolution. The Russian peasant, in Bakunin's view, was inherently communistic and revolutionary. The revolutionary intelligentsia had the task of inciting the peasantry to revolt, not for specific political ends but in order to achieve a state of anarchy in which peasant socialism would naturally triumph. In collaboration with his sinister young protégé, Nechayev, Bakunin composed a *Revolutionary Catechism* which stipulated that the revolutionary's role was one of complete, selfless dedication to the task of revolution, his one purpose being to destroy the existing state without thought for himself, his family or friends. This violent document reflected the violence and love of conspiracy in Nechayev's character. He is best known for the fact that in November 1869 he ordered the murder of a young student of the Moscow Agricultural Institute, Ivanov, who had apparently disagreed with his instructions. It was upon this incident that Dostoyevsky based the murder of Shatov in his novel, *The Possessed*. Shortly afterwards Nechayev went abroad, but the police arrested other members of his small revolutionary group; they were tried for the murder and sentenced to Siberia in Nechayev's absence. In 1872 he was himself arrested in Switzerland, handed over to the Russian authorities and tried at the beginning of the following year. He died in prison in 1882, faithful to his revolutionary principles to the end.

Nechayev's activities probably had a greater effect on Russian public opinion than Bakunin's words. Lavrov's *Historical Letters*, which appeared in book form in 1870, exerted a still greater influence. He called upon the intelligentsia as "critically thinking individuals" to realise that they were members of a privileged class who had incurred a grave debt towards the peasantry. The duty of the intelligentsia was therefore to identify their own interests with the interests of the peasantry in order to absolve themselves of this debt. The moral appeal of Lavrov's ideas, especially the importance which they attached to the role of the "subject" in history, served to unify many disparate elements amongst the intelligentsia under the banner of "going to the people". Tkachyov, as distinct from Bakunin and Lavrov, believed that revolution had to have specific political aims, that it required to be organised by trained and disciplined revolutionaries whose single purpose would be to overturn the existing political system in order to establish a new socialist order. The masses had to be led to revolution, in Tkachyov's opinion. Though this idea was later espoused by Lenin, Tkachyov's aim was not, as was Lenin's, to promote proletarian revolution at all costs, but to lead Russia away from capitalism to a socialism based on the peasant commune.

All these ideas had their part to play in what was to be known as Populism. But Populism, as a specific movement among the intelligentsia, did not come into being until the 1870s. The "sixties" were dominated, in the cultural sphere, by the ideas of the "new men", by nihilism.

Censorship, of course, left its mark upon the literature of the period, but there was a considerable relaxation in censorship regulations after the death of Nicholas I and in 1865 "temporary rules" were introduced which abolished preliminary censorship on original works of more than 160 printed pages and translated works of more than 200. The Minister of Internal Affairs was still empowered to ban books and journals on the slightest suspicion of anti-state activity. However, during the period of the 1850s and 1860s literature flourished more abundantly than ever, especially after 1855.

Gogol's death in 1852 marked the end of the "Gogolian" or first phase in the development of realistic prose literature. It also occasioned the arrest of Turgenev for an obituary notice on Gogol. Yet Turgenev was to become the major writer of the 1850s, both as the greatest novelist of the period and as chronicler of earlier phases in the development of the Russian intelligentsia. In his first novel, *Rudin*, of 1856, he portrayed a further type of "superfluous man", intellectual but weak-willed, who epitomised the failure of Turgenev's own generation of the "forties" to act upon their principles. Another portrait of a "man of the forties", this time of Slavophil persuasion, is to be found in Lavretsky, the hero of Turgenev's second novel, *A Nest of the Gentry* (1859). In 1860, with his novel *On the Eve*, Turgenev attempted to depict the more active and courageous social attitudes of the younger generation, but his portrait of the Bulgarian revolutionary, Insarov, was not a success and his heroine, Yelena, was portrayed too subjectively and sentimentally. Another prominent writer of the 1850s was Goncharov (1812–1891), whose most famous novel, *Oblomov* (1859), portrayed the slothful "dressing-gown existence" of the nobleman, Ilya Ilyich Oblomov, and prompted Dobrolyubov, in his polemical article "What is Oblomovism?", to interpret him as the final stage in the decay of the "superfluous man". The first part of the trilogy, *Childhood, Boyhood and Youth*, by Tolstoy (1828–1910) appeared in 1852. A notable work of the period was the long novel *A Thousand Souls* (1858), by Pisemsky (1820–1881)—a grim indictment of the morals of contemporary officialdom.

The tone for much of the literature of the 1860s was set by Turgenev's greatest novel, *Fathers and Children* (1862), which offered the first portrait of the "new man", the nihilistic Bazarov. The veracity of this portrait was such that it brought down upon Turgenev's head the wrath both of the radical younger generation and the right-wing conservatives. A year later there appeared the work by which Chernyshevsky is best known, his novel *What is to be Done?*, written while he was in prison and illustrating in fictional terms his ideas on the importance of co-operatives, female emancipation and the tasks of the "new men". His hero, Rakhmetov, disciplined himself both intellectually and physically into order to become, as Chernyshevsky expressed it, "the flower of the best people, the movers of the movers, the salt of the salt of the earth". With the exception of such poetic works as Nekrasov's famous *Red-Nosed Frost* (1863) or the publicism-cum-literature of Saltykov-Shchedrin (1826–1889), much of the literature of the 1860s was devoted to attacking the atheistic nihilism and "rational egoism" of Chernyshevsky and his adherents. The attack began with Pisemsky's *Troubled Sea* (1863), a novel of even less literary merit than Chernyshevsky's, and was followed in 1864 by another pamphlet-novel, *Nowhere (Nekuda)*, by Leskov (1831–1895), who was to become better known subsequently as the author of such brilliant short stories as *Lady Macbeth of the Mtsensk Region* (1865) and *Levsha* (1882). Meanwhile, Dostoyevsky, having returned from his Siberian exile in 1859, had begun to re-establish himself as a writer with his first important novel, *The Insulted and Injured* (1861), and his memorable record of his prison experiences, *Notes from the House of the Dead*. In 1862 he paid his first visit to Western Europe and this, combined with the discovery of Christian faith which he had made during his years of exile, turned him against European rationalism and socialism. Seeing such influences among the nihilists of the younger generation, he joined the crusade against Chernyshevsky with his *Notes from the Underground* (1864), which asserted that man was governed by the caprices of his will, not by his reason—an idea that he was to develop in his novel *Crime and Punishment* (1866), whose hero, Raskolnikov, murders a money-lender for nihilistic motives in order to prove that he is a man of self-will. Forced into a second exile, this time in Europe, in order to avoid his creditors, he wrote *The Idiot* (1868), which was intended to offer a portrait of a "positively good man" in the figure of the childishly Christ-like idiot, Prince Myshkin. Almost simultaneously, Turgenev, who had become Dostoyevsky's bitterest enemy, made his own attack upon both the younger and older generations, the radical and the liberal wings, of the Russian intelligentsia, in *Smoke* (1867). But the greatest work of the 1860s was to be Tolstoy's epic historical novel about the Napoleonic invasion of Russia, *War and Peace* (1869). Its panoramic sweep, its powerful, evocative characterisation which embraced both the nobility and the peasantry, its spaciousness, vitality and sense of movement, in which scenes of war on the battlefields of Austerlitz and Borodino blend with peaceful scenes on the estates of the Russian nobility, its concern with moral issues such as the search for God or its attempt to discover a theory of history—these, allied to the psychological and representational realism of Tolstoy's manner, lifted it above the polemics and animosities which had characterised most of the novels of the previous decade and gave it a unique place in world literature.

In the theatre, A. N. Ostrovsky (1823–1886) established himself as Russia's greatest dramatist during this period, especially with his pictures of the "dark Kingdom" of petty-bourgeois merchant life of which the finest example is *The Storm* (1860). In music, there was a similar burst of creative activity as in literature. Musical conservatoires were formed in St Petersburg (1862) and Moscow (1866). There also grew up round the composer, Balakirev (1837–1910), a group of young men who later became known as the most important Russian composers of the nineteenth century—Musorgsky (1839–1881), whose songs and instrumental works, particularly his opera *Boris Godunov* (1870, first produced 1874), brought new splendour and stature to Russian music; Borodin (1833–1887), whose opera *Prince Igor* was begun in 1869, though it remained unfinished at his death, and whose chamber music and symphonic works, even if thematically weak, are richly polyphonic; and Rimsky-Korsakov (1844–1908), who completed Musorgsky's operas and wrote such brilliant orchestral pieces as *Scheherezade* and *Sadko* and the opera *The Snow Maiden*. Standing outside Balakirev's group and one of Anton Rubinstein's pupils was the most famous of Russian composers, P. I. Tchaikovsky (1840–1893), whose first major work was his overture to *Romeo and Juliet* of 1870.

In painting such names as Perov, Kramskoy and Vereshchagin became famous during this period, though the most important place must be assigned to Repin (1844–1930); however, the Victorian earnestness of the Russian realistic school of painting makes it seem far more dated and unadventurous than the literature and the music of the time. More exciting was the scientific research, chiefly the work being done in the sphere of mathematics, physics, chemistry and biology, by such scholars as Chebyshyov, Stoletov and Mendeleyev (1843–1907), the last of whom achieved world fame with his *Fundamentals of Chemistry* (1869). In biology particular mention should be made of Sechyonov (1829–1905) who, with his pioneer work on brain reflexes in 1863, laid the foundation for the experimental work of Pavlov.

During the first ten years or so after the Crimean War, Russia's relations with her European neighbours were peaceable, if not amicable. Gorchakov, Russian Minister of Foreign Affairs for practically the whole of Alexander II's reign, favoured closer relations with France, but the hostility in St Petersburg towards Great Britain and Austria served, on the one hand, to prevent really friendly ties with France, owing to the French alliance with Britain, and, on the other, to strengthen Russian relations with Prussia. Bismarck, Prussian ambassador to St Petersburg from 1859 to 1862, played a considerable part in this process, and relations between Russia and France and Great Britain were not improved by Anglo-French verbal support for the Poles in their revolt of 1863. The subsequent unification of Germany caused certain apprehensions in Russia during the 1860s, but Russian troops were not committed at any stage during the unification process. The attention of Russia, militarily speaking, was drawn eastwards, to the colonisation of huge areas in the region of the Caspian, Central Asia and the Far East. Shamil, the militant leader of the Caucasian hill tribes, was captured in 1859; and by the middle of the 1860s Russian colonial expansion was extending beyond the Caspian into the khanates of Central Asia. Alma-Ata, Turkestan and Chimkent, towns to the east and north of the Central Asian area, were already in Russian hands by 1864. In 1865 Tashkent was stormed and captured by troops under General Chernyayev. In 1868 the khanate of Bokhara was subdued with the capture of Samarkand; simultaneously the khanate of Kokand became a Russian protectorate. By the mid-1870s Khiva had suffered the same fate, while Kokand itself, after an unsuccessful revolt which was brutally suppressed, became the Fergana Valley region of Russia. In the Far East, under the active leadership of Muravyov-Amursk, Governor-General of

Eastern Siberia, Russian colonisation had extended to Nikolayevsk by 1850, Sakhalin by 1852 and Khabarovsk by 1854. The occupation of Sakhalin first brought Russia into contact with Japan, but of more immediate importance was the infringement of Chinese sovereignty which such colonisation involved. After several local treaties, the Treaty of Peking of 1860 finally regularised the position of the Russians on the Pacific seaboard by recognising Russian sovereignty and granting trading rights. Vladivostok was founded in the same year.

Earlier in the century Russian expansion into the mainland of North America had taken the form of trading colonies run by the Russian-American Company. When the American Civil War ended, discussions on the transference of these trading colonies resulted in the American decision to buy Alaska from Russia for the sum of 7,200,000 dollars. The transaction was completed in 1867. In the light of twentieth-century events, it may appear to be one of the most important purchases ever made.

The Seventies

A CURTAIN-RAISER to all the events of the "seventies" was the Franco-Prussian War of 1870–1871. For the Russian government it provided an admirable opportunity to renounce, both *de jure* and *de facto*, the Black Sea clauses of the Treaty of Paris (1856) which denied Russia the right to station naval vessels in the Black Sea. The Western Powers and Turkey agreed to this change in a treaty signed in London in 1871. But for the Russian intelligentsia the Franco-Prussian War had a different meaning. It tended to prove what the intelligentsia had always liked to feel: that Europe was rotten, undermined by capitalism and imperialistic jingoism, and that Russia should therefore adopt a specifically Russian, or at least non-European, course in the future. This renewed concern for Russia's future led to a deepening of the rift between the intelligentsia and the government. Two policies—one unofficial, the other semi-official—dominated Russia in the period 1871–1881 : Populism and Panslavism. Both proved to be unworkable and both ended in pointless bloodshed.

The theories upon which Populism was based had been formulated by Herzen, Chernyshevsky, Bakunin, Tkachyov and Lavrov (to name only the most important "founders" of this movement) during the two preceding decades. In other words, by the beginning of the 1870s Popuism united many different strands of thought and feeling among the intelligentsia. The unity of purpose which brought so many disparate elements together was founded on the idea that the future of Russia lay with the peasantry. But such unity of purpose contained within it many different points of view about the precise future role of the peasantry. Some thought of them as the only revolutionary force capable of over-throwing the autocracy for the purpose of creating anarchism, federal-ism or peasant socialism, thus avoiding a capitalist phase in Russia; others wished to "repent" before the peasantry (the so-called "repentant noblemen"), to "simplify" themselves or "purify" themselves through physical labour. Certainly, it is true to say that whether under the in-fluence of Mikhaylovsky (1842–1904), whose theory of progress and "subjective" method of sociology laid such stress upon maintaining the freedom and integrity of the individual, or under the influence of the ideal of moral purity upheld in the Populist circle organised by N. V. Chaykovsky, the Populists of the "seventies" were guided, very largely, by a fervent desire to immolate themselves upon the altar of the people's freedom and thus to regenerate Russian society in the name of truth, justice and love. So great was the moral fervour of the younger intelli-gentsia for the idea of helping the peasantry to achieve freedom, so intense their mystical reverence for the suffering and travail of the people, that they tended to renounce political ends in favour of apolitical means, to enlighten rather than incite, to influence by example rather than in-flame by leadership. These features characterised the "going to the people" which occurred in the summer of 1874.

The movement was, it seems, spontaneous. Dressed in peasant clothes and carrying socialist tracts, about 3,000 young members of the intelligentsia, mostly students, left the universities and urban centres in order to live and work among the peasants. They hoped to tell the peasants the "truth"—that the Emancipation had not given them real freedom, that the land belonged to them alone and should be re-distributed among them, that all men were equal. The lack of organisa-tion among the Populists and the mistrust with which the peasants greeted their overtures had inevitable consequences. The government, seriously alarmed at the proportions of the movement, began to make arrests, in many cases assisted by the peasants themselves. In the end, 770 Populists were arrested and many remained in prison until 1877. Though there were other, smaller, movements "into the people" in 1875 and later, the failure of the first large-scale movement of 1874 showed the majority of the intelligentsia that it was a mistake to abandon conspiratorial methods in the struggle against Tsarism. But the failure of 1874 showed that the peasants were not the dry tinder of revolution which Bakunin, for instance, had represented them as being; on the contrary, they were conservative, intensely resentful of strangers and petty-bourgeois, rather than communistic, by instinct.

Economic changes in the post-Emancipation epoch were beginning to have a marked effect upon rural Russia by the 1870s. The building of railways was one very important new development. If at the time of the Crimean War Russia had only 1,000 *versts* of railway, then by the end of the 1870s the railway network had increased over twenty times, linking Moscow with Warsaw and Nizhny-Novgorod, with Vologda in the north and Sevastopol in the south. Yet the most significant feature of this development was the provision, especially during the 1870s, of rail links between the grain-producing areas of southern Russia and ports in the Baltic and Black Sea. This had the effect of leading to a rapid increase in grain exports. The area of ploughland in the black-earth belt increased by a third during the same period. The socio-economic effects of these changes were being felt among the peasantry, and there were signs of the emergence of a rich middle-class of peasant proprietors and a village proletariat. Such manifestations of capitalism in the countryside, however, have tended to be unduly exaggerated in Soviet research on the subject. It has to be borne in mind that by 1881, when redemption was made compulsory, approximately 14 per cent of the peasantry were still "temporarily obligated" to the landowners. Moreover, even though each peasant household might possess, on average, about thirty-five and a half acres by the late 1870s, the area of land still possessed by the nobility had not decreased as sharply as might have been expected. Peasant ignorance, the widespread use of the three-field system of cultivation which left one-third of the land fallow, the restricting effects of communal proprietorship (particularly in the repartitional communes), burdensome taxation, rent and redemption payments all served to delay or slow down the growth of agriculture. Increasing population pressure and consequent land hunger also contributed to the stagnation in the countryside. Despite this, the peasants could not be regarded either as the servile masses which they had been formerly or the budding socialists which the Populists hoped they would become in the immediate future. The peasants were simply nursing their age-old dream of being able to own land in the face of economic changes which were gradually forcing many of them to offer their labour for hire either as a village or an urban proletariat.

The Emancipation Act helped to create a class of "landless" peasants, particularly from among house serfs or those on "beggars' allotments". These and other former rural dwellers gravitated towards the factories, causing an increase in factory workers and mine workers of approximately one and a half times their number between 1865 and 1879. Behind the apparent modesty of this advance a very important process was occurring: the change-over from small-scale industrial enterprises employing under 500 workers to large-scale industrial plants employing more than 1,000. Unskilled labour, however, was cheap, in abundant supply and easily exploited, with the result that wages were low, hours of work long (seldom less than twelve hours a day) and working conditions appalling. Extensive use was made of female and child labour. So far as production was concerned, the most notable increases occurred in the textile and sugar industries, though progress was by no means at even rate. Industrial growth as a whole was accompanied by a succession of crises, the most important occurring in 1867 and 1873. The growth of heavy industry was slow, one indication of this being the slow rate of increase in Russian pig-iron production. Coal production in the Donbass began to increase rapidly after the building of railways, and there was a similar increase in Baku oil production, but these were simply the modest beginnings of an industrialisation process which was only to gather momentum in the last two decades of the century. Among the pioneers in this process mention should be made of the Welshman, John Hughes, who started the new metallurgical centre in the Donbass in 1869 and was later granted extensive mining concessions and loans by the Russian government. It was clear, then, that Russia was beginning to experience the first phases of capitalist development during the 1870s, but the political implications of this change were not as yet readily apparent.

The intelligentsia could hardly be blamed in these circumstances for remaining true to their Populist beliefs. Russia was a peasant nation and agriculture dominated the country's economy. Admittedly, with the growth of an industrial proletariat, isolated attempts were made to form unions of workers. A Southern Union of Workers, founded in 1875, was quickly destroyed by the police. Though a similar Northern Union was formed in 1878 and remained in existence until 1880, the decision of one of its founders, Khalturin, to engage in acts of terrorism tends to suggest that workers' political organisations were at this time little more than flashes in the pan of revolutionary discontent. The revolutionary movement among the intelligentsia had become centred in a new "revolutionary party", the second "Land and Freedom", which began its existence with a large demonstration outside the Kazan Cathedral in St Petersburg in December 1876. Plekhanov, later to found Russian Social Democracy, made his first public speech on this occasion. Having learned its lesson from the failure of 1874, "Land and Freedom" organised itself primarily as a secret society which, in the late 1870s, published its own paper and established settlements in several provincial areas in order to learn the peasants' needs at first hand and to disseminate Populist propaganda. Such methods had very limited success. The old controversy, which had been present in Ishutin's student group during the 1860s, between the advocates of propaganda and the advocates of terrorism, revived even more bitterly. But in 1877–1878 the Russo-Turkish War momentarily distracted the public's attention from domestic affairs.

Panslavism, which had a considerable influence upon Russian motives in the Russo-Turkish War, united a belief in Russia's role as unifier and liberator of the Slav peoples with hatred for Turkey as the arch-enemy of Orthodox Christendom. The most prominent adherents of Panslavism were members of the nobility, former Slavophils such as Ivan Aksakov or such publicists as Fadeyev and Danilevsky, and their views found particular favour with Ignatyev, Russian ambassador to Constantinople from 1864 to 1877. Slavonic Committees for the promotion of cultural, educational and religious exchanges between Russia and the Slav peoples had been formed in Moscow in 1858 and St Petersburg in 1867, though they did not begin to attract widespread popular support until the mid-1870s. The trouble with Panslavism was that it attempted to combine many contradictory features. Although there was in Panslav messianism an assumption of the superiority of Eastern Orthodoxy, such a view could clearly not be shared by the Poles or other non-Orthodox Slavs; similarly, the Panslav doctrine that Russia was destined to be the cultural and political leader of Slavdom not only aroused resentment among Slavs whose cultural attainments were clearly superior to Russian attainment in the same field, but was scarcely likely to appeal to Slav nationalist leaders who sought independence for their countries, not another kind of political dependence under the Russian autocracy. It was impossible to deny, for instance, that the Poles were Slavs, yet from whom were they to be liberated if not from the Panslav Russians?

In April 1877 Russia declared war on Turkey in support of the Serbian revolt against Turkish sovereignty. This so-called "war of liberation" was inspired by Russian hopes of freeing the Orthodox Slavs in Serbia, Bulgaria, Bosnia and Herzegovina, of regaining the areas of Bessarabia which had been lost as a consequence of the Crimean War and of reinforcing Russia's hold over Turkey. Agreement with Austria-Hungary ensured that Russia would have a free hand in the Balkans, while the Turks hoped that Britain, ever suspicious of Russian activities in the area of the Straits, would come to their aid. But the Turks, in their arrogant rejection of the terms for settling the Balkan problem agreed between the six major powers (Great Britain, Russia, Austria-Hungary, Germany, France and Italy), overplayed their hand and precipitated hostilities with Russia.

Although poorly equipped and not yet properly reorganised after the military reforms of 1874, the Russian armies were initially successful both in the Danubian area and in the Caucasus. However, after three disastrously unsuccessful assaults upon the Turkish fortress of Plevna, the Russian march on Constantinople was halted. From September until December 1877 Plevna was besieged. When it finally surrendered the Russians undertook a remarkable winter campaign which carried them beyond Adrianople to within a short distance of Constantinople itself. Turkey sued for peace and was obliged to sign the humiliating Treaty of San Stefano in February 1878, the terms of which, negotiated by Ignatyev, provided for the creation of a much enlarged autonomous Bulgaria. The implications of this treaty were not lost upon the Western Powers, especially Great Britain, who saw in the Russian victory a serious threat to the balance of power in the Eastern Mediterranean. War between Great Britain and Russia was averted by the Congress of Berlin, which Bismarck reluctantly convened in June 1878. By the terms of the resultant Treaty of Berlin, Russia regained the parts of Bessarabia lost in 1856, also Kars and Batumi in the Caucasus, but Bulgaria was divided into a relatively small autonomous principality of Bulgaria in the north and a new province of Eastern Rumelia in the south, under Turkish control. The diplomacy of Disraeli, by now Lord Beaconsfield, seemed to have seized the fruits of a victory won by the Russians at great cost in dead and wounded and to have left the messianic dreams of the Panslavists in ruins. Equally important, the Russian economy had been subjected to great strain and Russia's international prestige had not been noticeably enhanced.

Although Panslavism had proved to be a myth and the earlier idealism of Populism had had to be abandoned, this does not alter the fact that their influence had for a time been very strong. The literature of the "seventies" reflected this influence in all its major works, particularly in the novels of Dostoyevsky, Tolstoy and Turgenev. Dostoyevsky's *The Possessed* (1871), a novel of black comedy about the nihilists, is also an anatomy of Russia in which the three choices facing the Russian intelligentsia at the beginning of the "seventies"—atheistic socialism, Orthodoxy and Populism—are represented as choices between belief and non-belief, the ideal of Russia as a nation with a specific Christian mission or Russia possessed by the demon of European rationalism, of the God-man or the man-God. Tolstoy's interpretation of the dilemma facing Russia is also founded on a contrast between reason and faith. His *Anna Karenina* (1877) shows not only how Anna is forced tragically and inevitably into suicide by a society which denies her happiness and by her own inability to perceive the moral law which she has violated, but it also illustrates, in the story of Levin, how faith and perfectibility are to be attained through the discovery that life cannot be lived on reason alone. This great novel, more compact, topical and balanced than *War and Peace*, is equalled only by Dostoyevsky's last novel, *The Brothers Karamazov* (1878). Here, the three Karamazov brothers implicated in the murder of their father—Dmitry, Ivan and Alyosha—represent respectively three aspects of contemporary Russia: the undisciplined, licentious but "natural", unsophisticated Russia of the present; the Russia penetrated by atheistic, Western concepts of freewill, socialism and man as Superman or man-God; the Russia imbued with Christian charity towards all sinners, destined to build the Kingdom of Heaven on earth in a spirit of wisdom and humility. Dostoyevsky conceived his novels as Tragedies, fusions of the detective-story and mystery-play, in which man's earthly acts are invested with a transcendent and incalculable significance and his search for redemption becomes his search for God. Tolstoy's novels, more closely related to reality, are projections of his own search for a means of reconciling his Rousseauism with the immoral nature of contemporary society. For him, man's redemption is to be sought in social terms, his belief in God is to be a means of reconciling himself with the society about him. Both Tolstoy and Dostoyevsky were concerned to investigate God's ways to man on this earth and in this life; they were not concerned with eschatological solutions. In this respect, they reflected the desire of the Populists to achieve a moral regeneration of Russian society.

Virgin Soil (1877) was a deliberate attempt to depict the activities of the Populists in the Russian countryside, but Turgenev's lukewarm attitude to the Populist movement gave his novel an anti-revolutionary bias which was detrimental to the validity of the characters. One of the finest expressions of Populist sentiment in the literature of the period was Nekrasov's long poem *Who in Russia Lives Well*, which remained incomplete at the time of his death in 1878. Other notable works of the period were Leskov's *Cathedral Folk*, a picture of the life of the provincial clergy, and Saltykov-Shchedrin's study of the decay of a noble family after the Emancipation in his powerful but intensely pessimistic novel, *The Golovlyov Family*. In general, however, the 1870s are to be regarded as the end of the Golden Age of Russian literature. Dostoyevsky was to die in 1881, Turgenev in 1883 and Tolstoy was to abandon literature in favour of his religious philosophy. There were no contemporary writers of comparable stature to take their place.

The Russian intelligentsia may have been inclined to adopt a holier-than-thou attitude towards Europe at the time of the Franco-Prussian War. By the end of the "seventies" the Russian intelligentsia itself had blood on its hands. In 1877 those Populists who had been arrested in connection with attempts to "go to the people" in 1874 and later were brought to trial. Two large show trials—the trials of 50 and 197, so called owing to the number of the accused—were staged by the authorities, but such was public feeling at the time that the government's attempt to make an example of the young Populist detainees seriously misfired. The judicial proceedings resulted in mass acquittals and the imposition of only a few, relatively light, sentences. On the day after the trial of 197 ended, in January 1878, a young noblewoman of revolutionary convictions, Vera Zasulich, walked into the office of General Trepov, Governor of St Petersburg, and wounded him with a shot fired at point-blank range. It transpired that she had committed this act in retaliation for the brutal flogging administered to a student called Bogolyubov on Trepov's orders. She was later tried and, to the surprise and consternation of the authorities, acquitted, after which she succeeded in escaping abroad. Vera Zasulich's shot initiated a new phase of the Populist movement.

"Land and Freedom" proceeded to split into two parts, one forming the Black Partition group who hoped to promote the aims of socialism by propaganda, the other evolving into the party of the "People's Will" which comprised a group of terrorists acting under the orders of an Executive Committee. Yet even before "The People's Will" was formed, there had been acts of terrorism in the south of Russia. There had also been an attempt on the Tsar's life in the spring of 1879. The immediate reaction of the government was to increase the activities of the secret police and to appoint governor-generals in several of the largest cities empowered to govern virtually by military law. The answer of the revolutionaries was to strike at the centre of the governmental system itself, at the Tsar, for it was felt that this would be the most likely means of sparking the peasantry and the nation as a whole into revolt. After "The People's Will" was officially formed in June 1879, its members proceeded to make elaborate plans for attempts upon the Tsar's life. The story of Zhelyabov's, Sofya Perovskaya's and Khalturin's work in dynamiting railways and planting explosives in the Winter Palace is one of fanatical self-sacrifice. For a time, in 1880, it certainly seemed that the activities of the awesome Executive Committee of "The People's Will" were forcing the government to acknowledge the need for some kind of constitutionalism. On March 1st 1881, however, while the Tsar was driving along the road beside the Catherine Canal in St Petersburg, the second of two bombs flung by "throwers" of "The People's Will" succeeded in mortally wounding him. His death was the final success of "The People's Will" and the final act of the Populism of the "seventies". On the morning of his assassination the Tsar had signed a document prepared by Loris-Melikov, the new Minister of Internal Affairs, which envisaged the establishment of commissions of representatives from the *zemstva* and the large towns; these were to be the preparatory steps towards the granting of a constitution, or so it was thought at the time. Nothing came of Loris-Melikov's proposals. Also, within ten days of the assassination, all the prominent members of "The People's Will" had fallen into police hands, later either to be hanged or sent into exile. The end of the "seventies" was the end of what came to be known as the "epoch of great endeavours", but there was ultimately very little to show for all the sacrifice and all the bloodshed.

Chapter IV

1881 – 1905

The Reign of Alexander III

DURING the nineteenth century the Russian autocracy subsisted on the doctrine of unripe time : time was never ripe for change. Even the reforms of Alexander II's reign were undertaken with reluctance. Under Alexander III the autocracy found time ripe only for whittling down the reformative measures of the previous reign and for curbing the process of modernisation which had been inaugurated after the Crimean War. Alexander III, the last true autocrat of the Romanov dynasty, believed that patriotism should be equated with conservatism. Born in 1845, he was a man of upright character and strong will. Though taught by the eminent historian, Solovyov, to understand Russian history, he learned respect chiefly for the autocratic principle and took little account of public opinion. Before his accession to the throne in 1881 he had been a determined proselyte of Panslavist doctrines. After his accession his interest in such ideas cooled, largely due to the anti-Russian and anti-autocratic sentiments of the Balkan Slavs. He was much influenced in his political thinking by such extreme conservatives as Pobedonostsev, the Chief Procurator of the Holy Synod, and Katkov, the editor of *The Moscow Chronicle*. In short, his reign was notable for three things : a considerable measure of reaction in domestic policies, a momentous shift in foreign policy away from alliance with Germany towards alignment with France, and fairly rapid industrial expansion.*

The assassination of Alexander II and the accession of the new Tsar brought to an end Loris-Melikov's "dictatorship of the heart". During Loris-Melikov's brief period of high office, from February 1880 to March 1881, the notorious Third Section was abolished and its duties transferred to the Police Department of the Ministry of Internal Affairs; attempts were made to win over liberal opinion, especially in the *zemstva*; and proposals were framed for what was thought to be a constitution. When these latter proposals were discussed in March 1881, the new Tsar, under the influence of Pobedonostsev, decided to put them aside. Loris-Melikov resigned, to be replaced as Minister of Internal Affairs by Ignatyev, former ambassador to Constantinople and the originator of the Treaty of San Stefano. One of his first acts was the promulgation of a statute in August 1881 which gave far-reaching

* Economic developments will be summarised in the next section.

powers of preliminary arrest, trial by administrative process or military court and the right to impose severe fines both to the Ministry of Internal Affairs and to all levels of the administration in any area where a state of emergency might be declared. Ostensibly enacted for a temporary period of three years, this draconian statute became in practice a piece of permanent legislation until 1917. Later in 1881 some slightly more liberal measures were introduced. Redemption, for instance, was made compulsory for all "temporarily obligated" peasants and redemption payments were reduced by one rouble on each peasant allotment. In 1882 the *per capita* poll tax was abolished with effect from the beginning of 1887; 1882 also saw the creation of a Peasant Bank through which peasants could obtain loans at an annual 6·5 per cent interest rate for the purchase of land, though during the reign of Alexander III the purchases made through this bank accounted for less than a third of the total land bought by the peasantry. Meanwhile, government efforts to suppress sedition became more sinister. In many parts of Russia the police, taking a leaf out of the terrorists' book, provoked anti-Jewish pogroms. Support for such acts was officially condoned on the grounds that there had been Jewish participation in the assassination of Alexander II. Official consent was also given to a secret anti-revolutionary organisation called the *Sacred Company* which attempted to infilrate revolutionary organisations and to publish pseudo-revolutionary tracts as a means of undermining revolutionary propaganda. Ignatyev's final and most dramatic measure was the summoning of two commissions of "experienced men" to advise on peasant legislation; but this was simply a preliminary measure intended to lead to the summoning of a *zemsky sobor* or conclave of representatives from the whole of Russia. So shocked was Pobedonostsev by Ignatyev's curious proposal that he persuaded the Tsar to dismiss his new Minister of Internal Affairs. His place was taken, in May 1882, by the extremely reactionary former Minister of Education, Dmitry Tolstoy—"a quiet little man," as a British journalist reported, "middle-aged, with colourless, parchment face, like so many Russians, the result, largely, of living always in hot, dry rooms". Indeed, the legislation introduced by Tolstoy—and the whole of Alexander III's reign—had the closed atmosphere of a hot, dry room into which neither fresh air nor the sounds of the outside world were permitted to enter.

After the coronation of Alexander III in 1883 the tone for the future was set. Revolutionary sedition having been eradicated through improved police methods, the government was no longer prepared to flirt with liberalism, even fanciful liberalism on the Ignatyev pattern, but was determined to rely on the conservative loyalties of the nobility. One of Tolstoy's earliest measures as Minister of Internal Affairs had been to introduce new "temporary rules" for the press (August 1882) which obliged all publications which had received three official warnings to submit to preliminary censorship on the eve of publication. In 1884 the most famous radical journal, *Annals of the Fatherland*, was suppressed. University autonomy was abolished in the same year : all appointments to senior university posts were made by the Ministry of Education, the power of the inspectors was increased and all student societies were prohibited. In 1885 a first important step was taken towards enhancing the prestige of the nobility with the creation of a Nobles' Bank which offered substantial loans at a favourable 4·5 per cent interest rate in an effort to abate the increasing indebtedness of the landowners. The powers of the judiciary, already curtailed by Ignatyev's statute of 1881, were further modified in 1885 by increasing the Minister of Justice's disciplinary authority over judges; other legislation empowered the Minister of Justice to conduct closed hearings if the dignity of the state was involved, increased the property qualification for jury service, prescribed trial without jury for offences against state officials and virtually prohibited Jews from holding posts in the legal profession. In 1886 peasants who violated their work agreements with the landowners could be arrested and tried as criminals; similarly, in an attempt to retain the patriarchal character of the peasant household, the division of peasant property was made conditional upon the agreement of the head of the household and a two-thirds majority in the commune assembly.

These encroachments upon peasant independence were followed in 1887 by more discriminatory legislation in the sphere of education. Admission to Gymnasiums was seriously curtailed for children of poor parents, or "cooks' children" as they were called in official parlance; university entrance was made more discriminatory; fees at both Gymnasium and university level were increased (at university level from ten roubles to fifty roubles annually) and Jews were only to be admitted to establishments of higher education on a quota basis (10 per cent of intake within the Pale*, 5 per cent outside and 3 per cent in Moscow and St Petersburg). Higher education for women suffered a setback with the closure of the only medical school for women in 1882 and the suspension of all university courses in 1886, though these were renewed in a limited form at St Petersburg University in 1889. One of the most pernicious aspects of all this legislation was its anti-Semitic bias. Apart from the instances already mentioned, Jews were not permitted to move from their place of residence, to engage in the sale of spirits or to buy,

* The area of the Pale was not properly defined. It consisted of south-western Russian and the Ukraine.

rent or manage estates, or to take work in local or municipal government. It is hardly surprising in view of these and many other administrative restrictions that Jews should later come to be among the most prominent and bitter opponents of Tsarism.

Reactionary legislation was intensified in the late 1880s and early 1890s. In a serious attempt to restore the pre-1861 authority of the nobility over the peasantry, a law of 1889 provided for the appointment of Land Captains by the Minister of Internal Affairs. Land Captains were to be chosen from members of the hereditary nobility and were empowered to wield both administrative and judicial authority over the peasant regional divisions. It was in their power to choose the peasant elders, supervise membership of their courts and the activities of the commune assemblies, impose fines up to five roubles, order arrests of up to seven days, and in general to have control over the lives of the peasants. The Land Captains also took over the functions of the justices of the peace (a post which was abolished); they were answerable to a regional assembly composed of the local marshal of nobility and other Land Captains, above which was a provincial body presided over by the provincial Governor. In the final resort, they were subject only to the control of the Minister of Internal Affairs; and in certain cases their power was absolute. In this way, even such modest independence as had been granted to the peasantry by the Emancipation Act was reduced and the power of the state apparatus at rural level correspondingly strengthened. The peasants' freedom was further limited in 1893 by laws which prohibited a peasant from withdrawing from the commune without the consent of a two-thirds majority in the commune assembly, forbade the mortgaging of communal lands and prevented the sale of such land to anyone outside the commune; and by a law of 1894 no peasant could obtain a passport to leave his commune without the consent of the assembly or, if he were under age, the head of his household.

In 1890 and 1892 legislation was introduced modifying the autonomy of, respectively, the *zemstva* and the municipal governments. All members of *zemstva* boards became virtually government officials, subject to the Governor's approval, while both the Minister of Internal Affairs and the provincial Governor could exercise the power of veto over *zemstva* decisions and could punish board members. More significantly, peasant representatives on the *zemstva* were to be appointed by the Governor from lists submitted by the peasant electors, which ensured a decrease in peasant representation, and only landowners were allowed to be chairmen of *zemstva* boards. If this guaranteed a predominance of the nobility in local government, then in municipal government a predominance was ensured to property-owners, the representation of tradespeople and businessmen being either eliminated or drastically curtailed.

A similar reactionary course was pursued in the sphere of religion and among the subject nationalities of the Russian Empire. Religious discrimination was practised against Roman Catholicism in Poland and Protestantism in the Baltic provinces; there was also serious persecution of such non-Orthodox sects as the Skoptsy, Stundists and Dukhobors. Russification, affecting all areas of social and cultural life, was promoted relentlessly in Poland, to a lesser extent in Finland and among the Bashkirs, but everywhere in the subject territories the dominant policy was that of Greater Russian nationalism.

In this period of administrative reaction and political obscurantism the prevailing atmosphere among the intelligentsia was one of despondency. The literature reflected it most clearly in the work of Garshin (1855–1888) and Chekhov (1860–1904). Garshin's miniaturist works, whether in allegorical form or in the luminous intensity of such short stories as *Red Flower* (1883), reflected not only his own hypersensitivity but the morbid despair of the whole generation of the "eighties". Chekhov, through his medical training, had a more objective, diagnostician's view of the comedy and melancholy of Russian life. His early, comic stories were designed primarily to entertain, but with such longer works of the late 1880s as *Steppe* and *A Dull Story* he developed the special "Chekhovian" quality of evoking mood and atmosphere which was to inform all his later work. The ephemeral nature of life and human experience, the melancholy that is both comic and tragic, the lyricism and the realism blended in Chekhov's stories of the 1890s—particularly in *The Wife, Ward No. 6, The Teacher of Literature, Three Years, The House with the Attic, My Life* and *Peasants*—to offer pictures of different aspects of life in what has been called "the epoch of small endeavours", meaning the period of reaction after the assassination of Alexander II when work in the *zemstva* or the pursuit of such ideals as Tolstoyanism were the only outlets for the intelligentsia. Tolstoy himself, after his conversion to Christianity described in his *Confession* (1882), preached throughout the remaining years of the century his own brand of Christian philosophy based on the doctrine of "non-opposition to evil by violence" and the morally regenerating effect of physical labour. His literary work was limited to stories illustrating his philosophical precepts, the most famous of which were *The Death of Ivan Ilyich* (1886) and *The Kreutzer Sonata* (1889), though mention should also be made of his largest, if not his most successful, work of this period, *Resurrection* (1899), which was written in order to help the Dukhobors to escape from Tsarist persecution. Otherwise during the 1880s the literary scene was remarkable only for the modest beginnings of a poetic revival which was to lead, in a decade or so, to Russian Symbolism. Although Russian poetry since the death of Lermontov had been dominated by the civic poetry of Nekrasov, the lyrical tradition had not been extinguished completely. Tyutchev (1803–1873) had written philosophical and nature lyrics of great beauty; minor poets such as Maykov, Polonsky, Alexey Tolstoy and Fet had also kept the spirit of poetry alive; and in the "eighties" the deeply pessimistic, though courageous, poetry of Nadson (1862–1887) was in vogue. By the end of Alexander III's reign a harsher and more forceful note had been sounded in Russian literature with the arrival of Maxim Gorky (1868–1936), born in Nizhny-Novgorod (which has since been named after him), whose first work, the semi-Romantic tale of the gipsy *Makar Chudra*, appeared in a Tiflis journal in 1892.

Apart from Tolstoyanism, the most important philosophical influence of the period was the work of Vladimir Solovyov (1853–1900), the son of the historian. His *Lectures on Godmanhood* (1878) and his *La Russie et l'église universelle* (1889) expounded his views on the need to reintegrate philosophy and Christian belief. He was fascinated by the idea of a universal church and by mankind redeemed through the divine Logos or "Sophia". A prophet and visionary, who claimed that he had encountered his Eternal Feminine on three occasions (once, somewhat surprisingly, in the British Museum), he was a man of profound aesthetic sensibility, whose mysticism and asceticism were to influence some aspects of the later Symbolist movement. But the greatest contribution to the cultural life of Russia at this time was made by the composer, P. I. Tchaikovsky. His ballet music for *Swan Lake* (1876), *The Sleeping Beauty* (1889) and *Nutcracker Suite* (1892), his operatic works *Eugene Onegin* (1878) and *The Queen of Spades* (1890), along with his Piano Concerto and Violin Concerto, not to speak of many other brilliant orchestral pieces, gained him lasting popularity throughout the world. Moreover, Tchaikovsky was the only nineteenth-century Russian composer to achieve real success in the field of symphonic composition, the finest and certainly the best known example of which is his Sixth Symphony or *Pathétique* (1893), composed shortly before his death.

The *fin-de-siècle* melancholy which pervaded Russian literature and music during Alexander III's reign was heightened — if it was not exactly caused by — the prevailing reaction in domestic policies. There was a similar quietism in Russia's foreign relations. The Tsar was wise enough either to heed the counsel of caution offered by his Minister of Foreign Affairs, Giers, or to refuse to be provoked into embarking on costly foreign adventures. This was a wisdom no doubt dictated by expediency rather than considerations of statesmanship, but it was at least to have the effect of keeping intact the ramshackle edifice of Tsarism.

Russia's position as a European Power was consolidated in 1881 by a renewal of the *Dreikaiserbund* between Russia, Germany and Austria–Hungary which had been initiated in 1873. Apart from ensuring Russian neutrality in the event of a Franco–German war, the 1881 alliance encouraged the preservation of the *status quo* in the Balkans. Russian responsibilities in this sphere were confined to Bulgaria, but the Bulgarians, though "liberated" by the Russians as a consequence of the Russo–Turkish War, turned out to be prickly friends. Prince Alexander of Battenberg, who had been elected Prince of Bulgaria under the constitution granted to that country by Alexander II in 1879, soon found himself at loggerheads both with the constitution and with his Russian advisers. In May 1881 he succeeded in establishing himself as dictator. Had the conservative Bulgarians and the Russian army personnel upon which his dictatorship depended been able to work amicably together, his régime might have lasted longer. As it was, the Bulgarian members of the government soon resigned and in 1883 Prince Alexander was forced to restore the constitution. This was a serious blow to Russian prestige; it also caused intense hatred of Prince Alexander in St Petersburg. When, in 1885, Eastern Rumelia was suddenly annexed by Bulgaria, this precipitate act in violation of the Treaty of Berlin caused Russia to withdraw military support for Alexander. Despite this, the Bulgarian army succeeded in repulsing an attack by Serbia, but Russian influence in Bulgarian affairs had meantime practically ceased. With the abdication of Prince Alexander in 1886 and the election of Prince Ferdinand of Saxe-Coburg in his place, Bulgaria passed for a time out of the Russian sphere of influence.

In 1885 Russia and Great Britain came within a hair's breadth of war over the Russian threat to Afghanistan. After a month or so of crisis, it was agreed that the work of the Anglo–Russian border commission, set up in 1884, should be resumed. An important factor in this crisis had been Bismarck's insistence that the Straits should be closed in the event of hostilities between Russia and Great Britain. The Russian reaction, though favourable towards Germany at the time, was complicated by the failure of Russian policy in Bulgaria, which under Prince Ferdinand had begun to draw closer to Austria–Hungary. Renewal of the *Dreikaiserbund* including Austria–Hungary seemed, from the point of view of St Petersburg, to be unwarrantable. Consequently, in June 1887, a secret re-insurance treaty was signed with Germany which recognised Russian interests in Bulgaria and guaranteed the "benevolent neutrality" of Germany if Russia had to defend the entrance to the Black Sea.

Although this new treaty was stipulated to remain in force for three years, both Russian and German public opinion were becoming hostile to the idea of alliance between the two countries. With the accession of Kaiser Wilhelm II to the German throne in June 1888 and the resignation of Bismarck two years later, the Russo–German alliance, so long a feature of European power politics, was allowed to lapse by mutual consent. Russia now looked to France. Assisted by closer economic relations, French loans and military assistance, absolutist Russia and democratic France began to find, however paradoxically, a basis for joint action in face of the German threat. The first steps were taken in 1891 after the visit of a French fleet to Kronstadt. By a secret military agreement of the following year it was decided that in the event of mobilisation by the Triple Alliance (of Germany, Austria–Hungary and Italy) French and Russian armies would mobilise simultaneously and military action would be coordinated between the two general staffs. This agreement, eventually ratified in 1894, prepared the way for the alignment of Powers which was to precipitate the First World War twenty years later. It was to be the most momentous legacy of Alexander III's reign, for he died in October 1894, to be succeeded by the last of the Tsars. It was to be no less momentous, as it turned out, for the German Kaiser and the Habsburgs. The end of the era of European stability, founded on the balance between the Great Powers, was already in sight.

Economics and Politics

THE economic changes which occurred in Russia during the last two decades of the nineteenth century were more effective in changing the nature of the opposition to Tsarism than in changing Tsarism itself. The politics, therefore, which will be discussed in this section, were not the politics of Tsarism so much as the politics of the opposition.

In 1860 the Russian Empire, excluding Finland, had approximately 74,000,000 inhabitants; by 1900 this figure had increased to 133,000,000, partly as a result of the annexation of territories in Central Asia and the Caucasus but chiefly through a remarkable increase in the birth-rate. According to Lenin's calculations based on the census of 1897, the peasant population at that time numbered about 97,000,000. Though no detailed statistics are available, it is clear that peasant society had become stratified into the rich *kulaks*, who had substantial land holdings, and a mass of poorer peasantry who either worked on inadequate allotments or hired themselves out for work on the holdings of the *kulaks* and the nobility. Of the land sold by the nobility between 1877 and 1905 approximately a third was bought by the *kulaks*, a third by poorer peasants and a third by town dwellers or various kinds of cooperative society. Yet such a redistribution of the land had little effect upon the widespread poverty and stagnation in the countryside, even though it was upon agricultural production that Russia depended almost exclusively for exports. The fall in world grain prices, which began in the 1870s and continued until the mid-90s, seriously depressed rural living standards. Although Russian grain exports increased in volume by nearly 70 per cent between 1880 and 1897, the monetary value of such exports increased little. The peasants, forced to produce more for less money, were obliged to eat less and had less purchasing power for the products of industry. It is not perhaps without significance, as a mark of the physical deterioration, that in 1899–1901 more than a fifth of all youths called for military service were found temporarily or permanently unfit. The annual death-rate for European Russia at the beginning of this century was 31·2 per thousand (as against 19·6 in France and 16 in Great Britain).* The famine of 1891–1892 which affected practically the whole black-earth area brought death and untold suffering to millions of peasants. The government on this occasion, unable to do anything for itself, reluctantly permitted *zemstva* organisations to help with famine relief. Moreover, the burden of taxation fell more heavily upon the peasantry than upon the wealthier classes. *Zemstva* rates were twice as high for peasant land as they were for the land of the nobility, and although the peasants only paid half as much in direct taxation as did the wealthier classes, even this half constituted a heavy burden, added to which was the more diffuse but nonetheless heavy weight of indirect taxation, amounting in 1897 to 452,000,000 roubles or considerably more than a third of total government revenue. Such depressed living conditions in European Russia gave rise to large-scale migrations to Siberia and the Far East, which in the late 1890s achieved an annual average of more than 100,000. The government took some hesitant steps to ameliorate conditions for the peasantry by reducing interest rates on loans from the Peasant Bank in 1894 and by extending the period for redemption payments in 1896, but the real problem of peasant poverty remained untouched.

The number of workers employed in the manufacturing and mining industries and on the railways in European Russia rose from approxi-

---

* "The statistics on the death-rate in the villages—what empty things they are, unless one remembers a certain village near Tambov, a certain house with broken windows and rotted thatch, and the sound of wailing that went on all night." Robinson, *Rural Russia under the old Regime*, New York, 1949, 117.

mately 1,189,000 in 1879 to 2,208,000 in 1903, though if the rest of the territory of the Russian Empire is included this latter figure might well be in the region of 2,800,000. The reason for this increase is to be traced chiefly to the influx of share capital from the West, particularly from France and Belgium. This process was encouraged by the protectionist tariff of 1891, the advantageous interest rates offered by the Russian government to foreign investors and the unusually enlightened policies of a succession of Tsarist Ministers of Finances : Bunge (1881–1886), Vyshnegradsky (1887–1892) and, most remarkable of these, Witte (1892–1903). During the twenty years or so that these Ministers were in charge of Russian finances, government revenue increased two-and-a-half times, the national debt only by a third and in 1897, through a currency reform instituted by Witte, Russia adopted the Gold Standard. These measures encouraged industrial expansion, but a more practical inducement was the building of new railways. Among the most significant developments in this sphere was the government's policy of bringing the railways under state control—a course dictated by strategic and financial reasons. In 1881 more than 95 per cent of Russian railways were privately owned; by 1902 this figure had fallen to about 33 per cent. Apart from expanding the railway network in western Russia, the government promoted rail links between the Black Sea and the Caspian, into Central Asia, and in 1891 embarked on the building of the Trans-Siberian railway, though the rail loop round Lake Baykal was not completed until the Russo–Japanese War of 1904–1905. Probably the most important line to be built during the 1880s was the railway linking the Donbass with the iron-ore deposits at Krivoy Rog, and the most important piece of railway legislation was the law of 1885 which regularised tariffs for the carriage of freight and passengers on privately-owned lines.

For the greater part of the 1880s industrial expansion developed at a fairly slow rate, but certain branches of heavy industry advanced much more rapidly. Coal production in the Donbass more than doubled between 1880 and 1892, as did the production of ferrous metal, while oil production increased more than fourteen times. By 1900 Russia had become the fourth largest metal-producer in the world, having overtaken France and being surpassed only by Germany, Great Britain and the United States. Oil production more than doubled by 1900, and for a short time Russia was the world's leading oil-producing nation. The manufacture of machinery increased correspondingly, especially locomotives and rolling-stock, and there was a significant increase in the output of the simpler kinds of agricultural machinery. The manufacture and consumption of consumer goods made less striking increases. In general it can be said that the total output of industry during the boom years 1893–1900 almost doubled.

The boom was followed by a depression in 1900–1903. The industries hardest hit were those which supplied rails and equipment to the railways, for railway building declined sharply. Many firms went bankrupt, factories were closed and about 30 per cent of the labour force was put out of work.

Throughout this period there had been a tendency for industries to unite in large industrial complexes, which was accompanied by the creation of monopolies tending to eliminate competition and to keep prices at an artificially high level. Such, for instance, was the *Prodameta* monopoly formed in 1902 which eventually controlled about 75 per cent of total Russian pig-iron production, 78 per cent of sheet-metal production and just under half the production of rails. Similar monopolies grew up in the production of pipes, nails, cement, sugar, Donbass coal and rolling-stock. It is not very surprising, therefore, that about 50 per cent of the entire labour force should be concentrated in these large industrial complexes, giving rise to the existence of an hereditary proletariat which was both closely-knit and freed from most former connections with the land. The majority of these workers were, of course, employed in light industries, such as textile manufacture (in which the labour force was 40 per cent women), or in food production—industries, in other words, which were usually close to the large urban centres of population and which contributed in no small part to the doubling of the urban population in European Russia during the latter half of the nineteenth century. It was here, not in the country-side, that revolution was to begin.

Soviet scholarship lays much emphasis on the increasing frequency of strikes and industrial disputes during this period, but just as much emphasis has to be laid on the fact that only a small minority of such strikes were due to political agitation. Workers came out on strike very largely as a result of insufferable working and living conditions, inadequate wages, irregular payment of wages, the imposition of heavy fines and other "economic" grievances. The most serious and organised of such strikes during the 1880s was the Morozov strike of 1885, which caused widespread interest, especially as it had to be suppressed by the army, and elicited indignant protests from many quarters at the inhuman treatment to which the strikers had been subjected. Industrial unrest of this kind obliged the government to introduce factory legislation. A Factory Act of 1882 prohibited the employment of children under twelve and limited the working day of children between twelve and fifteen to eight hours. A further law in 1885 forbade the employment of women and juveniles under seventeen on night work, initially in textile mills and later in other industries; but this prohibition was lifted in 1890. These could hardly be regarded as momentous pieces of legislation. More important was a law of 1886 which laid down rules for work contracts, stipulated that wages should be paid at least monthly and in money, not in kind, and introduced into the management of industry a certain measure of advisory control by the government through factory boards; but it also imposed heavy fines for strikes and made refusal to work punishable by arrest. Needless to say, trade union organisations were strictly forbidden. A further advance in factory legislation occurred in 1897 when laws were passed imposing a maximum eleven-and-a-half-hour working day and a ten-hour maximum for night work, though factory-owners were not automatically penalised for violating these limits; and in 1903 a law obliged employers to pay compensation for accident injuries, while another law made provision for the election of factory "elders" who were given very limited representative powers. Industrialists tended in the main to resent such legislation, which, however, fell short of the legitimate demands of the workers, and the government factory inspectors were for the most part too few in number to ensure that it was universally enforced.

During the period 1881–1905 Marxist Social Democracy began to replace Populism as the revolutionary opposition to Tsarism. Its beginnings were modest and its voice sounded only very faintly in the stagnant Russia of the 1880s. The first consistent and fully committed exponent of Marxism was Plekhanov (1856–1918). When "Land and Freedom" split in 1879 into the terrorist organisation of "The People's Will" and the propaganda group "Black Partition", Plekhanov became the acknowledged leader of the latter group. At the beginning of 1880 he was forced to flee abroad in order to escape police persecution. He took up residence in Geneva, where his earlier peasant socialism soon yielded to an interest in Marxism. In 1882 he translated the *Communist Manifesto* into Russian and in the following year organised the first Russian Marxist group, Liberation of Labour, for the dissemination of Marxist literature. His chief collaborators were Vera Zasulich and Akselrod, but Plekhanov himself was the group's leading polemicist.

In his first political pamphlet, *Socialism and the Political Struggle* (1883), Plekhanov attacked the Populists, particularly the Bakuninist wing, for assuming that socialism was incompatible with politics. He also attacked "The People's Will" for having damaged the Populist movement by resorting to terrorism without being able to justify such activities with a doctrine, certainly not with the doctrine of scientific socialism. The Populist notions that Marxism was not applicable to Russia because it was based on Western European developments and that Marx was more concerned with economics than with politics were refuted by pointing out that, in Marx's view, all class struggle was political struggle. The economic liberation of the working class could only be achieved through political struggle, and yet this struggle was not to be conducted by a group of political conspirators but by the working class itself. The task of the Social Democrats was therefore to make the proletariat aware of their political role as the *avant-garde* in the struggle against capitalism. But capitalism was a bulwark of Tsarist absolutism; the social, economic and political aims of the proletariat were only to be achieved through the overthrow of Tsarism, during which process the proletariat would become a politically conscious and organised revolutionary force.

Plekhanov's second pamphlet, *Our Disagreements* (1884), was an elaboration and clarification of his first attack upon Populism. He criticised the views of certain Populist economists who underestimated the significance of capitalist developments in Russia and believed that Russia could still achieve socialism through the peasant commune. Plekhanov was able to demonstrate that capitalism had taken root not only in the industrial centres but also in the countryside. With the growth of capitalism and the emergence of an industrial proletariat, the Communist struggle would become centred not in the increasingly petty-bourgeois rural commune but in the industrial areas. Social Democrats should welcome the decay of the rural commune and actively engage in propaganda and organisational work among the industrial workers, thereby inculcating into the working class an awareness of its political task. At the same time, the Social Democrats in Russia should set about organising themselves into a Workers' Socialist Party.

To many intellectuals in Russia during the 1880s Plekhanov's talk of Social Democracy, capitalism and an industrial proletariat seemed either premature or wholly unreal. Gorky, for instance, in the third part of his autobiographical trilogy, *My Universities*, describes the heated controversies which Plekhanov's *Our Disagreements* aroused in a revolutionary group at Kazan in 1887. Yet Plekhanov could declare quite confidently at the International Socialist Congress in Paris in July 1889:

"The task of our revolutionary intellectuals . . . amounts, in the opinion of the Russian Social Democrats, to the following: they must master the views of modern scientific socialism, spread them among the workers and, with the help of the workers, take by assault the citadel of autocracy. The revolutionary movement in Russia can triumph only as the revolutionary movement of the workers. There is not, and cannot be, any other way out for us. . ."

This declaration, his earlier pamphlets and his most important "legal" publication *In Defence of Materialism*, which was published in Russia late in 1894 under the pseudonym Beltov and a clumsy title, *Concerning the Question of the Development of a Monistic View of History*, designed to avert the suspicions of the censorship, served to educate a whole generation of Russian Marxists. Several small Marxist groups sprang up in Russia during the 1880s, chief among which were the Blagoyev group founded in 1883, which succeeded in organising political groups among St Petersburg workers, the Tochissky group of 1888 and the larger "Social-Democratic Commonwealth" organised by Brusnev in 1889. But these did not constitute a Social-Democratic Party; it was left to Lenin to become the organising genius of the workers' movement.

Vladimir Ilyich Ulyanov, later to be known as Lenin, was born in Simbirsk (now renamed Ulyanovsk) in April 1870. Until 1887 his life was lived calmly in this undistinguished provincial backwater on the Volga.* His family was respectable and respected; thoughts of revolution, it seems, were not even entertained, let alone countenanced, by his father, the school inspector, who in 1873 became a recognised member of the bureaucratic nobility, which entitled his children to attend the local Gymnasium. By a curious coincidence, the headmaster of the Gymnasium was named Kerensky, father of Alexander Kerensky, born ten years later than Lenin though destined to pass out of history at the moment that Lenin assumed power. Lenin proved to be an exemplary pupil and finished his Gymnasium course by obtaining a gold medal. But in 1887 his elder brother, Alexander, then a student at St Petersburg University, was arrested for attempting to assassinate the Tsar and hanged. The Ulyanovs were ostracised by Simbirsk society, even by those of ostensibly liberal views; perhaps it was at this time that Lenin acquired the distrust of liberals which remained with him for the rest of his life. In the autumn of 1887 he entered the law faculty of Kazan University, but was expelled after student disorders in December of that year and exiled to a distant village outside Kazan. Though permitted to resume his studies in 1890, he was not permitted to re-enter a

---

* Though undistinguished as a township, Simbirsk could lay claim to fame as the birthplace of both Karamzin and Goncharov. It is worth noting, as one of the ironies of Lenin's story, that his native heritage combined the monarchist sympathies of Russia's first major historian with that epitome of Russian inertia which is commonly known as "Oblomovism", the decayed romantic ideal of a decaying nobility.

university and sat the external examination for a diploma in law while living in Samara, in 1891. During his stay in Samara he became a convinced Marxist; it may also have been at this time that he became acquainted with conspiratorial techniques of the members of "The People's Will", several of whom were in exile in Samara at that period. Certainly, for Lenin, Marxism and conspiratorial organisation were to become practically synonymous. After practising for a short while as a lawyer, he moved to St Petersburg in 1893 and at once began to participate actively in a Marxist group. His first pamphlet, an attack on the Populists, appeared in 1894. In the spring of 1895 he went abroad to visit Plekhanov in Geneva, in the hope of arranging closer liaison between the Liberation of Labour group and the Marxists in St Petersburg, but was dismayed to find Plekhanov advocating the view that the working class should look for allies among the liberals. Upon his return to the Russian capital he and Martov became the leaders of a new Marxist organisation called The Union of Struggle for the Liberation of the Working Class which conducted agitational work among strikers at several St Petersburg factories during the autumn of 1895. Attempts to organise a workers' paper ended, as did The Union of Struggle itself, when Lenin and his associates were arrested. Lenin was subsequently sent into administrative exile in Siberia, from which he did not return until 1900. During his exile he married Krupskaya, wrote among other things his famous economic study, *The Development of Capitalism in Russia*, and became convinced of the need for strict organisational discipline in the working-class movement.

Lenin had not succeeded before his exile in organising a specific Social-Democratic party, but his activities had set in motion unifying processes which were to lead, in March 1898, to the first congress of an All-Russian Social-Democratic Workers' Party at Minsk. The congress was organised by Pyotr Struve, who composed the Party manifesto, but it was attended by only nine delegates who were all shortly afterwards arrested. Moreover, in the absence of an active leadership, the Social-Democratic movement quickly fell under the influence of "economists" who believed that it was not the duty of Social Democracy to engage in a political struggle with Tsarism but simply to assist the workers in their spontaneous or elemental "economic" struggle against capitalism. The newspaper *Workers' Thought* became the mouthpiece in this new trend in Social-Democratic thinking, known as Economism. Lenin disagreed violently with this revisionist tendency. When he was permitted to return from his Siberian exile in 1900, he at once took the opportunity of emigrating abroad to join up with Plekhanov, Akselrod and Vera Zasulich. Largely as a result of his determined organisational work a new Social-

Democratic paper The *Spark* (*Iskra*) was launched in opposition to the emigré Economist paper *Workers' Cause*. Broadly speaking, Lenin's aim was now to attack Economism, assemble as many *Iskra*-supporters as possible for a new Social-Democratic Party congress and organise a highly disciplined, conspiratorial, monolithic party, directed from an emigré centre abroad.

A recital of the salient facts in Lenin's story cannot really give a picture of this extraordinary man's character. Lenin was a professional revolutionary. His writing, his organisational ability, his tactical prowess, his strength as an orator, his capacity for intrigue, his singlemindedness in pursuit of clearly defined ends were all integral parts of Lenin, the revolutionary. In addition, it required a cold anger, a chill and detached view of humanity, not compromised by notions of fair play or a sentimental attitude toward "friends", and a strength of mind made cynically realistic by defeat and contemptuous by success, in order to achieve revolution in Tsarist Russia. Lenin possessed this anger, coldness and strength of mind to a degree which had no precedent among the earlier Marxists or the Social Democrats of his own generation.

His first trial of strength as a leader of the Russian Social-Democratic movement came in 1903 at the time of the second congress of the All-Russian Social-Democratic Workers' Party, held in Brussels and London. Before the congress, in 1902, he had made clear his own position in the important pamphlet *What is to be Done?* (named after Chernyshevsky's novel). Here Lenin attacked Economism as "wagging the tail" of the working-class movement, whereas the real role of Social Democracy was to act as the vanguard of the working class in the struggle against capitalism. For this reason two things were essential, in Lenin's view : centralised control and ideological homogeneity. A working-class organisation which was not centrally controlled would soon be broken up by the Tsarist police, and the working class itself, if left to its own devices, would soon be dominated by bourgeois liberalism. "Give us an organisation of revolutionaries," said Lenin, "and we will overturn the whole of Russia." When the second congress assembled in Brussels in July 1903, Russia was in the grip of a strike-wave after three years of industrial depression. Another opposition party, the Socialist Revolutionary Party, or SRs, was already in existence. Its programme combined an agrarian socialism on Populist lines with terroristic activities modelled on the methods of "The People's Will". The liberals in the *zemstva* had not been inactive during this period. Shipov, a leading liberal, had organised a congress of *zemstva* chairmen in 1896. Professional elements in the *zemstva* administrations, known as "the third element", had begun to organise congresses, and by 1901 their discussions had become concerned primarily with political issues. In 1902 Struve, having abandoned Marxism for left-wing liberalism, began to edit a liberal journal *Liberation* in Stuttgart, where in the following year a Union of Liberation was formed by a group of liberals and socialists. Thus it was clear that Social Democracy had serious rivals among other opponents of Tsarism and it had become all the more urgent for the Social Democrats to combine forces, agree on Party aims and determine what future action should be taken.

Lenin had taken great care to ensure that a majority of the fifty-seven delegates who assembled in Brussels were his supporters. Not all the delegates had votes, but those who did steam-rollered through item after item of the agenda which Lenin had prepared, until the time came to vote on the first paragraph of the Party statutes which defined Party membership. By this time Lenin's arrogant tactics and the fact that the Belgian authorities had forced the congress delegates to move from Brussels to London were beginning to tell. Lenin insisted that Party membership should be conditional on "personal participation" in one of the Party organisations; Martov, hitherto Lenin's most ardent supporter, wanted this to be emended to read "regular personal cooperation under the direction of one of the Party organisations". The issue at stake was a choice between a close-knit, centrally directed organisation of professional revolutionaries and a broad-based Party with many loosely affiliated members. When put to the vote, Lenin's draft was defeated by twenty-eight votes to twenty-three, Martov having voted against him. Such a defeat represented a frontal challenge not only to Lenin's leadership of the congress, but also to the Party as he conceived that it should be organised. In order to recover his prestige in the congress he now made a brilliant tactical move. Though Lenin was assured of a solid bloc of twenty-three or twenty-four votes, Martov had been supported by delegates of the Jewish Bund (the Jewish Social-Democratic organisation) and by the Economists of the *Workers' Cause*. When the question of the autonomy of the Jewish Bund was put to the vote, it was defeated by a majority of the congress delegates and the representatives of the Bund naturally walked out; similarly, when *Iskra* was recognised as the Party organ, the representatives of *Workers' Cause* followed suit. Martov's majority had now been reduced by seven votes. In all the subsequent voting Lenin could always command a majority of at least three votes. He exploited this tactical advantage brilliantly by calling his supporters Bolsheviks ("those in the majority"), while his opponents had to be content with the title of Mensheviks ("those in the minority"). The split between Bolsheviks and Mensheviks was never satisfactorily healed, though it was patched up for a time at later congresses. In fact, this split meant that at the very outset the All-Russian Social-Democratic Party became divided into two organisations of Bolsheviks and Mensheviks, which often engaged in separate activities and frequently indulged in mutual recrimination. More often than not the Mensheviks were in the actual majority at Party congresses, in the Workers' Soviets and in other Social-Democratic organisations. Nevertheless, Lenin had ensured that they would be branded with the psychologically and politically inhibiting title of "those in the minority". At the historic second Party Congress of 1903 Lenin and his Bolsheviks achieved an ascendancy in the Social-Democratic movement which—if history can be said to have portents—portended the eventual seizure of power by Lenin and the Bolsheviks in 1917.

The Turn of the Century

WHATEVER may be the role of determinism in history, Lenin and the Bolsheviks would not have seized power with such ease had the last Tsar, Nicholas II, not been so brainless, incompetent and insipid. History is nothing if not personalities. Nicholas II's personality was not dominated by the need to rule, as was Lenin's by the need to achieve revolution; it was dominated by his German-born and English-educated wife, Princess Alice of Hesse, or "Alix" as she was affectionately known, whom Nicholas married in November 1894 shortly after his accession to the throne and with whom he led an exceptionally happy married life. Her love of the autocratic principle, her passionate espousal of Orthodoxy and her reliance upon such religious charlatans as Rasputin were all manifestations of her essentially unbalanced character, which shunned contact with "them", meaning chiefly the opposition elements in the Duma, though it could also mean anyone outside the tight circle of sycophantic mediocrities with whom she surrounded herself at court. One gains the impression that the last Tsar was a mediocre amateur, whose continual answer to the professional political standards demanded of him by life was : "If only I could be allowed to be an autocrat"; but an autocrat by profession cannot afford to remain a political amateur.

Born in 1868, Nicholas received the usual wide-ranging education and military posts accorded to the heir to the Russian throne. No amount of preparation, however, could have made much difference to the fatal combination of spinelessness and charm of which he was composed. As it was, he ascended the throne largely unprepared, possessed of no administrative experience and almost entirely ignorant of affairs of state. According to his diary, which he wrote up with meticulous care, he enjoyed outdoor games, the sport of shooting, paddling in a canoe; he was fond of reading in the evenings, though what he read is not detailed; he adored his family; and he was always careful to note the state of the weather. As for politics, to judge from his diary they seem to have occupied a scarcely more prominent place in his life than would the doings of menials in the life of a nineteenth-century English milord: they were beneath him and he was more or less indifferent to them. Such insensitive, callous, well-meaning, healthy, ignorant and charming people are usually the most despicable authoritarians. Let us leave it to Trotsky to pass the most ruthless judgment on this weak man who was the last of the Tsars: "This 'charmer', without will, without aim, without imagination, was more awful than all the tyrants of ancient and modern history."

Nicholas II was reputed to be a fatalist. Certainly, his reign began inauspiciously. A stampede at his coronation in May 1896 resulted in the death of about 1,300 people with many more injured. Otherwise the first half-dozen or so years of his reign were fairly quiet on the surface. Beneath the surface, accompanied by strikes, student disorders and sporadic peasant uprisings, a wave of political activity was developing which was to culminate in the revolution of 1905. In the main, the government's answer to such "sedition" was temporising and underhand. Apart from summarily arresting and exiling strike leaders, the authorities took the strange step of organising official trade unions. These were the brain-child of Zubatov, head of the Moscow security police, who hoped that they would act as political lightning-conductors, and in the era of what was known as *Zubatovshchina* so-called trade union organisations sprang up in many industrial centres. At first they attracted a widespread following, until the dimensions of the movement began to alarm the government. In 1903 Zubatov was sacked. The movement quickly collapsed, leaving the workers more than ever disillusioned and all the more ready to listen to revolutionary agitators. Police provocations and the use of spies alienated public opinion, discredited the régime and ensured that the revolutionaries strengthened their organisations and redoubled their vigilance. In the early 1900s the "combat organisation" of the Socialist Revolutionary Party succeeded in carrying out a number of "executions". In April 1902 the Minister of Internal Affairs, Sipyagin, was assassinated; his successor, Pleve, suffered a similar fate in 1904 and Grand Duke Sergey in February

1905. These later terrorists acts had been engineered by Azev who, it later transpired, was both police-agent and terrorist.

Stated quite simply, the government of Nicholas II pursued the same reactionary policy in domestic affairs as had been pursued in the previous reign. The hopes entertained by the *zemstva* liberals of some form of constitutionalism were dashed at Nicholas's accession. By 1903, with the introduction of a regulation which prohibited *zemstva* revenues from increasing by more than 3 per cent annually, it seemed that the government was intent upon abolishing the autonomy of local government. The peasant problem, though considered at length by a number of government committees, was only tackled in earnest by a conference sponsored by Witte which gathered information about conditions in the countryside. A salutary feature of these activities was the widely expressed opinion that the communal system should be abolished. However, the commune was declared to be "inviolable" in an imperial proclamation of 1903. In 1904 a law was passed prohibiting the regional courts from ordering corporal punishment. The *status quo* was being maintained in domestic affairs, but only just.

Culturally, Russia at the turn of the century was dominated by innovations in the theatre, by Symbolism, a review known as *The World of Art* and the work of Maxim Gorky. The state monopoly of the theatres in Moscow and St Petersburg had been abolished by decree in 1882. This permitted the organising of private theatres, the most famous of which was to be the Moscow Arts Theatre, founded in 1897–1898 under the direction of Stanislavsky (1863–1938) and Nemirovich-Danchenko (1859–1943). Chekhov's plays—*The Seagull* (1896), *Uncle Vanya* (1899), *Three Sisters* (1901) and *The Cherry Orchard* (1904)—were all given their first successful productions by the Moscow Arts Theatre under Stanislavsky and in each case their dependence upon atmosphere and their abrogation of dramatic action met Stanislavsky's wish to create a theatre without stars, of equal excellence in all its parts. For all their static quality Chekhov's plays, and Stanislavsky's productions of them, were earthquakes which have since shaken apart former theatrical conventions; they were also pre-echoes of the coming revolutionary earthquake which was to destroy forever the world of small endeavours to which Chekhov's characters belong. Chekhov himself died in 1904. "I have not drunk champagne for a long time" were his last words; there is no need to underline their prophetic and wistful irony.

Symbolism in literature was energetically promoted at the turn of the century by Valery Bryusov (1873–1924), whose *Russian Symbolists* (1894) was a dishonest, though bold, attempt to prove that a school of Russian Symbolism existed. Later he acquired a deservedly high reputation as a poet and a man of wide erudition. Accompanying the Symbolist movement there was a revival of literary criticism, the most remarkable examples of which were Rozanov's *The Legend of the Grand Inquisitor* (1890) and Merezhkovsky's *Tolstoy and Dostoyevsky* (1901), though both these writers had axes to grind in the sphere of religion which gave them reputations as *savants* – now, alas, rather tarnished by time. The most outstanding figures in Russian Symbolism were Alexander Blok (1880–1921), whose mysterious, melodious and fragile lyrics to his Beautiful Lady appeared in 1904, and Andrey Bely (1880–1934) who first became known for his prose *Symphonies*, elaborate, semi-serious orchestrations of words. In prose literature at this period mention should be made of Korolenko (1853–1921), whose studies of Siberian life (*Makar's Dream*, 1885) and stories describing, in poetic and humorous terms, the lives of the poor made him popular as a "radical" writer.

The World of Art was a review organised by Serge Diaghilev (1872–1929) in 1898 to encourage interest in art. It quickly became the centre of an aesthetic revival, promoted exhibitions of paintings, encouraged the rediscovery of both European and Russian traditions of art in protest against the academic staleness of much nineteenth-century realism and therefore had the effect of making Russian painters and public aware of contemporary movements. It was through this review that impressionism became popular in Russia. With it were associated such notable artists as Levitan, Serov, Grabar and Vrubel and such scenic designers as Benois and Bakst; from it sprang such remarkable and original painters as Larionov, Marc Chagall and Kandinsky.

The work of Maxim Gorky stands in opposition to the "art for art's sake" attitude represented by Symbolism, the aestheticism of *The World of Art* and the *fin-de-siècle* world of Chekhov. Throughout the 1890s he wrote short stories, first published in collected form in 1898, which gave an increasingly realistic picture of Russian petty-bourgeois provincial life. His heroes of this period were mostly drawn from among the *bosyaki* or those "bare-foot ones" who had left the villages in search of work on the railways or in the factories, shipyards and workshops. The fact that such *bosyaki* were not tainted by bourgeois acquisitiveness made them superior to, and freer than, their petty-bourgeois surroundings. Yet Gorky was searching for some concrete image of revolution which would correspond to his belief that literature itself should have a revolutionary purpose. The *bosyaki* proved to be less revolutionary than he had supposed; similarly, his studies of recalcitrant members of bourgeois society in his first novel *Foma Gordeyev* (1898) and his first play *Meshchane* (1902) served only to reveal the ineffectual character of bourgeois and liberal ideology. His greatest play, *The Lower Depths* (1903), a picture of destitutes at the bottom of society, opposed the idea of man as a creature continually in need of some comforting illusion to the idea of man liberated by truth and capable of remaking the world. Gorky had early been influenced by Marxism; he was an active supporter of the Bolsheviks and was arrested on several occasions. His allegiance to Marxism is expressed most openly in his most revolutionary work, the novel *Mother* (1907), which laid the basis of what has since come to be known as Socialist Realism—reason enough, it seems, for Western tastes to reject the book as no more than a political pamphlet. But Gorky was greater than his politics. His work has vigour, breadth and power of a kind which far surpasses anything done by his contemporaries. Although he found his concrete image of revolution in the proletarian mother and son of his novel, Gorky himself probably best represents that spirit of revolutionary change which emerged in Russia at the turn of the century.

In foreign affairs Russian attentions were directed towards the Far East. By the end of the nineteenth century China had become the playground of the Great Powers. Apart from the concessions made to Great Britain, France and Germany, the Sino–Japanese War of 1894–1895 had also obliged China to recognise the independence of Korea and to cede to Japan the Liaotung peninsula with Port Arthur, though after protests from Russia, France and Germany these ceded territories were later handed back. Russia stepped in at this point to aid the defeated Chinese and received in return the concession to build a Chinese Eastern Railway across Manchuria from Chita to Vladivostok. Russian expansion in northern China had now brought her into direct contact with Japanese interests in Korea. In 1898 this process was accelerated by the Chinese decision to grant Russia a twenty-five-year lease to the Liaotung peninsula, including Port Arthur and Dairen, and a concession to build a Southern Manchurian Railway linking Kharbin with these ports. Japan at once demanded that her rights in Korea should be respected in return for Japanese recognition of Manchuria as a Russian sphere of influence, but the Russian government would not agree to this. The Boxer Rising of 1900 gave the Russians the chance to strengthen their hold over Manchuria. In 1902, however, the Japanese alliance with Great Britain was a setback to Russian plans for expansion in the region of northern Korea. Nicholas II, urged on both by the unscrupulous adventurer Bezobrazov and Kaiser Wilhelm II, continued to have designs on Korea, although for a time he was willing to countenance a more moderate policy which involved an evacuation of Russian troops from Manchuria in three stages. The evacuation was halted after the first stage by a renewal of the Russo–Japanese conflict over their respective interests. Russian obduracy and foolhardiness, on the one hand, Japanese sense of hurt and aggressiveness, aided by the knowledge that she had the support of Great Britain on the other, turned a rather academic controversy into an excuse for war.

The Japanese seized the initiative at once by a surprise attack upon the Russian naval vessels in Port Arthur on the night of February 8th–9th (NS) 1904. The Russians, ill-prepared for war, were never able to recover from this initial shock. Port Arthur was besieged by the Japanese and extensive fighting broke out in Manchuria. In August 1904, after heavy fighting, the Russians were forced to retreat to a position south of Mukden. A big offensive mounted against the Japanese in September failed to break the Japanese lines and, after the surrender of Port Arthur in December, two enormous Japanese and Russian armies (each numbering more than 300,000 men) became locked in combat outside Mukden, which finally fell into Japanese hands in February 1905. Meanwhile, in order to replace the Russian Far Eastern fleet, which had not only suffered at the outset of the war but had been rendered more or less useless in attempting to break out of Port Arthur in August 1904, a hastily re-equipped Baltic fleet had been despatched to the Pacific. One peculiar feature of this disastrous episode in Russian naval history was the mistaken Russian belief that British fishing vessels sighted in the North Sea were Japanese torpedo boats. The sinking of one of the British vessels almost precipitated a war between the two countries. When, in May 1905, the Russian fleet eventually reached the coast of China it was engaged in the Straits of Tsushima by a Japanese fleet under Admiral Togo and virtually wiped out. So ended major operations in the Russo–Japanese War, which had been a series of disasters for Russia from start to finish; so ended, also, Russian expansion in China.

By the Treaty of Portsmouth, New Hampshire, negotiated by Witte, and signed on September 5th (NS) 1905, the territories leased by China to Russia—the Liaotung peninsula, Dairen and Port Arthur—and the railway concession in southern Manchuria were handed over to Japan. Korea was recognised as a Japanese protectorate and northern Manchuria remained a Russian sphere of influence. The only seriously disputed territorial concession was the island of Sakhalin, which was eventually divided between the two Powers.

The Tsarist government's main aim in embarking on such a "little war" with Japan had been to distract public attention from the revolutionary situation that was brewing in European Russia. The disastrous outcome of the Far East campaign had precisely the opposite effect: it exacerbated the existing tensions and laid bare all the flaws both in the government's prosecution of the war and in the Tsarist administration. By the time the Treaty of Portsmouth was signed, Russia was seething with revolution.

CHAPTER V

1905 — 1917

The Revolution of 1905–1907

THE appointment of Prince Svyatopolk-Mirsky as Minister of Internal Affairs in place of the reactionary Pleve, assassinated in July 1904, gave promise of a more liberal régime. But the disastrous reverses suffered in the Russo–Japanese War had, by the autumn of 1904, already led to considerable restiveness among the peasantry, who objected to recruitment for the army and began to default in large numbers. At the beginning of 1905 the Putilov works in St Petersburg came out on strike. A petition giving expression to the workers' grievances was drawn up by the priest Gapon, who had been responsible for organising a police union among the factory workers. On January 9th 1905, a Sunday, Gapon led a demonstration of some 150,000 workers through St Petersburg with the object of presenting the petition to the Tsar. The authorities, forewarned of this demonstration, had taken care to ensure that it would be met with armed force. As the workers approached the Winter Palace (the Tsar was not in residence at the time), the troops opened fire, killing more than a thousand and wounding a further three thousand. This was "Bloody Sunday". It marked the beginning of the Revolution of 1905. In retrospect it may be said to have marked the end of Tsarist absolutism in Russia, for after such a savage dispersal of what was essentially a peaceable demonstration neither workers nor peasants were ever again to be duped into believing—as Gapon, it seems, had misguidedly believed—that the Tsar, the "little father", would be willing to listen to the complaints of his humble subjects. The image of a benevolent autocracy was irrevocably shattered by the events of "Bloody Sunday". The use of force against unarmed workers could only provoke them into using armed force against Tsarism. The revolutionary struggle had now taken a new turn: liberal hopes of moulding Tsarism to a more liberal pattern by peaceful means were in effect jeopardised, if not rendered totally invalid, by the government's recourse to mass murder; and Lenin's view that Tsarism had to be destroyed at all costs by a politically conscious, militant proletariat received a striking endorsement. The more bitter and protracted the revolutionary struggle, the greater the likelihood that Lenin's view would prevail; the easier the struggle, the greater the likelihood that liberal opinion would exert a dominant influence upon the administration and wring liberal concessions from the government. But the facts now seemed to prove that Svyatopolk-Mirsky's quasi-official liberalism was doomed to failure. The killing of the demonstrators on "Bloody Sunday" was to set in motion a terrible process of blood-letting that culminated in the civil war of 1918–1921.

Svyatopolk-Mirsky resigned. Trepov, the son of the General whom Vera Zasulich had attempted to assassinate in 1878, was appointed Governor-General of St Petersburg with dictatorial powers to suppress the general strike in the capital which was the workers' answer to the "Bloody Sunday" massacre. In this appointment the government showed its mailed fist; in the appointment of Bulygin as Minister of Internal Affairs and the Tsar's rescript of February 18th announcing the creation, under Bulygin's chairmanship, of a commission to prepare a law on a consultative State Duma a more liberal line was adopted. Meanwhile, a commission had been appointed under the senator Shidlovsky to hear the workers' grievances, but the workers' delegates walked out of the commission when their demands were rejected. Another commission under the Minister of Finances, Kokovtsov, was sabotaged by the employers, who refused to make any major concessions. Yet the wave of strikes continued unabated. Particularly serious, owing to the political demands made by the workers, were the strikes in Ivanovo-Voznesensk and Lodz, in Poland, both of which had to be suppressed by armed force. The situation grew graver still in June 1905 when a mutiny broke out on the battleship *Potyomkin*, then in Odessa harbour where a general strike was in progress. The mutiny ended when the crew sailed for Roumania and surrendered at Constanţa. Simultaneously peasant riots occurred in the central black-earth regions and Latvia.

With Tsarism in full retreat before the revolution the time was ripe for the revolutionary forces to state their case openly. The extreme left wing of the revolution was occupied by the Socialist Revolutionary Party, though it was not properly organised until its first congress in December 1905–January 1906. The Social Democrats were the most important left-wing force in the revolution. At the third congress of the All-Russian Social-Democratic Workers' Party, which Lenin and the Bolsheviks convened in London in April 1905, it was agreed that the situation demanded an alliance between the working class and the peasantry, the armed overthrow of the autocracy and the establishment of a provisional revolutionary government. The Mensheviks, who held a conference in Geneva, paid lip service to the idea of armed revolt, but believed that the working class should look for allies among the liberals in the struggle to achieve a bourgeois democratic régime; once bourgeois democracy had triumphed, then would be the time for the working class to come out in opposition to liberalism in order to bring about a socialist revolution. The Menshevik view was more orthodox in the Marxist sense than was Lenin's, but Lenin's view was more daring. He wished to forestall the bourgeois stage of the revolution and jump at once from autocracy to a dictatorship of the proletariat. Politically the central position in the revolutionary movement was occupied by the *zemstva* liberals and the professional intelligentsia who comprised "the third element". In May 1905 a congress in Moscow organised by the Union of Liberation combined these liberal and professional elements into a Union of Unions. By October this amalgamation had led to the founding of the Constitutional Democratic Party, or Kadets, under Struve and Milyukov. Its liberal platform made demands initially for the summoning of a Constituent Assembly, but it was prepared to work within the framework of the proposed Duma in order to make that body more effective as a constituent part of the legislature. Also supposedly of the revolutionary centre was the Peasant Union, founded in May 1905, but at its second congress in November demands were made for a Constituent Assembly and the transference of all land to national ownership. Its political aspirations were subsequently represented by the Socialist Revolutionary and Trudovik parties and proved to be unexpectedly radical. On the right wing of the revolution were the Octobrists, formed in October 1905, who united the right wing of the *zemstva* liberals with the business classes. More to the right was the Russian Monarchist Party and far to the right was the Union of the Russian People. This latter organisation combined loyalty to the Tsar with a refurbished version of Uvarov's triadic formula of Orthodoxy, autocracy and nationalism, the last item being a cover for anti-Semitic agitation which adumbrated some of the worst features of Nazism.

In August the Bulygin commission made known its proposals for a Duma. The franchise, however, was to be so limited, excluding most of the intelligentsia and all workers, and the Duma's powers were to be so restricted that the proposals found no support. There were immediate demands for a Constituent Assembly. Peasant uprisings began to occur in many parts of the Empire. In September strikes began in Moscow and led to serious street fighting. This was followed by a strike of railway workers, which quickly spread to St Petersburg and brought the Russian railway network almost to a standstill. By October 12th St Petersburg was in the grip of a general strike which included not only workers but the professional classes as well. The granting of autonomy to the universities, which had occurred in August, meant that they quickly became centres of revolutionary agitation. Still more important was the fact that on October 13th the St Petersburg Soviet of Workers' Deputies was formed and soon became almost the equivalent of a second seat of government. Under the chairmanship of the Menshevik, Khrustalev-Nosar, the Soviet put forward political demands; yet the firebrand of the Soviet was the young Jewish Social Democrat, Bronstein, better known as Trotsky, whose fiery, demagogic oratory stirred in the strikers a feeling of revolutionary working-class solidarity, though his lone voice was not sufficient to make the workers of St Petersburg take up arms against the government.

Faced by such solid opposition, the government back-pedalled still further and on October 17th the Tsar issued a manifesto granting freedom of the press, opinion, assembly and association and announcing that a legislative Duma would be elected on an indirect but much wider franchise than had been contemplated by the Bulygin proposals. A Council of Ministers was formed, roughly equivalent to the British cabinet, the presidency of which was entrusted to Count Witte, newly returned from America where he had been Russia's chief negotiator in framing the Treaty of Portsmouth.* Thus, on the face of it, Russia seemed about to become a constitutional monarchy, with a cabinet, a prime minister and an elective legislative assembly. To the liberals it seemed that the revolution had very largely achieved its object. The manifesto of October 17th inaugurated a period known as "The Days of Freedom" when moderate opinion was triumphant and extremist opinion made desperate efforts to reassert its influence.

Extremist elements of the right, supported by the Minister of Internal Affairs, Durnovo, organised "black hundreds", gangs of hooligans, criminals and other social dregs, who attacked revolutionaries and conducted ruthless and despicable pogroms against Jews in many parts of Russia. On the left wing, the new freedom enabled the Bolsheviks to come out in the open. At the beginning of November Lenin returned to Russia and at once advocated a continuation of the struggle. The legal Bolshevik organ *New Life*, which Lenin edited, called upon the workers to make an armed uprising against the autocracy. The St Petersburg Soviet preferred to call for a general strike in favour of an eight-hour working day. It soon became clear that a position of stalemate had been reached in the revolution. Moreover, although there were mutinies of sailors at Kronstadt and Vladivostok, a serious uprising of soldiers and sailors at Sevastopol, led by a Lieutenant Schmidt, and further rebellions among garrison troops in Kiev, Kharkov, Turkestan, Azerbaydzhan, Irkutsk, Rostov-on-Don and Moscow, the government under Count Witte was beginning to reassert its authority and on November 27th

* Witte was created Count in recognition of his services as negotiator at the Russo-Japanese peace talks.

arrested Khrustalev-Nosar, chairman of the St Petersburg Soviet. At the beginning of December the Soviet itself was dispersed. The revolution seemed to be petering out. However, throughout the Russian Empire, especially among the subject nationalities, the revolution had left its mark, whether by increased activity among the socialist parties or in the formation of liberal and nationalist parties which combined demands for social reform with calls for autonomy. Revolutionary activities were widespread in Poland, the Ukraine, among the Armenians and Georgians, the Moslems of Central Asia and even as far afield as Buryat-Mongolia and Yakutia. The most notable successes were enjoyed by the revolutionary movement in Finland, where the policy of Russification, pursued with energy previously, was abandoned and the Diet was re-modelled so as to permit an electoral system based on proportional representation and a considerable measure of universal suffrage, which included giving the vote to women. The final episode in the revolutionary year of 1905 was the Moscow uprising. After the suppression of the Bolshevik organ *New Life*, the Moscow Soviet of Workers' Deputies called for a general strike which, chiefly as a result of Bolshevik agitation, soon developed into an armed uprising of workers which lasted for almost a fortnight (December 8th–20th). The Semyonovsky regiment had to be called from St Petersburg to put down the insurrection in the Presnya district with artillery fire. At the cost of a thousand dead and great destruction to property the Moscow uprising was eventually quelled. It was the last desperate fling of the left wing and its failure marked the end of the revolution of 1905.

Nevertheless, the government had been forced to concede a constitution and certain important civil liberties. Trade unions could now be openly organised, though it is worth bearing in mind in this connection that the trade union movement in Russia tended to follow in the wake of the political organisations of the working class and it is not therefore so surprising that trade-unionism in Soviet Russia should always play second fiddle to the political leadership. Employers' organisations also came into existence. The press enjoyed in general more freedom than it had ever known. Expectations of a liberal-democratic future for Russia were not wholly without foundation, but with the noise of the revolution still in everyone's ears it was hardly likely that a humiliated autocracy would listen to sweet reason or that the newly formed political parties would at once assume the responsibilities of a mature opposition.

The electoral law for the Duma, worked out by Count Witte, envisaged indirect elections through electoral *curiae* or colleges based on social classes. Property-owners or tax-payers over twenty-five received the franchise, but women, the armed forces, landless peasants and students were excluded. Deputies to the Duma were chosen on the basis of 1 per 2,000 in the landowning colleges, 1 per 7,000 in the urban colleges, 1 per 30,000 in the peasant colleges and 1 per 90,000 in the workers' colleges. A very high proportion of the seats in the Duma were awarded to the peasants' deputies in the belief that they would comprise a conservative bloc. The State Council was made into an upper chamber, half of the members being appointed by the Tsar and half being elected by the *zemstva*, the nobility, the clergy, the Academy of Sciences, the universities, commercial interests and the Finnish Diet. According to the "fundamental laws" of April 1906 Russia was to remain an autocracy, with a Tsar empowered to appoint and dismiss ministers at will and to exercise a veto, but no legislation could be passed without endorsement by the State Council and the Duma. The Duma, however, had no power of veto and article 87 of the fundamental laws empowered the Tsar to introduce whatever legislation he wished when the Duma was not in session. By this means the Duma, upon which so much hope had rested, was rendered almost useless as a legislative body. Count Witte, the architect of this embryonic, though deformed, constitutional scheme and the only notable statesman of the period capable of putting it into effect, never enjoyed the Tsar's confidence. Having succeeded in raising a French loan of 2,250,000,000 francs in order to keep Russia afloat financially after the Russo-Japanese War and the internal disorders, he was forced to resign. His place as president of the Council of Ministers was taken by the aged and inept Goremykin; and Durnovo's place as Minister of Internal Affairs was taken by the able but ruthless administrator, Stolypin, who had acquired a certain notoriety for his suppression of peasant riots in the Saratov region.

The elections to the Duma, conducted in March and April 1906, were boycotted by the Socialist Revolutionaries and the Social Democrats. At the unificatory congress of the Social Democrats, held in Stockholm in April, Lenin continued to argue in favour of an armed uprising, but the revolutionary tide in Russia had already receded and it was the agrarian question which became the central point at issue. Earlier Lenin had thought that all the peasants required was the return of the land they lost as a result of the Emancipation of 1861 ; now he advocated nationalisation of the land. The Mensheviks proposed "municipalisation" of the land, i.e. the transference of landowners' holdings to self-governing municipalities from which the peasants could rent allotments. Lenin's advocacy not only of an armed uprising but of bank hold-ups as a means of obtaining party funds discredited him in the eyes of the congress delegates and the Mensheviks, who commanded a majority, were able to gain approval for their views.

In the event, the Duma elections gave a substantial majority to the Kadets (over 150 seats), with the Trudoviks representing the peasantry and working class (over 100 seats) occupying second place, and the right-wing parties, chiefly the Octobrists (17 seats), coming a poor third. Even though it might not be a real legislature, the Duma had become a forum of public opinion. The Social Democrats, Lenin especially, were quick to realise that they had been wrong to boycott this new institution.

A dignified ceremony in the Winter Palace on April 27th 1906 officially opened the Duma, but the radical complexion of the Duma's membership and the radical demands for expropriation of the land-owners' estates which the Duma addressed to the Tsar soon reduced the dignity of all concerned. The Tsar and the government attempted to remain aloof from the unruly democratic infant which they had allowed to occupy the Tauride Palace. Yet the Kadets were doing no more than asking for such legitimate rights as universal suffrage, parliamentary government and direct votes. To the government the Duma seemed to be a revolutionary tribunal. When Goremykin rejected all the Duma's demands, all chances of cooperation came to an end. Though efforts were made to invite certain moderate Kadets and Octobrists to partici-pate in the government, the Tsar decided that the only way out of the situation was to dissolve the Duma, to which effect a manifesto was issued on July 9th. Goremykin's place as president of the Council of Ministers was taken by Stolypin. So ended the first Duma, the first remotely democratic institution in the history of Russian government.

The immediate reaction of the Kadet and Trudovik deputies was to cross into Finland and issue an appeal to the Russian people urging non-cooperation with the government in recruitment for military service, payment of taxes and deposits in savings accounts—all to little effect, except that the instigators of the appeal were made ineligible for mem-bership of future Dumas. Stolypin retaliated by setting up military courts which could order the death sentence. They were designed to deal with peasant rioters and in the first six months of their existence ordered about 950 executions; but it should also be noted that the Socialist Revolutionaries undertook 1,500 terrorist "executions" during 1906 and many more in 1907. In August 1906 they also attempted to take Stolypin's life, but succeeded only in killing twenty-seven other persons who were in his house at the time. The anti-revolutionary Council of the United Nobility, formed in May 1906, was used by Stolypin as a means of nurturing pro-government feeling in the country at large. Indeed, the government actively participated, through the various right-wing parties, in the campaigning for the second Duma; the Socialist Revolutionaries and the Social Democrats also dropped their boycott.

Meanwhile, Stolypin introduced legislation on November 9th 1906 which radically reversed previous government policy on peasant land tenure. Earlier legislation had already halved, and then abolished, as from 1907, all redemption payments; the peasants had been very largely freed from the authority of the Land Captains, could obtain passports on the same terms as other citizens, could elect their own representatives to the *zemstva* without the sanction of the provincial Governor and were no longer collectively responsible for the payment of taxes. Now, by the November legislation, they were free to leave the communes. The arable land allotted to a peasant in a commune with repartitional tenure could now become that peasant's individual property; in a commune with hereditary tenure the hereditary holdings could become hereditary property. By such means Stolypin hoped to create, and to a certain extent succeeded in creating, a class of peasant landowners who were able to make their own farmsteads either on the English or American pattern (the so-called *khutor* which meant that the peasant had his farmhouse on his own enclosed farmlands) or on the so-called *otrub* system, which meant that the peasant lived in a settlement but worked enclosed stretches of arable land in the locality. Land organisation commissions were set up to conduct surveys and to consolidate the boundaries of peasant properties. Some measure of individual dignity was also given to the peasant proprietor by the abolition of joint family ownership.

The first Duma had shown that the Tsar's fond notion of the peasantry as loyal, conservative supporters of the régime was groundless. The second Duma, which opened on February 20th 1907, showed that the government's land laws, though more in keeping with peasant needs than any previous legislation, were unacceptable to the left-wing parties. Despite vigorous government campaigning and persecution of the opposition parties, especially the Kadets, the second Duma had an even more left-wing complexion than the first. Of the 516 deputies there were 104 Trudoviks, 65 Social Democrats and 37 Socialist Revolutionaries, while the number of Kadet deputies dropped to 98. The government, on the other hand, could rely on only 90 votes. The remainder of the deputies were either representatives of nationalities, who were concerned chiefly with autonomy, or those without any clear party affiliations. There was thus even less likelihood of this second Duma cooperating with the government; and it was a foregone conclusion that the government's legislation on peasant land tenure would not receive the Duma's approval. At this point the fifth Social-Democratic congress,

convened in London at the beginning of May, once again reite
need for an armed uprising. Stolypin, whether on the basis of a f.
or on concrete evidence it is difficult to say, accused the Social
cratic deputies of preparing to overthrow the state; 55 of
were arrested and on June 3rd the Duma was dissolved. Simultanᵤously
a new electoral law was unconstitutionally introduced which increased
the number of Duma deputies who could be elected by the landowning
nobility and bourgeoisie (just under 50 per cent of the deputies) and
reduced the number who could be elected by the peasants and workers
(about 25 per cent). These, and other, provisions ensured that future
Dumas would show a more conciliatory attitude towards the government.

Stolypin's arbitrary treatment of the one democratic institution
which had been born out of the bloodshed and public disorders of the
revolution of 1905 was evidence enough that the revolutionary impetus
in the country had already drained away. The mood of public opinion
had quietened, the government seemed to be once more in firm control
and reaction appeared to be everywhere triumphant.

Reaction and War

INEVITABLY, during the revolutionary period 1905-1907, many issues
became tangled together. It would be wrong to try and present them as
coherent or consistent. In the ensuing period of reaction — 1907-1912 —
it becomes possible to see that these issues were beginning to resolve
themselves into some kind of pattern, the central thread of which was
a right-wing semi-constitutional monarchy aimed at preserving the interests of a rich rural and industrial bourgeoisie in a country of overwhelming peasant and working-class poverty. Such a division between
rich and poor was to have the political effect of forcing the bourgeoisie
into a position of dependence upon the governmental authority and of
making the peasant and working-class masses into a largely disenfran-
chised reservoir of potential revolution. So long as the armed forces and
the police were controlled by the government, the bourgeoisie could be
hopeful of retaining and increasing their authority; once such government control ceased, the bourgeoisie would be virtually without authority and power would most likely pass into the hands of the insurgent
peasant and working-class masses. This latter possibility was the most
important lesson taught by the revolutionary period 1905-1907. It

remained a possibility throughout the ten years 1907–1917; and yet it might never have been more than that had not imperial Russia suffered at German hands more humiliating and devastating defeats than it suffered at the hands of the Japanese in 1904–1905. These blows at the outer fabric of the Russian Empire, coupled with the internal tensions, burst asunder the imperial edifice.

To state the position thus is not to discount the importance of personalities. The government's success in stabilising the position after 1907 was due in very large part to the decisiveness and political acumen of Stolypin; the government's failure to pursue its policies with the same thrust and perspicacity after Stolypin's assassination in 1911 must be said to be due to the Tsar's temporising and feeble handling of state affairs. Stolypin realised that what imperial Russia most needed after 1907 was an era of stability: "Give the state twenty years of domestic and foreign peace and you will not recognise present-day Russia." But Russia was to enjoy only five years of what passed, in Stolypin's view, for "domestic peace" and it is significant that only about a quarter of the government's peasant policy was to be fully implemented, in the sense that between 1906 and 1916 only about two million peasant households, or a quarter of the total number of communal households, had left the communes and received legal title to their own lands. The vast majority of peasants still remained in the communes, which were chiefly of the repartitional tenure type. Even though, by further legislation of 1910, repartitional tenure was officially abolished and by a law of 1911 a peasant wishing to establish himself on his own land could demand a portion of the undivided communal lands, the communal system was still the preponderant system of land tenure in Russia before the revolution of 1917. The government's attempt to create a grass-roots conservatism among the vast mass of the peasantry did not have time to succeed, and would probably never have succeeded. Stolypin's "gamble on the strong", as he himself described his policy of officially encouraging individual peasant land tenure, tended to increase tensions in the countryside not only by failing to lessen peasant resentment of the landowning nobility but also by intensifying the poorer peasants' hostility towards the "strong" *kulaks* or those peasants who could afford to secede from the communes. One is left with the impression that for Russia to have become a "modern" agricultural country on the pattern of the United States the process of homesteading should have begun at latest in 1861. It did not begin then; twenty years after it began and had reached its crescendo (in 1908–1909) the Soviet government was to put the process ruthlessly into reverse with the collectivisation programme of 1928–1932.

The third Duma, which opened on November 1st 1907, showed, as Stolypin had hoped, a distinct right-wing bias. The extreme right wing, composed chiefly of the Union of the Russian People, the Council of the United Nobility and various nationalist deputies possessed about 150 seats. The left wing, including Kadets, Progressives, Trudoviks and Social Democrats (of whom only four were Bolsheviks) could muster about 120. The biggest single group of deputies were the Octobrists, who had 154 seats, insufficient for a majority but enough to ensure a balance between the right and the left wings. Although the third Duma was even less democratic and representative of the mass of the Russian people than its predecessors, it could number among its members several able men, such as Milyukov, leader of the Kadets, or Guchkov, leader of the Octobrists, who represented broad sections of liberal or liberal-conservative opinion. Moreover, although the Duma tended to remain a rubber-stamp legislature, it became a forum for discussing such important state matters as the budget, military expenditure and organisation, education and railway construction. The Duma also reflected, to some extent, the desire for stability among the people at large.

Revolution was clearly in retreat during this period. The Socialist Revolutionaries boycotted the third Duma. As for the Social Democrats, although their fifth congress (May 1907 in London) had given a majority to the Bolsheviks, the tiny Bolshevik representation in the Duma tended to be dwarfed by the Menshevik representatives and this gave rise to demands that the conspiratorial form of the All-Russian Social-Democratic Workers' Party should be "liquidated" in favour of a legal party pursuing Economist aims. Lenin, of course, objected bitterly to such a proposed abandonment of what was for him primarily a political struggle. He was equally opposed to those who wished to withdraw the Bolshevik deputies from the Duma and thus to boycott the Duma along with the Socialist Revolutionaries. After much manoeuvring by Lenin, who had to deal not only with political revisionism among both Bolsheviks and Mensheviks but also with the deviation from Materialism of the "God-Builders" (which Lenin scathingly attacked in his *Materialism and Empirio-criticism*), the split between Bolsheviks and Mensheviks finally became an acknowledged fact in Prague in 1912, when Lenin claimed, as might have been expected, that only the Bolsheviks were the true Social-Democratic Party. Such a fragmentation of the ranks of Social Democracy during the period of the third Duma was a result of the general lowering of the revolutionary temperature in Russia. "Domestic peace" was the last thing that Lenin wanted.

After 1907 Russia entered upon a period of modest economic revival. There was an improvement in the standard of living of peasants in the main food-producing areas owing to an increase in food prices, though peasants in other areas who had to buy food suffered correspondingly. The government attempted to alleviate the pressure of population in European Russia by encouraging migration to Siberia and the Far East, the high-water mark of which was reached in 1908 with more than 650,000 such migrants. But in subsequent years the number fell away sharply and a considerable proportion returned, having found that the harsh climatic and living conditions of the resettlement areas were too much for them. Nevertheless, Siberia began to become an important grain-producing area. There was a 15 per cent increase in the area of land under cultivation in European Russia between 1901 and 1913. Cotton-growing expanded rapidly in Turkestan; the production of flax, sugar-beet and potatoes also increased, and animal husbandry expanded, but there was a tendency throughout the period towards regional specialisation. Grain exports, predominantly wheat, increased substantially between 1890 and 1913, although there were considerable fluctuations. The Peasant Bank played an important part both in helping the peasants to purchase their own land and to buy agricultural machinery. There was also a sharp increase in the number of agricultural cooperatives after 1907. Even so, except for a small proportion of *kulaks* and bigger, more progressive, landowners, the average peasant farmer was abysmally ignorant and inefficient. Manual labour predominated in all branches of agriculture. It has been calculated, for example, that in 1913 there were no more than 166 tractors in the whole of Russia, all of them imported. The average annual income of a peasant household was probably between 200 and 500 roubles, and in the majority of cases much nearer the lower than the higher figure; if 250 roubles is taken as the average, this would mean about £26 per annum.

The average industrial wage in 1910 was about 240 roubles per annum (= £25). The number of workers employed in factories subject to the control of factory inspectors rose from approximately 1,800,000 in 1909 to 2,300,000 in 1913. However, if miners, railway workers and building workers are included, then the total industrial labour force might have been in the region of 6,000,000 by 1913. Between 1908 and 1913 the production of pig iron and manufactured iron and steel rose considerably; as did oil output, and to a lesser extent coal output. Despite this, it is worth noting that Russia, with a population equal to, if not more than, the total population of Great Britain, France and Germany, produced, in industrial terms, thirteen times less per head of population than did Germany in 1913, fourteen times less than Great Britain and more than twenty times less than the United States.

The two most important incentives to increased industrial production in the years immediately before the First World War were foreign investment and the growing military expenditure. By 1914 the total capital of foreign firms in Russia amounted to 1,343,000,000 roubles, or a third of the total capital invested in Russian industry. There was also considerable foreign investment in Russian banking and commerce. Military and naval expenditure meanwhile rose to about 30 per cent of total budget expenditure, a considerable proportion being allocated after 1912 for rebuilding of the Baltic fleet destroyed at Tsushima. Strategic considerations also dictated the building by the state of new railways on the western and southern borders of the Russian empire, but about 75 per cent of the railways built between 1911 and 1913 were controlled by private companies. Throughout this immediate pre-war period there was an increase in syndicates and monopolies, which tended to have a stagnating effect upon industrial growth.

Foreign trade showed a steady upward trend. The average annual value of exports was growing fast, but the contribution of manufactured goods amounted to less than 6 per cent of the total. Imports also increased significantly, amounting in 1913 to 1,375,000,000 roubles. Russia's chief foreign customers were Germany and Great Britain, though Germany dominated in total trade by providing more than 45 per cent of Russian imports. A highly protectionist tariff policy increased government revenues, but placed a heavy strain upon consumers. In raising revenue not only for state expenditure but also for servicing the national debt, which in payment of interest on foreign loans, etc. amounted to about 13 per cent of budget expenditure in 1913, the government relied heavily on indirect taxation, which provided 47 per cent of state income. In other words, it is not difficult to see that the Russian economy depended upon the poorest section of the population, the peasants, who grew the wheat which comprised 55 per cent of Russian exports and paid the indirect taxes which provided almost half the revenue.

The picture of Russian economic development before 1914 is thus by no means wholly dark, but it is not particularly bright. The prospects for constitutional freedom, however, tend to darken noticeably. Stolypin, for instance, deliberately flouted the constitutional powers of the State Council and the Duma in March 1911 when he obliged the Tsar to prorogue both chambers for three days under article 87 of the fundamental laws in order to introduce legislation establishing Russian-dominated *zemstva* in the six western provinces of Russia where the landowners were predominantly Polish. The Greater Russian nationalism inherent in this legislation was repeated in several enactments under the third Duma which whittled away the autonomy of Finland and reintroduced a policy of Russification. Jews, though not subjected to pogroms, were persecuted by further educational restrictions and by mass deportations (over a thousand were suddenly deported from Kiev in 1910). The most serious example of anti-Semitism, deliberately engineered, it seems, by the government, was the affair of the Jewish workman, Mendel Beilis, who was accused of ritually murdering a Christian child. He was eventually acquitted in 1913 for lack of evidence after the case had lasted more than two years. More sinister, however, was the apparent connivance of the security police in the assassination of Stolypin, who had incurred the Tsar's disfavour over his handling of the legislation for the *zemstva* in the western provinces. On September 1st 1911, while attending a gala performance in the Kiev opera house, at which both the Tsar and Tsarina were also present, Stolypin was assassinated by an agent of the security police. His successor as Premier was Kokovtsov, formerly Minister of Finances. Still more sinister was the growing influence of the dissolute holy man, Rasputin, who had won the esteem and morbid affection of the Tsarina for his ability, apparently hypnotic, to stop the bleedings of the haemophilic Tsarevich (born in 1904). For all his licentiousness and drunkenness, Rasputin gained such a hold over the Tsarina, the well brought-up and religious-minded "Alix", that he became, despite his obscure and humble beginnings, a real power behind the Russian throne. From 1912 onwards his scandalous behaviour became a matter for press comment, attacks in the Duma and extravagant rumours, none of which reflected any credit upon the Tsar or the government.

In 1912 the period of "domestic peace" came to an end. The shooting of 270 strikers in the Lena gold-fields on April 4th 1912 sparked off a wave of strikes throughout Russia involving more than a million workers, a figure which increased in 1913 and rose to almost one-and-a-half million in the first seven months of 1914. *Pravda*, the first legal Bolshevik newspaper, began publication in St Petersburg on April 22nd 1912 and played an important part in giving political direction to the strikes. *Pravda* also denounced the workers' accident and sickness insurance scheme which was introduced by the third Duma shortly before its dissolution. Such left-wing agitation had no effect on the elections to the fourth Duma, which were held in the autumn of 1912. The Octobrists were obliged to yield ground to the extreme right-wing parties, but even with a reduction in their seats from 154 to 97 they were still able to hold the balance between the 184 seats obtained by the right wing and the 126 seats obtained by the Progressives and Kadets. The socialist parties were represented by 10 Trudoviks, led by Kerensky, and 14 Social

Democrats, of whom only 6 were Bolsheviks and one of these, Malinovsky, turned out to be a police agent. An Octobrist, Rodzyanko, became the president of the fourth Duma; but, one of the most influential deputies was the textile manufacturer, Konovalov, a leading spokesman of commercial interests and a staunch advocate of constitutional legality. The government under the fourth Duma showed a certain leniency. Justices of the Peace were re-instituted and an amnesty in 1913 on the tercentenary of the Romanov dynasty permitted political offenders to return to Russia (though this did not affect Lenin), but there were no official attempts to liberalise the régime. Indeed, the relatively liberal Kokovtsov was dismissed as Premier in 1914 and the aged reactionary Goremykin took his place. Kasso, Minister of Education from 1910 to 1914, pursued an unenlightened policy of repression towards the universities which antagonised both professors and students and led to serious student unrest. By the eve of the First World War the government enjoyed little confidence in the Duma, where a weighty liberal opposition had come into being, and was faced in the country at large by growing agitation among the workers which, in July 1914, in St Petersburg had assumed the proportions of incipient revolution with street demonstrations, shootings and the building of barricades. In such an unsettled and divided condition imperial Russia, under the feeble rule of an ineffectual Tsar, embarked upon war.

The cultural scene prior to the war was not dominated, as was so much of the nineteenth century, by great individuals or great issues. In 1910 Tolstoy, the last great nineteenth-century personality, left Yasnaya Polyana on a journey of escape which ended in his death at the railway-station of Astapovo. His place as the leading Russian writer of the twentieth century had already been taken by Maxim Gorky, but Gorky's work during his exile on Capri (1907–1913) had neither the fervour nor the colourfulness of his earlier writing. Cut off from Russia, he drew his inspiration chiefly from his own memories of Russian provincial life, the squalor of which he depicted with vivid, though monotonous, realism in *Okurov Town* and *The Life of Matvey Kozhemyakin* (1911); yet the final work of his Capri period, *Childhood*, was probably the greatest work he ever wrote. A writer of lesser talent than Gorky, but in the same realistic tradition, was Ivan Bunin (1870–1953), whose stories in *The Village* (1910) and whose study of death, *The Gentleman from San Francisco* (1916), brought him considerable fame, including the Nobel Prize for literature in 1933. More experimental and influential was Leonid Andreyev (1871–1919), who published in 1908 an impressive and awesome story, *The Seven Who Were Hanged*, describing the last hours of political prisoners awaiting their deaths. Fyodor Sologub's novel about the eruption of the demonic into everyday life, *A Little Devil* (1907), enjoyed great popularity, as did Kuprin's *The Duel* (1905), about army life, and his salaciously sentimental study of prostitutes, *The Pit* (1910). A pornographic novel which had a great vogue during this period was Artsybashev's *Sanin* (1907). The literary-cum-political tone of the time, especially during the third Duma when anti-revolutionary ideas predominated, was set by the compendium *Signposts* (1909) which urged the intelligentsia to turn from politics to religion as a basis for their philosophy of life.

In poetry Symbolism began to give way to Futurism, the lyricism of Blok's fine cycles of poems *On the Field of Kulikovo* (1908) and *Italian Poems* (1911) being paralleled by the stridency of Mayakovsky's first works. In music the melodiousness of Rimsky-Korsakov, who died in 1908, was succeeded by the tempestuous work of Stravinsky (*b.* 1882), whose music for *The Firebird* ballet (1910), *Petrouchka* (1911) and *Le Sacre du printemps* (1913) has echoed in all quarters of the musical world. The innovations of Stravinsky and Scriabin (1871–1915) must be set beside the classical manner of Glazunov (1865–1936) and Rachmaninov (1873–1943). For Europe and the world at large that brilliant combination of music, choreography and scenic design which is Russian ballet made its first overwhelming impact in 1909 when Serge Diaghilev took his *corps de ballet* to Paris. The names of Fokine, Nizhinsky, Pavlova and Karsavina have since become legendary. Even if certain aspects of Russian cultural life in the decade before the First World War may have shown signs of degeneracy, it was a degeneracy accompanied and shot through by an abundant vitality, whether expressed in brash experimentation, naïve pornography or the splendid innovations of Diaghilev's ballet and Meyerhold's theatre, which proclaimed the beginnings of a revolution in art as all-embracing and profound as any that might occur in life itself.

In appraising the last years of Tsarist Russia, mention should be made of such famous scholars as the historian Klyuchevsky (1841–1911), the philosopher Berdyayev (1874–1948), the chemist Mendeleyev (1843–1907) and the physiologist Pavlov (1849–1936), who first experimentally demonstrated the conditioned reflex. These names, along with many others, are a part of universal scholarship. They are evidence, if any evidence is needed, of the fact that Tsarist Russia, for all its isolationist tendencies, neither shut itself off from the rest of the world nor became so preoccupied with its own political image that it could not recognise virtue in others. Under Tsarism Russian cultural and scientific standards were the cultural and scientific standards of the rest of the world; and if Russia led the world in certain branches of culture and science, it was not because Tsarist Russia was politically superior, nor was it because the social or economic conditions of Russian life were naturally conducive to the creation of great literature, music, art or ballet. It was simply that Tsarism, unlike the Soviet brand of Communism, did not wilfully place barriers in the way of cross-fertilisation between Russia and the West. There may have been a great deal less political freedom in Tsarist Russia than in the Western democracies, and less economic freedom for the workers than there was to be in Soviet Russia; but in the last years of Tsarism Russia enjoyed more cultural freedom than it ever enjoyed before, more perhaps than it has ever enjoyed since. In any epitaph to Tsarism this point is worth remembering.

*   *   *

By 1914 Russian relations with Japan had improved so much that they were on a generally amicable footing. Russian relations with Great Britain in Asia and the Near East, especially in Persia, had been regularised by the Anglo-Russian convention of 1907. The crisis-points were once more, as they had been for the greater part of the nineteenth century, the Balkans, the Straits and Turkey.

Under Izvolsky, appointed Foreign Minister in 1906, Russian diplomacy attempted to achieve what military action had demonstrably failed to secure : the opening of the Straits to Russian warships. Diplomatic overtures to Austria-Hungary were accompanied by the emergence of neo-Slavism or a new kind of Russian Panslavism, the need, in the Russian view, to protect the Balkan Slavs from Austro-Hungarian aggression being reinforced by Russian misgivings over the increasing influence of Germany in Turkey. In the autumn of 1908 Izvolsky's diplomacy suffered a severe rebuff when Austria-Hungary, after a rather free interpretation of tentative agreements reached between the Austrian and Russian Foreign Ministers at Buchlau in mid-September 1908, suddenly annexed Bosnia and Herzegovina. Serbia at once demanded compensation, but Germany brought pressure on Russia to recognise the Austro-Hungarian annexations and Russian military unpreparedness left her little choice but to accept. In 1910 Izvolsky was forced to resign and Sazonov was appointed in his place. Germany had meanwhile made several attempts to break up the 1907 Entente between Russia, France and Great Britain, but without success. With the Straits as its ultimate objective, Russian diplomacy now succeeded in forging a short-lived alliance between Serbia and Bulgaria which in 1912 led to war with Turkey. Bulgarian and Serbian armies quickly overran most of the European territory still in Turkish hands and by the Treaty of London, signed on May 30th (NS) 1913, Turkey surrendered to the Balkan allies all her former possessions west of the Midye-Enos line. But squabbles over the division of Macedonia quickly brought about the collapse of the Serbo–Bulgarian alliance. Bulgaria attacked Serbia and Greece and was defeated, losing practically all her recently-won gains. The success of Serbia in both the wars of 1913 aroused such hostility in Austria-Hungary that it became clear that the Austro-Hungarian Empire would let slip no opportunity to humiliate its Serbian neighbour.

Relations between Russia and Germany were aggravated in December 1913 by the appointment of a German General, Liman von Sanders, as commander of the first Turkish army corps, then stationed in Constantinople. Sazonov became alarmed by the potential diplomatic and military threat which such an appointment entailed. Although Great Britain and France gave Russia no active support, the German General was transferred to the post of Inspector-General of the Turkish Army and the threat of German control over Constantinople was temporarily removed. Sazonov could claim that he had won a minor diplomatic victory, but he could scarcely have known that it was to be the last victory in the annals of Tsarist diplomacy.

On June 28th (NS) 1914 Archduke Francis Ferdinand, heir to the Austrian throne, was assassinated while visiting Sarajevo. It transpired that his assassin, G. Princip, was a Serbian nationalist. This fact, though the complicity of the Serbian government in the assassination was not proved, offered the opportunity for which Austria-Hungary had been waiting. On July 23rd (NS) Berchtold, the Austrian Foreign Minister, with the consent and connivance of the German government, issued an ultimatum to Serbia, the terms of which were so humiliating as to be clearly unacceptable. After forty-eight hours, despite a very conciliatory Serbian reply, Austria-Hungary broke off diplomatic relations with Belgrade. The Russian government decided to support Serbia and the mobilisation of armies began throughout Europe. On August 1st (NS) Germany declared war on Russia and on August 3rd (NS) on France. On the next day German expectations that Great Britain would remain neutral were ended with the British declaration of war against Germany in defence of Belgian neutrality. So began the First World War, desired by none of the Entente Powers, least of all by Russia, and of ultimate benefit least of all to the Central Powers which had done so much to provoke it.

The beginning of hostilities brought to an end the wave of strikes which had been growing in Russia throughout 1914. The nation appeared to present a united front to the Teutonic threat, one minor manifestation of which was the official change in the name of the capital

from the German-style St Petersburg to the Russian-style Petrograd.
Though ill-prepared and ill-equipped, the Russian first and second
armies, under Rennenkampf and Samsonov, embarked upon a "steam-
roller" invasion of East Prussia. The campaign was at first successful.
The first army in the north advanced, though slowly, towards Koenigsberg; the second army to the south began to advance without any
proper sense of direction, lost contact with the first army and became
dispersed. The Germans, alarmed nonetheless by the threat to their
rear, called upon Hindenburg to take command. With the aid of two
corps and a cavalry division transferred from the western front, where
the first Battle of the Marne was in progress, Hindenburg trapped the
Russian second army at Tannenberg, rendering it useless as a military
force, and within a fortnight was pursuing the first army back across the
East Prussian border. This defeat cost the Russians more than 200,000
men and 500 guns and caused widespread demoralisation in the Russian
ranks. In Galicia, on the other hand, the Russian offensive launched
simultaneously with the advance in East Prussia brought hard-won but
significant gains. The Austrians, faced by the Russian onslaught, retreated; huge numbers surrendered. By late September Austrian losses
totalled close to 400,000 men and the Austrian military machine had
been dealt a crushing blow. In an effort to relieve the pressure on
Austria, Hindenburg launched an attack towards Warsaw, but after
heavy and confused fighting, especially round Lodz, the German
advance was halted and the front stabilised. At the end of 1914, despite
the defeat at Tannenberg, the Russian position was militarily satisfac-
tory, even if it gave no cause for rejoicing. France and Great Britain
could well be thankful that Russian pressure in the east had helped to
prevent the collapse of the allies in the west; 1940 was to tell a different
story.

The position worsened radically, however, in 1915. The extreme inefficiency of the War Minister, Sukhomlinov, corruption in high places
and wartime profiteering brought down upon the government the indignation of broad sections of public opinion. A powerful German
offensive launched in the spring of 1915 drove the Russians from
Galicia. Shortage of arms and ammunition had by this time become
so acute that 30 per cent of the Russian troops committed in battle
were without arms, and field guns were rationed to a couple of shells a
day. In Poland the Russians were forced to abandon Warsaw; Brest-
Litovsk and Vilna fell; by September the Germans had advanced to
within sight of Riga. Though the attempt to force Russia out of the war
had not been successful, this series of military defeats, which had cost
the Russians more than three million men and incalculable losses in

material and property, was a crippling blow. Apart from unsuccessful offensives on the western front and the hideous fiasco of the Dardanelles expedition, which had the object of opening up a southern route between Russia and the West, the Franco–British forces did little to alleviate the position of their hard-pressed ally. Indeed, in 1915 the Russian armies bore the brunt of German military might. Total defeat was avoided only by a very narrow margin—that margin, in terms of military strategy, being the extent to which the Russian armies could retreat and the German armies advance without either the one or the other losing viability as a military force.

In September 1915 the Tsar himself assumed supreme command of all Russian forces. General Alekseyev became the new chief of staff—a competent administrator, though hardly an outstanding military mind. The Ministry of War was reorganised under General Polivanov. This last change, and the increase in allied shipments of supplies, ensured that the Russian troops were better equipped in 1916 than at any stage in the war. But morale was already very low. Moreover, save for a few exceptional individuals, the personalities who had been involved in governing wartime Russia had proved themselves wholly inadequate to the task. Ministerial offices were filled by a succession of mediocrities; and after September 1915, with the Tsar absent from the capital, many appointments to senior posts were made on the recommendation of Rasputin, aided and abetted by the Tsarina. The surprising fact in these circumstances is that Tsarist Russia was able to survive the strains and stresses of total war for more than two and a half years. This fact is much less easily explicable than is the eventual revolution.

In March 1916, in order to relieve the pressure on the western front, the Russians mounted a hastily prepared offensive in the region of Vilna which was repulsed with heavy losses. Again, at the end of May, in answer to pleas from the Italians, whose army was about to be encircled at Trentino, General Brusilov attacked on the Austrian front. This offensive had an unexpected and timely success. The Austrians collapsed, yielding more than 400,000 prisoners and huge areas of Galicia. The pressure on the Italians was relieved and Roumania was brought into the war on the side of the allies. Yet these were hollow victories. They cost Russia stupendous losses in manpower, lengthened the front and, though they can be said to have sounded the death-knell of the Habsburg Empire, they cannot be said to have brought Russia demonstrably closer to ultimate victory.

The forces of discontent were now steadily building up both at the front and at the rear. The rise in the cost of living, dislocations of supplies, government mismanagement, inept generalship and a universal

abhorrence of the protracted, wasteful and apparently senseless war ga
rise to outspoken attacks upon the Tsar at all levels of society. A wav
of protest strikes began, involving in 1916 more than a million workers.
The peasants, who formed the bulk of the recruits to the armed forces,
had shown resistance to recruitment from the beginning and now began
to desert in large numbers. Vociferous attacks were made in the Duma
on the "dark forces" behind the throne. In December 1916 Rasputin
was murdered by a clique of aristocrats. By the turn of the year it was
widely acknowledged that the Tsar would have to go if the mounting
political tension was to be controlled and the war prosecuted to a successful conclusion.

But when the February revolution of 1917 actually occurred, it took
practically everyone by surprise; and the important events which comprise the Russian Revolution of 1917 occurred for the most part in
Petrograd. This is not to deny that the effects of the revolution were felt
throughout the territory of the former Russian Empire. But it is worth
bearing in mind that the Russian people as a whole suffered far more
grievously in the struggle against the Central Powers than they did
during the events of 1917. Russian losses in dead, wounded and
prisoners during the war years numbered more than seven million. The
collapse, not so much of formal authority, as of the traditional authority
of the nobility, the depletion of the officers' corps, the recruitment of
about fifteen million men, mostly peasants, into the armed forces and
the consequent breakdown of the economy—these events of the war
years were in themselves revolutionary changes which fundamentally
affected the life of every citizen of the Russian Empire. Petrograd in
1917 became the stage on which the political revolution was acted out
before a nation which had had revolution in its heart since 1905 and
had been driven to an extremity of despair by the terrible privations and
losses of the First World War.

The February and October Revolutions of 1917

STRIKES, mutinies, street demonstrations and peasant revolts had been
occurring sporadically throughout the autumn and winter of 1916–
1917, but it is generally acknowledged that the February Revolution of
1917 began on International Women's Day, February 23rd 1917. On
that day serious bread riots broke out among the Petrograd workers. The
government, in anticipation of civil disorders, had increased the Petro-

grad garrison to 160,000 troops, the majority of whom, however, were raw and untrained recruits. A further special force of 120,000 soldiers, gendarmes and police had been created to meet emergencies. These large bodies of armed men were quartered in Petrograd and its environs for the purpose of maintaining order chiefly among the 400,000 workers in the capital's factories. What the government had not envisaged was the rapidity with which the army battalions would melt away once the workers' movement had gathered momentum. On February 24th the crowds from the workers' settlements in Vyborg began to attack the police while the cossacks maintained a temporary neutrality. On February 25th a general strike was declared in Petrograd. The Tsar, at the supreme army headquarters in Mogilyov, ordered General Khabalov, commander of the Petrograd garrison, to suppress the disorders by force. On February 26th, a Sunday, police fired on workers who had broken through the cordons into the Nevsky Prospekt and by the evening of that day General Khabalov could report to the Tsar that the situation was under control. But by the evening of the 27th the Petrograd garrison had already gone over to the revolution. Ostensibly loyal detachments sent to quell the mutiny joined forces with the workers. General Khabalov retreated to the Admiralty building. On the morning of the 28th this last outpost of government power gave up and Petrograd was entirely in revolutionary hands.

But whose hands guided the revolution at this stage? The question is not easily answered, nor was it really to be answered until October. The February revolution threw up no outstanding leaders. Indeed, it looked to leadership from two bodies which sprang into existence almost simultaneously on February 27th. The first of these was a Temporary Committee of the Duma representing all the parties in the fourth Duma except the extreme right wing and the Bolsheviks (the five Bolshevik deputies had been arrested in November 1914 and exiled to Siberia). The second was the Temporary Executive Committee of the Petrograd Soviet of Workers' Deputies, organised in the Tauride Palace on the pattern of the Soviet of 1905. The real power of the revolution, in the shape of the armed workers and the soldiers who had joined the revolutionary cause, was vested in this second body, which on March 2nd was renamed the Soviet of Workers' and Soldiers' Deputies. But the Executive Committee of the Soviet, composed chiefly of Mensheviks and Socialist Revolutionaries, was not prepared to assume governmental power. On the assumption that this was to be a liberal-bourgeois revolution, it preferred to see governmental authority devolve upon the Duma Committee with the Soviet acting as the revolution's socialist conscience.

On February 28th the Tsarist ministers were arrested and the Duma

Committee appointed commissars to take their place. Rodzyanko had meanwhile attempted to obtain the Tsar's permission for the formation of a new responsible government. The Tsar was slow to realise the seriousness of the situation. He despatched to Petrograd from Mogilyov a force under General Ivanov in the hope that these crack troops would bring the situation under control; but when they arrived in the capital on March 1st the troops mutinied. Supreme army headquarters was by this time firmly of the opinion that it was useless to send further troops. On the morning of the 28th the Tsar left Mogilyov for Petrograd, but was delayed in reaching the capital by having his train re-routed via Pskov. Rodzyanko now demanded the Tsar's abdication. The Tsar, after consulting with his generals, decided on March 2nd to abdicate in favour of his son, though when the two Duma representatives, Guchkov and Shulgin, reached him at Pskov on the evening of that day, he had changed his mind in favour of his brother, Grand Duke Michael. With little ceremony and with no one to regret his decision, Nicholas II signed a document of abdication which terminated his reign and became the death warrant of Tsarism. Simultaneously with the Tsar's abdication, the leading liberal in the Duma, Milyukov, announced in the Tauride Palace the possible accession of the Tsarevich with Grand Duke Michael as regent. His announcement was howled down. Similarly, when Guchkov and Shulgin returned to the capital with the abdication document, Guchkov was arrested for a time by a group of armed workers at the railway station when he shouted: "Long live the Emperor Michael!" As Trotsky puts it: "The country had so radically vomited up the monarchy that it could never crawl down the people's throat again." The liberal dream of a constitutional monarchy ended at that point. And when, on March 3rd, members of the Duma Committee approached Grand Duke Michael with an invitation to accept the throne, he refused on the grounds that he would only accept such authority from a Constituent Assembly and that, in any event, his personal safety could not be guaranteed. So ended the Russian monarchical tradition. The imperial family remained under house arrest at Tsarskoye Selo until the summer of 1917. Afterwards they were moved first to Tobolsk and later to Yekaterinburg where they were murdered on July 16th (NS) 1918.

By March 3rd a Provisional Government had come into existence under the premiership of Prince G. E. Lvov. Milyukov took charge of foreign affairs, Guchkov of the war ministry; Tereshchenko, a wealthy industrialist, became responsible for finances, Konovalov responsible for trade, and Nekrasov, a member of the Kadet Party, for communications; the only member of the Provisional Government who was also a member of the Executive Committee of the Petrograd Soviet was Kerensky, the new Minister of Justice. The Provisional Government was given the mandate to act in the name of the revolution until the summoning of a Constituent Assembly. But it could only act in consort with the Petrograd Soviet, and Soviets or "councils" of workers' and soldiers' deputies had begun to spring up all over Russia, both in the main urban centres and in the armed forces. Moreover, by Order Number 1 issued by the Petrograd Soviet on March 1st, the control of all arms was handed over to the elected soldiers' and sailors' committees, which were not permitted to give them to officers even if demanded. This famous Order Number 1 not only undermined discipline in the armed forces but also rendered useless the authority of the Provisional Government and made it virtually impossible for Russia to undertake a vigorous prosecution of the war against Germany, as the Provisional Government had intended. There grew up as a result a kind of dual power : the Provisional Government was on the face of it the new government of Russia, recognised as such by America, France, Great Britain and Italy, but the power to implement the government's orders rested with the Soviets.

This strange state of affairs was not destined to last long. The liberal bourgeoisie, having assumed nominal power, had little means of exercising it. On the other hand, the revolutionary workers and peasants, poorly and haphazardly organised in Soviets, adopted a wait-and-see attitude which was out of keeping with the actual facts of the situation. Why? Primarily because the socialists who dominated the executive committees of the Soviets could not bring themselves to grasp the power at their fingertips for fear that a socialist revolution might be premature. Lenin had no such qualms. On March 27th (OS) he left Switzerland and travelled across Germany in a sealed train, arriving in Petrograd from Sweden on the evening of April 3rd. Chkheidze, the Menshevik leader of the Petrograd Soviet, greeted him as a fellow socialist with an exhortation to support the unity of the revolution. Lenin replied by addressing the crowds who had gathered to welcome him outside the Finland Station with the words : "Long live the socialist revolution!" The distinction was important. For Lenin the revolution was not the Provisional Government and he had no time for the conventional Marxist view that there could be no socialist revolution until the bourgeoisie had triumphed. In his April theses, which he enunciated to a Bolshevik meeting on the day after his arrival, he stated that "the special characteristic of the current moment in Russia is the *transition* from the first stage of the revolution which has given power to the bourgeoisie as a result of the political immaturity and lack of organisation of the proletariat *to the second* stage, which must place the power in the hands of the proletariat and the poorest sections of the peasantry."

Before Lenin's return Bolshevism had not been a major force in the revolution. *Pravda* had restarted publication, under the editorship of Molotov, on March 5th, but with the return of Kamenev and Stalin from Siberian exile on March 13th, its initially hostile policy towards the Provisional Government had been changed to one of conditional support for the government in its prosecution of a defensive war and in granting an eight-hour working day. Lenin's April theses swept aside such an opportunistic, compromise policy. He violently repudiated any Bolshevik support for the Provisional Government, dismissed the idea of a parliamentary republic and offered in its place a Republic of Soviets. "All Power to the Soviets!" became his slogan. He envisaged confiscation of all landowners' estates, nationalisation of the land, the creation of new model farms under the control of peasant Soviets, the establishment of a single national bank, the elimination of the army, the police and the officials. These proposals seemed to be too revolutionary even for the revolutionaries. But history has proved that Lenin judged the mood of the revolution better than his contemporaries. The revolution was not finished: it was in a state of *transition*. So long as the Provisional Government stood for continuation of the war while Lenin demanded peace, or upheld the rights of the landowners while Lenin demanded the confiscation of the estates, the revolution would continue in a state of transition. The transitional period could only end with the final removal of either Lenin or the Provisional Government. It is not right perhaps to ascribe too much prescience to Lenin; but it would be just as wrong to deny the clarity of his thinking or the force of his personality. Lenin gave a purpose and direction to the left wing of the revolution, to the Bolsheviks and their Socialist Revolutionary sympathisers, which they had not had previously and which eventually proved historically decisive when the tide of the revolution began to flow strongly towards the left.

Lenin's April theses may have been couched in abstruse Marxist terms; their intent was simple in the extreme: he offered the workers and peasants peace and land. The programme of the Provisional Government, though embellished with glowing appeals to the "wisdom" of the Russian people, was based on concepts of legality which may have seemed boldly revolutionary in the parliamentary setting of the Duma but seemed irrelevant, even archaic, in the lawless streets of revolutionary Petrograd. The ineffectiveness of the Provisional Government was emphasised by the almost total collapse of discipline in the army, the anarchy in the countryside, the wholesale seizure of factories by workers' committees and the break-up, with the granting of independence to Poland and Finland and the separatist movement in the Ukraine, of the former Russia. At the beginning of May the Provisional Government itself suffered a crisis over foreign policy questions. Guchkov and Milyukov resigned. In the ensuing government reshuffle six socialists received ministerial posts, a leftward swing which appeared to bring the Provisional Government and the Petrograd Soviet closer together, though all the major decisions were taken by a triumvirate of Kerensky, now responsible for the war ministry, Tereshchenko, the new Minister of Foreign Affairs, and Nekrasov. The appointment of Victor Chernov, leader of the Socialist Revolutionaries, as Minister of Agriculture produced tensions in the cabinet which were eventually to rend it apart.

By this time Kerensky's star was clearly in the ascendant. As a lawyer, experienced in forensic oratory, he had been the only member of the Provisional Government in the early stages of the revolution who had been able to sway the mobs with electrifying speeches. In June, after dismissing General Alekseyev and appointing General Brusilov commander-in-chief, he even succeeded in arousing sufficient fervour among front-line troops for the mounting of an offensive in Galicia. There were street demonstrations in Petrograd in his honour. By the beginning of July, however, the offensive had turned into a rout and Petrograd (July 4th) swarmed with Bolshevik-led demonstrators who marched to the Tauride Palace and demanded that the Petrograd Soviet become the new government. This, the first organised attempt by the Bolsheviks to seize power, petered out very largely, it seems, because Lenin was not as yet prepared for a *coup*. Nonetheless, the enormous demonstration effectively exhibited the powerlessness of the government. The government's response gave rise to the most curious episode in the revolution. Documents were published on the authority of the Minister of Justice allegedly incriminating Lenin as a German agent. There is no doubt that he travelled to Russia with the active connivance of the German government, but there is no concrete evidence to show that he ever acted under German orders although he may have received funds at this stage from official German sources. Yet the probability remains. Recent research suggests that a considerable proportion of Bolshevik funds may have derived from a certain Jacob Fuerstenberg, who profiteered during the First World War in medical supplies and contraceptives.* Whatever the truth of the matter, these revelations provoked strong anti-Bolshevik feeling. *Pravda* was raided and shut down, and Lenin, Zinovyev and Kamenev narrowly evaded arrest by escaping into Finland (July 6th).

* See Futrell, M., *Northern Underground*, London, 1963. The evidence in this book is marshalled with care and ingenuity, but no conclusive proof is offered.

But this period of crisis also had repercussions within the Provisional Government. Prince Lvov, unable to accept the socialist views of Victor Chernov, resigned and Kerensky became Prime Minister. Briefly, for a period of little more than a month, between mid-July and late August, Kerensky enjoyed unparalleled popularity And it seemed that the influence of Bolshevism was ebbing.

The turning-point came with the Kornilov revolt. General Kornilov, a cossack of humble origins, had been appointed commander-in-chief after the failure of the offensive in Galicia. He advocated "iron rule", the reintroduction of discipline and the death penalty (abolished in March). There was little love lost between Kerensky and Kornilov. Though they were in general agreement on the need to strengthen the government, in political outlook few people could have been more dissimilar. At a State Conference, convened on Kerensky's initiative in Moscow (August 13th–15th), Kornilov had been given an ovation by the right-wing delegates which may have encouraged him to regard himself as being cast in the role of saviour of Russia. When, on August 24th, news reached him in Mogilyov that a Bolshevik uprising was planned in Petrograd, he despatched a cavalry corps to the capital. This precipitate action by a general of avowedly monarchist sympathies immediately aroused fears that the revolution was in danger. The Petrograd Soviet set up a committee for struggle with the counter-revolution and proceeded to organise armed workers into units of Red Guards. Equally alarmed, Kerensky dismissed Kornilov, appealed to the Bolsheviks, appointed himself commander-in-chief and assumed dictatorial powers. The Kornilov revolt was of little significance in itself; yet it had the effect of producing a wave of pro-Bolshevik feeling which gave rise to Bolshevik majorities in the Petrograd Soviet (August 31st) and in the Moscow Soviet (September 6th).

To Lenin, temporarily exiled in Finland, an armed insurrection by the Bolsheviks now became a matter of urgency. The slogan "All Power to the Soviets!" could now imply "All Power to the Bolsheviks!", but for the slogan to have any meaning the power would have to be seized by an armed insurrection. The sixth Bolshevik Party Congress, at the end of July, had supported this policy in principle. Yet the Bolshevik Central Committee, when faced with letters from Lenin demanding that an insurrection should be prepared, was undecided. The Provisional Government meanwhile underwent a further reshuffle, which gave it an even more socialist complexion than its predecessor. A large Democratic Conference was also summoned (September 14th–22nd), which spawned a consultative body of 550 members, known as the Council of the Republic. This was designed to act as a pre-parliament before the summoning of a Constituent Assembly. Trotsky, recently emerged from prison, denounced the Council of the Republic; the Bolsheviks, who had been vociferous participants in the Conference, walked out of the pre-parliament. Like many other Social Democrats, Trotsky had earlier found himself out of step with Lenin; now he gave himself over whole-heartedly to the Bolshevik cause. On September 23rd he was elected chairman of the Petrograd Soviet, which was situated at that time in the former girls' school in Smolny, also the headquarters of the Bolshevik Party. Trotsky, as chairman of the Soviet and a member of the Bolshevik Central Committee, expressed in his person the ascendancy which pro-Bolshevik feeling had achieved in the Soviets. It also fell to Trotsky, as the leading organiser of the newly formed Military Revolutionary Committee of the Petrograd Soviet, to head the armed insurrection.

On October 10th Lenin arrived secretly in Petrograd to attend a session of the Bolshevik Central Committee at which the issue of armed insurrection was hotly debated. The resulting vote showed a majority of ten for Lenin's proposals, but two of the committee members, Zinovyev and Kamenev, who were among Lenin's most longstanding supporters, voted against him. Despite this dissension, Trotsky energetically proceeded with plans for a revolt. All units of Red Guards were brought under the control of the Military Revolutionary Committee, arms were procured, commissars appointed. The uprising was widely anticipated in the press, largely because Zinovyev and Kamenev had gone on record as disagreeing with the Bolshevik Central Committee's decision. In their view it would have been better to wait until the summoning of the Constituent Assembly, but such advance publicity for the revolt made little difference. By October 21st commissars of the Military Revolutionary Committee had taken charge of the Petrograd garrison. The government's attempt to suppress the Bolshevik newspapers and to arrest the Bolshevik leaders came to nothing; and the cruiser *Aurora*, which had anchored in the Neva opposite the Winter Palace, instead of putting to sea as ordered, offered its services to the insurgents. On the night of October 24th units of Red Guards occupied the State Bank, the post office, telephone exchange, bridges and railway stations. On the morning of October 25th, after vainly striving to obtain reinforcements, Kerensky left for the northern front in a car commandeered from the American embassy. The Provisional Government, under the temporary premiership of Konovalov, remained in session in the Winter Palace protected by a motley collection of cossacks, cadets and members of a women's battalion. This farcical situation continued until nine o'clock in the evening of the same day, when a blank shell fired by the *Aurora* led to the dispersal of most of the defenders. Later that night and in the early morning of the 26th, after some firing from both the *Aurora* and the Peter and Paul fortress, an attack led by Antonov-Ovseyenko penetrated the Winter Palace. The members of the Provisional Government were arrested. The October Revolution, a deliberately planned *coup d'état* by Lenin and the Bolshevik-controlled Petrograd Soviet, had been successfully accomplished.

Chapter VI

1917 – 1936

Soviet Power and Civil War

WHY did the October Revolution occur with such apparent ease? Primarily because Lenin knew what he wanted and no one else did. But there are secondary issues of great importance which explain, to some extent, the lack of opposition encountered by the Bolshevik *coup d'état* in Petrograd. Bourgeois liberalism, for instance, deliberately inhibited in its growth under Tsarism, proved when Tsarism was overthrown that it had neither sufficiently resolute political leaders nor a sufficient political following in the country at large to be able to retain the power which passed into its hands at the time of the February Revolution. In general the revolution, sparked off by street demonstrations, had a left-wing complexion and took a leftward course from the start. This meant that real power was likely to remain with the Soviets, which had come into existence spontaneously with the upsurge of the revolutionary tide. The power of the Soviets could only have been curbed, as was generally recognised in the summer of 1917, by strong government. But the Provisional Government, under Kerensky's dictatorship in the autumn of 1917, enjoyed little public confidence and even less real power. Moreover, the Provisional Government, enmeshed in its own divided policy of attempting to prosecute the war with Germany in the allied cause while promising and decreeing domestic reforms which could only be effectively implemented in time of peace, ultimately abandoned itself to placing all its hopes in the Constituent Assembly. In other words, it was a provisional government which had never been elected into power, had only provisional policies and exercised a semblance of provisional authority. When the testing-time came, it collapsed like a house of cards. Although Kerensky succeeded in persuading General Krasnov to lead a detachment of cossacks from the northern front, those reinforcements for the Provisional Government were decisively driven back by armed workers when they reached the outskirts of Petrograd. Kerensky eventually succeeded in escaping abroad.

What were Lenin's aims? Lenin aimed to achieve by armed force a "dictatorship of the proletariat" which would be a signal for world proletarian revolution. However, "dictatorship of the proletariat" meant dictatorship by Lenin and the Bolshevik Party through the Bolshevik majority at the second All-Russian Congress of Soviets which first met late on the evening of October 25th just before the final assault on the Winter Palace.* Of the 670 "elected" delegates to this Congress 390 were Bolsheviks, 160 Socialist Revolutionaries and 72 Mensheviks; the remainder belonged to smaller groups. Lenin would claim that the Soviets were a higher type of democracy than parliamentarianism, that "Soviet power was a million times more democratic than the most democratic bourgeois republic". The point is that Lenin aimed at power for Bolshevism—a power which was to be exercised exclusively by Bolsheviks for Party ends, on the basis of a network of Soviets, in the name of the proletariat and the poorer peasantry. What Lenin did not aim at was individual freedom, that precious ideal which it has been the aim of Western democracies to preserve by never allowing exclusive and unconditional power to accrue for an unlimited period to any one party or section of the population. Western democracy may be bourgeois-capitalist by Communist standards, but at least it curbs political power and allows the free expression of responsible political opinion; Communism will never be democratic by Western standards so long as political power remains exclusively and unconditionally in the hands of the Communist Party, even though such power may be wielded in the name of the proletariat. The October Revolution posed the most important question of twentieth-century politics: whether democratic ends are ever achieved by dictatorial means without dictatorship becoming an end in itself.

When news of the fall of the Winter Palace reached the Congress of Soviets in the early morning of October 26th, the Menshevik and right-wing Socialist Revolutionary delegates walked out in protest against the Bolshevik *coup*. Lenin, neatly freed by this walk-out from all opposition to his policies, made the transition from revolutionary plotter to government leader with the *sang-froid* of one to the manner born. "It makes one's head spin," he admitted, using the German expression *"es schwindelt"*; but the immediate problems facing the new Soviet government gave no cause for celebration. At the second and final session of the Congress, which met at nine o'clock on the evening of October 26th, Lenin introduced two pieces of legislation in fulfilment of his earlier revolutionary pledges: these were the decrees on peace and land. The decree on peace demanded an end to hostilities with Germany, universal peace based on democratic principles and—its most startling aspect in allied eyes—the abolition of secret diplomacy. The decree on land was makeshift and muddled. Owing more than a little to the programme of the Socialist Revolutionaries, it declared that all private estates,

* The first All-Russian Congress of Soviets had been held in June and was dominated by Socialist Revolutionaries and Mensheviks.

appanage and church lands were henceforth nationalised; they were to be handed over to regional land committees and local peasant Soviets for reapportionment on an egalitarian basis. This decree on land was the severing of a Gordian knot which the peasants themselves had very largely unravelled through their plundering of estates during the summer and autumn of 1917. The final act of the Congress was the election of an All-Russian Central Executive Committee, or VTsIK as it came to be known, consisting of 101 members of whom 61 were Bolsheviks and 29 left-wing Socialist Revolutionaries. At the same time the Congress elected a "cabinet" under the title of Soviet of People's Commissars of the Russian Republic, known as Sovnarkom for short. Lenin was elected chairman of this Sovnarkom, Trotsky became Commissar for Foreign Affairs, Rykov for Internal Affairs, Shlyapnikov for Labour, Lunacharsky for Education and Stalin for Nationalities. So was established the first Soviet government in Russia, the first and essential step in bringing the whole of Russia under the hegemony of Soviet state power.

But Soviet power was not established in Russia overnight. In Moscow the Soviet gained control only after a week's fighting. Elsewhere, though a semblance of Soviet control may have been established in the major urban centres by the end of November, in the countryside Socialist Revolutionary, rather than Bolshevik, sentiment was dominant. Within six months of the October Revolution civil war had broken out in Finland, concluding with the defeat of Bolshevism; anarchy was to prevail in the Ukraine for more than three years; and in the Baltic provinces nationalist movements were to gain control. There were also strong nationalist parties in Azerbaydzhan and Armenia; Menshevism had a strong following in Georgia and parts of Central Asia. Moreover, there still remained the threat of German invasion to contend with; and Soviet power appeared in many people's eyes to remain provisional so long as there was no Constituent Assembly.

The Sovnarkom, meeting regularly in Smolny, proceeded to issue a series of decrees. Among the most important of these were the institution of an eight-hour working day in all factories (October 29th), the declaration of universal free education (November 1st), the abolition of social classes and ranks and national inequality (November 10th), the establishment of workers' control in factories (November 14th) and the formation of a Supreme Soviet of the National Economy or VSNKh (December 1st) which was designed to regulate and control all industrial enterprises. Banks, syndicates, consumers' societies were nationalised during December; the payment of dividends was prohibited. On December 19th civil marriage became the only recognised form of marriage, illegitimate children received the same rights as those born in wedlock and women enjoyed equal rights with men. Two very significant decrees were also passed in December 1917. The first, of December 7th, after the abolition of the Petrograd Military Revolutionary Committee, established under Dzerzhinsky an All-Russian Extraordinary Commission, the notorious *Cheka*, which was empowered to suppress all manifestations of counter-revolution or sabotage against the Soviet state. The terror that was unleashed by this organisation against guilty and innocent alike probably damaged as much as it enhanced the power of the Soviet government and contributed in a large measure to that breakdown of "legality" which became such a marked feature of Soviet administrative procedure. Equally significant, though the issue of "legality" in this instance took another form, was the other decree (of December 20th) which announced the summoning of the Constituent Assembly for January 5th 1918.

Voting for the Constituent Assembly, based on a rather unwieldy system of proportional representation, had begun on November 15th 1917. There is little doubt that, although the Revolution from its inception had proclaimed the summoning of a Constituent Assembly as its ultimate aim, the events of October had rendered such an aim virtually meaningless. Lenin knew this only too well, but the shakiness of Soviet power forced him to honour the Bolshevik pledge to summon such a body. Whatever the weakness of the voting system, the Constituent Assembly, when it met in the Tauride Palace on January 5th, was the most truly representative body to have emerged from the Revolution. Of the just over 700 delegates 168 were Bolsheviks (25 per cent), but the largest single bloc consisted of right-wing Socialist Revolutionaries (380). In other words, the Constituent Assembly contained a large anti-Bolshevik majority, which included Mensheviks, Kadets and other "bourgeois" groupings. After the rejection of a Bolshevik motion supporting Soviet power, the Bolsheviks and their sympathisers walked out, leaving the Assembly, under Chernov's chairmanship, to fritter away the night of January 5th–6th in an endless succession of speeches. The Constituent Assembly was finally dispersed by a sailor, Zheleznyakov, who announced that "the guards were tired". It was never to meet again. The dissolution of the Constituent Assembly, ordered by VTsIK, was approved by the third All-Russian Congress of Soviets at its meeting on January 10th. Russia was now declared to be "a republic of Soviets" organised on supposedly federal principles, in which the highest organ of power was the Congress of Soviets or, in intervals between Congresses, the VTsIK, both of which were empowered to elect the Sovnarkom or government of the republic. By this means the Soviet government and its Bolshevik leadership "legalised" themselves, though such "legality" was in fact achieved by the simple process of dispersing the anti-Bolshevik opposition in the Constituent Assembly.

But a far more serious threat than any contained in a Constituent Assembly had now arisen. Peace overtures had been made to all the allied Powers early in November, though without result. Simultaneously cease-fire negotiations had been opened with the German military authorities on the eastern front and on December 9th a Soviet delegation, headed by Joffe, arrived in Brest-Litovsk to discuss peace terms. The German and Soviet delegates soon found themselves at cross-purposes. Trotsky, who took over from Joffe as head of the Soviet delegation, refused to sign any peace treaty which included annexations or denied the right of self-determination, whereas General von Hoffmann, the leading representative of the Central Powers, insisted upon the right to determine what should happen to the Russian territory in German hands. Frantic debates over this question broke out in the Bolshevik ranks. Meanwhile, the Central Powers proceeded to recognise the independence of the Ukraine and to conclude a peace treaty with the Ukrainian Rada (a parliament similar to the Polish diet), despite the fact that on February 8th (NS)* Bolshevik troops under Antonov-Ovseyenko had occupied Kiev. Annoyed by the procrastination of the Soviet delegation and Trotsky's declaration that, though no longer at war with the Central Powers, Russia would not sign an annexationist peace treaty, the Central Powers launched an offensive along the entire eastern front. Realising the imminent danger that now threatened, Lenin urged immediate acceptance of the German terms. For five days, between February 18th and 23rd, the troops of the Central Powers advanced and no word came from Berlin. When the German peace terms became known, they proved to be harsher than those demanded at the Brest-Litovsk negotiations. Even so, the Soviet government accepted them and on March 3rd, at Brest-Litovsk, a Soviet delegation quietly signed away more than 1,300,000 square miles of former Russian territory, including Poland, Belorussia, the Baltic provinces, the Ukraine, Finland, Bessarabia (ceded to Roumania) and areas in the Caucasus, comprising a total population of more than 60,000,000. The Peace of Brest-Litovsk saved the day for the Soviet government, but it was a peace bought at a terrible price. Ironically, some of the territorial losses suffered at Brest-Litovsk were to be recouped by the Soviet government, particularly in the case of the Ukraine, largely through the defeat of the Central Powers in November 1918 by the "capitalist" allies.

* On February 1st 1918 the Soviet government adopted the New Style calendar. From now on all dates in this book will be given in New Style.

After Brest-Litovsk Petrograd was too exposed as a seat of government, its connections with Tsarism too strong, and the capital was transferred to Moscow. There now began what has been called "the second Moscow period of Russian history". Few periods in history can have opened less auspiciously. The new Soviet government inherited chaotic conditions which rapidly deteriorated into the anarchy of civil war in many parts of Russia. Embattled in a country that was economically crippled, its hold upon the reins of power at best tenuous, the Soviet government strove to establish a socialist state while engaged in a desperate struggle for survival. Such measures as the introduction of a new calendar and a new orthography, the creation of a Workers and Peasants Red Army (organised by Trotsky) and a Red Fleet, the separation of the church from the state and the schools from the church, the annulment of all foreign loans, the nationalisation of the merchant marine and foreign trade—all enacted during the first four months of 1918—illustrate not so much the consistent pursuit of a socialist policy as an attempt to combine socialist rationalisation with the exigencies of the moment. The nationalisation of all large-scale industry, for instance, decreed in June, was prompted in part by the fear that certain industrial enterprises might fall into German hands. In view of the anarchy prevailing in industry as a result of "workers' control", Lenin insisted on the need for efficiency, proper accounting, the introduction of a form of state capitalism as a step towards socialism and the employment of former bourgeois specialists and administrators.

Such compromises with socialist doctrine, combined with the acceptance of the Brest-Litovsk terms, led to extreme friction within the ruling party. At the seventh Party Congress (March 6th–8th), which renamed the Party the "Russian Communist Party (Bolsheviks)", there was opposition among the so-called "Left Communists" to the Brest-Litovsk Peace; and at the fourth Congress of Soviets, which convened in Moscow on March 14th, the left-wing Socialist Revolutionaries who had been associated with the Bolsheviks in the Soviet government refused to accept the Brest-Litovsk terms and resigned. The Socialist Revolutionaries were also incensed by Lenin's attitude toward the peasantry. With the collapse of normal trade and distribution facilities between town and country, the peasants, now virtually the sole masters in the countryside, had little inducement to supply foodstuffs to the urban centres. But the pressures of the civil war, the need to supply the Red Army and the urban populations, obliged the Communists to enforce a system of compulsory requisitioning. Armed detachments from the towns were sent into the countryside to seize food supplies. At the same time, "committees of the poor" were formed in the villages in order to stimulate a class-war against the richer peasantry and *kulaks*. Barter took the place of money; centralised control replaced former marketing arrangements; rationing in the towns and egalitarian wage scales in the factories became features of this process. An enormous and inefficient bureaucracy grew up. The period of War Communism, as it came to be known, which extended from mid-1918 until 1921, was, despite its supposed egalitarianism, a period of the survival of the fittest. The Constitution of the RSFSR (Russian Socialist Federal Soviet Republic), which was adopted at the fifth Congress of Soviets in July 1918, based its attitude to labour on the principle that "he who does not work, does not eat"—a principle which was more of an ideal than a reality under War Communism. Such disparities between socialist ideals and the policies pursued by Lenin not only alienated the Socialist Revolutionaries, but drove them to resort to their former terrorist methods. Having protested in vain against the dictatorial methods adopted by the Communists, especially the establishment of "committees of the poor" in the villages, the left-wing Socialist Revolutionaries walked out of the fifth Congress. Two Socialist Revolutionaries killed the German ambassador, Count Mirbach —in the hope that such an act would provoke war with Germany—and on July 7th there was an attempt by the Socialist Revolutionaries to stage a *coup d'état* against the Soviet government. The incident was a symptom of the times : Lenin, who had come to power by armed force, had to face enemies who used armed force against both his government and his own person. On August 30th two poisoned bullets, fired by the Socialist Revolutionary Dora Kaplan, seriously wounded him and contributed to that breakdown in his health which was to make him a semi-invalid from 1922 onwards.

Civil war had by now broken out in the south. After Generals Kornilov and Alekseyev succeeded in escaping from Bykhov, where they had been detained after the seizure of the Mogilyov supreme headquarters by the Bolsheviks, they made their way south to join up with General Kaledin who had established a nationalist cossack régime in the Don area. By January 1918 General Alekseyev had managed to organise a Volunteer Army composed in the main of former Tsarist officers and cadets. Simultaneously Red units under Antonov-Ovseyenko launched a two-pronged attack against the Ukraine and the Don. The attack upon the Don brought about the collapse of Kaledin's régime and forced the Volunteer Army to retreat towards the Kuban on what was known as its "icy expedition" owing to the wintry conditions in the steppe. Its small force of 3,000 men survived this experience despite being defeated by the Reds and losing General Kornilov during an unsuccessful attack on Yekaterinodar in April. The Red attack on the Ukraine led to the

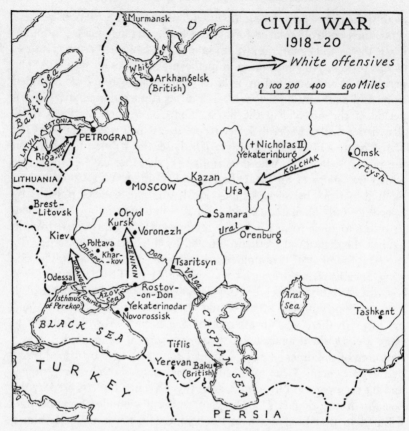

CIVIL WAR
1918–20
White offensives
0 100 200   400   600 Miles

capture of Kiev in February but it was driven back by the Germans, who dispersed the Rada and installed Skoropadsky as *Hetman*. The German occupation of Rostov in early May and the appointment of General Krasnov as cossack *Ataman* allowed the Volunteer Army to return to the Don area where it could re-equip and replenish its forces. The Volunteer Army now became a rallying-point for all supporters of the White, or anti-Soviet, cause.

At the end of May the Czech army corps of about 40,000 troops which was being moved along the Trans-Siberian Railway under nominal French command—the ultimate object of this exercise being the transportation of the Czechs to the western front via Vladivostock—seized control of all major stations, with the exception of Irkutsk, and set up anti-Soviet governments. In June an allied force, consisting chiefly of British troops, landed at Murmansk and subsequently took over Arkhangelsk where a northern Provisional Government was established under N. V. Chaykovsky, the prominent Populist of the early 1870s. British troops also intervened in Transcaspia in July and landed at Baku in August, at the same time as United States and Japanese troops were landing in Vladivostok. The allied intervention, though justified in part on the grounds of defending allied stores and equipment, served to raise the hopes of the various anti-Soviet groupings but made little active contribution to the White cause and gave the Soviet government every reason for representing their defeats in the civil war as the consequence of allied support for the Whites and their ultimate victory as a victory over capitalist imperialism.

During the summer of 1918 a Socialist Revolutionary government, known as *Komuch* (Committee of Members of the Constituent Assembly, so named because it consisted of former CA delegates) was set up in Samara and a more right-wing government in Omsk, both dependent for their existence upon the support of Czech troops. At a State Conference in Ufa in September an uneasy anti-Soviet compromise was reached between these two governments. During this time General Denikin, commanding the reconstituted Volunteer Army in the south, had captured Yekaterinodar and Novorossisk, but a huge army under General Krasnov failed to take Tsaritsyn, the defence of which had been organised by Stalin (hence the later renaming of Tsaritsyn as Stalingrad). Earlier Kazan had been captured by Czech and Socialist Revolutionary forces—a capture which gained them half a billion roubles' worth of Tsarist bullion, which had been sent to Kazan for safekeeping during the First World War. But on September 10th the fifth Red Army recaptured the city and in early October entered Samara. In late November Admiral Kolchak became Supreme Commander of the Whites in Omsk, supported by the Czechs and the British; the Socialist Revolutionaries were forced to go underground. More important, however, was the fact that the war in Europe had come to an end. The Germans relinquished their hold over the Ukraine and a Red Army was able, early in 1919, to re-establish partial Soviet control. The Ukrainian Socialist, Petlyura, who had ousted Skoropadsky, was in turn obliged to flee and his troops joined forces with those of the peasant revolutionary Makhno.

1919 was to be the decisive year in the civil war. If, during 1918, the issues at stake between the Reds and the Whites had been partially obscured by the fact of the allied intervention and the presence of German troops in the Ukraine, by the spring of 1919, with the allied decision not to intervene further, both the issues and the course of events became more clearcut. The Soviet government could rely on a Communist Party which, in its discipline and firmness of conviction, provided political guidance and cohesion to the largely peasant Red Armies which fought for the cause of the new Soviet state. Kolchak and Denikin had no such political instrument at their command; in political terms, the White cause stood for a return to past values, to monarchy and a "great, united, undivided Russia". In terms of military strategy, the Red Armies had the advantage of relatively short interior lines of communication, whereas the White armies, on the southern and eastern limits of European Russia, failed very largely because, in advancing towards Moscow, their lines of communication became over-extended. Yet the forces on both sides were fairly evenly matched, the numerical superiority of the Red Armies being offset by the greater military skill and experience—due to the backbone of former Tsarist officers—displayed by the White forces. The excesses of both sides were appalling; centuries of accumulated class, national and racial hatreds gave rise to vendettas of incredible savagery. The revolutions of 1905 and 1917 may have wrought the fundamental political changes in the Russian scene, but the bloodletting of the years of civil war was the final, cathartic stage in revolutionary process.

With the defeat of the Central Powers, Lenin could tear up the Brest-Litovsk treaty and the boundaries of Russia could once more be remade. In March 1919 the Third International, or Comintern, convened in Moscow and proclaimed the coming "dictatorship of the proletariat" throughout the world. This demonstration of the international character of Communism was overshadowed at the time by the success of Kolchak's armies advancing from Omsk. In mid-March Ufa fell to the White troops and by mid-April it seemed that Kolchak would be marching on Moscow, but he dissipated his efforts by attempting a two-pronged advance towards Arkhangelsk in the north, in the hope of joining up with the British, and towards the Volga in the south, in the hope of joining up with Denikin. At the end of April Red forces under Frunze counter-attacked and by mid-July Kolchak's armies had been driven back. Meanwhile, in the south, White armies under the command of Denikin captured Kharkov on June 25th, Tsaritsyn a week later, Poltava in late July and Odessa and Kiev in August. With the collapse of Kolchak's armies, Denikin struck northwards with the aim of capturing Moscow. Kursk was captured on September 20th, Voronezh on October 6th and Oryol, within 250 miles of the capital, on October 13th. A new threat now developed in the north. General Yudenich, with a force of some 20,000 men, advanced on Petrograd from Estonia and almost succeeded in encircling the city. The defenders were rallied by Trotsky and by the middle of November Yudenich had been forced to retreat behind the Estonian border. Simultaneously Denikin had been driven back from Oryol. By this time Kolchak's Siberian Empire had crumbled away. Less than a year after he had proclaimed himself Supreme Commander, Red troops entered his "capital" of Omsk (November 14th 1919). Kolchak himself travelled eastwards along the Trans-Siberian Railway in the company of Czech units and allied staff officers until, at Irkutsk, he was handed over to the left wing Political Centre which was in temporary control of the town. He was executed on the night of February 6th 1920 and his body was pushed under the ice of the frozen Angara. Throughout the winter of 1919–1920 Denikin's forces were pursued southwards and on March 27th 1920 Novorossisk, Denikin's last outpost, was captured. He handed over his command of the White armies to General Wrangel, Denikin himself and many of his followers being evacuated with British assistance. British troops had meanwhile been withdrawn from Arkhangelsk in September and by April 1920 all the American troops in the Russian Far East had been evacuated. The allied intervention was at an end, with the exception of Japanese troops who finally left the Russian mainland in 1922. The White threat, though in the autumn of 1919 it seemed as if both Moscow and Petrograd might fall to White armies, had been effectively dealt a blow from which it was never to recover.

Early in 1920 peace treaties were signed between the Soviet government and the newly-independent states of Estonia, Latvia and Lithuania. But Soviet Russia's western borders were still not properly defined. Finland's independence had been grudgingly recognised by the Soviet government at the end of 1917 and was confirmed in a peace treaty of 1920. Relations with Poland, on the other hand, were far from happy. With allied aid and encouragement, Polish troops under General Pilsudski advanced into the Ukraine and on May 6th 1920 occupied Kiev. Pilsudski's intention was to establish an independent Ukraine under the leadership of Petlyura. A counter-attack launched by Budyonny's Red Cavalry broke through the Polish lines and on June 12th Kiev was recaptured. At this moment General Wrangel broke out of his base in the Crimea and invaded parts of the southern Ukraine, thereby threatening the rear of the Soviet armies. Yet Budyonny's breakthrough in the south-west and the advance of Soviet forces under Tukhachevsky on a more northerly front had been so successful that the Poles were obliged to fall back in disorder. For a time, during July 1920, while the second Congress of the Comintern was taking place in Petrograd, it seemed as if victorious Soviet armies would sweep through Poland and carry the banner of international proletarian revolution into the heart of Europe. However, in mid-August Pilsudski managed to halt Tukhachevsky outside Warsaw, the Soviet troops were forced back and on

October 12th an armistice was signed in Riga. The ensuing Treaty of Riga of March 1921 regularised the Soviet–Polish border by placing large areas of the western Ukraine and Belorussia under Polish sovereignty. Peace with Poland allowed the entire Soviet military effort to be directed towards defeating Wrangel. A more intelligent and politically enlightened man than either Kolchak or Denikin, Wrangel had succeeded in forging a disciplined and efficient army, but it could not withstand the numerical superiority of the Soviet forces under Frunze which were now turned against it. After a series of bitter rearguard engagements Wrangel's army was forced back into the Isthmus of Perekop, which was finally stormed on November 11th 1920. Wrangel and 150,000 surviving Whites were evacuated in ships of the former Black Sea Fleet.

By August 1921 Makhno had been forced to flee into Roumania and the last serious opposition to Soviet rule had been removed. Except for Finland, the new Baltic states and an independent Poland, which were assumed to be a kind of *cordon sanitaire* between a capitalist West and a socialist East, Soviet Russia had by 1921 brought within its orbit practically all the territory of the former Russian Empire. Azerbaydzhan and Armenia were both invaded by the Red Army in 1920 at the invitation of Communist Military Revolutionary Committees which had seized control from the separatist, nationalist governments in the respective countries. The Menshevik government in Georgia was ousted, again by armed force, in February 1921. The Bashkir, Tatar and Kazakh peoples of the Caucasus were all brought within the confines of the RSFSR, as were the nationalities of Central Asia. A Far Eastern Republic became part of the RSFSR in November 1922 after the withdrawal of Japanese troops had caused the collapse of the White government in Vladivostok. Stalin can be said to have played the leading role in remaking Russia after the civil war. It is possible that his experience as Commissar for Nationalities may not only have taught him the simple lesson that armed force, not socialist talk, makes empires but also have given him that taste for power which was eventually to become his obsessive preoccupation, with consequences of such magnitude for Russia and the world that it will be impossible for many years to estimate their full extent.

The Period of NEP

In August 1921 the poet Alexander Blok died. His own testament, and the greatest testament in literature to the October Revolution, was his poem *The Twelve* about twelve Red guards marching through Petrograd in the winter of 1917. The concluding lines of the poem, with their reference to Christ at the head of the twelve revolutionary disciples, have puzzled commentators and have given rise to many and various interpretations :

> "So they stride imperiously,
> A hungry mongrel at their heels—
> A blood-red flag ahead of them,
> And through the swirling snow unseen,
> And from all bullets now redeemed,
> Softly above the storm's violence,
> Loftily through the snow-pearl radiance,
> Wearing a white crown of roses—
> Leading the way is the Lord Jesus."

There is perhaps an incongruity about associating Christ with a revolution engineered by Bolsheviks for avowedly atheistic ends. Yet the socialist egalitarianism of the Bolsheviks was manifestly closer to Christ's teaching than the ideas of rank and privilege upon which the Tsarist autocracy had been based. Although, in retrospect, it may seem that the revolution of October 1917 and the ensuing civil war were a matter more of taking life than giving it, of humanity degraded rather than ennobled, with brutish power politics everywhere the vanquisher of Christian principles, it may also seem in retrospect that from the holocaust of such terrible events there emerged perhaps a better, at least a new, Russia. Whatever the moral implications of such events, the events themselves cut deep into the experience of all those who survived them. In the literature of Russia since 1917 the consequences of these events persistently reverberate and one writer after another, Communist or non-Communist, has given expression to them. One of the earliest prose works to be devoted to the civil war was *The Iron Flood* (1924) by Serafimovich (1863–1949) which made use of some of the techniques of the cinema to describe the perilous journey of an army of refugees down the eastern shore of the Black Sea and through the Caucasian mountains. Another work, less a novel than a diary describing the struggle of partisans fighting against Kolchak, was *Chapayev* (1923) by Furmanov (1891–1926). *The Defeat* (1927) by Fadeyev (1901–1956), the first Soviet novel to make an obvious return to the traditional Tolstoyan manner of psychological portraiture, was concerned with the civil war in the Far East. *The Badgers* (1924) by Leonov (b. 1899), a racily written novel about the struggle between town and countryside, or the more experimental *Naked Year* (1922) by Pilnyak (1894–1937), or *Red Cavalry* (1926) about Budyonny's cavalry in Poland by Babel (1894–1941)—all three describe the changing allegiances, passions and violence of the civil war years. A quieter and more intellectual approach to the problems confronting the younger generation was offered by Fedin (b. 1892) in *Cities and Years* (1924) and *Brothers* (1928). The most monumental, and perhaps the greatest works of literature to come from Russia since 1917 have been concerned with the upheavals of 1917–1921 : such are the four-part epic novel *Quiet Flows the Don* by Sholokhov (b. 1905), the three-part novel *Road to Calvary* by Aleksey Tolstoy (1883–1945) and—the finest of them—*Doctor Zhivago* by Boris Pasternak (1890–1960).

By 1921 Russia was economically devastated. The industrial labour force had dropped to half its pre-war figure and industrial production was barely 14 per cent of the 1913 total. To the damage inflicted by seven years of war should be added the losses sustained as a result of inefficiency, ignorance and abysmally poor management, especially in the nationalised industries. In agriculture the labour force had probably been reduced by as much as 14,000,000 men; sown areas and yields had also steadily decreased. Then, in 1920, a drought affected the Volga area and yields were halved. A further and more terrible drought occurred in 1921, involving not only the Volga, but also the Urals, parts of Asia and almost the whole of the black-earth belt. In addition to the sufferings already visited on the people of Russia there now came the worst scourge of all—famine and, following famine, epidemic. In 1921–1922 the famine may have affected as many as 33,000,000 people, of whom 19,000,000 were in danger of dying of starvation. Relief work was organised by the government on an enormous scale and help poured into Russia from the United States (through the American Relief Commission organised by Herbert Hoover) and from other parts of the world, much of this aid being due to the unflagging efforts of the Norwegian explorer Nansen. In the end it has been calculated that perhaps 2,000,000—or as many as 10,000,000—people may have perished as a result of famine and epidemic. And on top of such natural catastrophe was the economic catastrophe of a spiralling inflation which culminated in the "scissors" crisis of 1923.

The Soviet government and the Communist Party survived the civil war only by a narrow margin. Notwithstanding its successes, Soviet power was not strong. Moreover, the anticipated proletarian revolutions in Germany and elsewhere in Europe, which Lenin had confidently assumed would occur once the proletariat had come to power in Russia, did not materialise. Soviet Russia was isolated as the only socialist state in a capitalist world. Fear both of reprisals by the capitalist nations against Soviet Russia (chiefly because the Soviet government had seized so many foreign assets in Russia) and of popular revolt against Soviet rule (chiefly due to the highly unpopular, repressive measures which had been employed against the peasants in an effort to ensure grain deliveries) tended, on the one hand, to foster a cynical realism in Communist ranks and, on the other, to emphasise the need for unity within the Party, making dissent of any kind appear to be hardly less than treason. Power for the Communist Party was the dominant issue; policies might be changed, but power for the Communist Party, both on a national and—ultimately—on a world scale, remained the grand strategy. Power within the Party itself also became a matter of supreme importance. From 1919 onwards most of the important decisions were being taken by a Politburo consisting of Lenin, Trotsky, Stalin, Kamenev, Zinovyev (from 1921), Rykov and Tomsky (both from 1922). Although Lenin was the acknowledged leader, he permitted discussion of policy and other issues at Politburo and Central Committee level. Opposition to the Party from other political parties, however, was being ruthlessly repressed by 1921, when the Menshevik and Socialist Revolutionary leaders were forced into emigration; and in 1922 the first Soviet political trial occurred, which eventually concluded, after Lenin's death, in the execution of fourteen of the Socialist Revolutionary defendants.

The civil war may have ended by 1921, but early in that year opposition to Communism began to take a more serious form. Six days before the tenth Party Congress was due to meet, a mutiny occurred (February 28th 1921) among the sailors of the Baltic Fleet garrisoned at Kronstadt at the same time as a wave of strikes was spreading throughout Petrograd. Both sailors and strikers were manifesting political as well as economic grievances against Soviet rule; and it was soon obvious that the Kronstadt mutiny was an example of sailors with revolutionary proletarian sympathies rising in revolt against Lenin's "dictatorship of the proletariat". The Soviet government did not take kindly to such revolutionary comrades. Soviet troops under Tukhachevsky stormed the Kronstadt fortress and the mutiny ended in mass executions. But the implications of the mutiny were not lost upon Lenin. He realised that the Communist Party had gone too far in pursuing the restrictive and repressive policies of War Communism. Concessions would have to be made to the general desire for a relaxation of tension if the Communist Party was not to be swept away by a rising tide of revulsion against its policies.

At the tenth Party Congress in March 1921 the policy of War Communism was abandoned and its place was taken by what was called a New Economic Policy or NEP. NEP was designed primarily to encourage the peasants to produce more food. In place of the practice of enforced requisitioning of foodstuffs which had been common under War Communism, a free market in foodstuffs was introduced. As NEP progressed, the peasants had to surrender in tax only 10 per cent of their produce and were free to sell their surpluses as they wished; they were also permitted to regard their holdings as their own private property, to lease their land and to engage hired labour. On the other hand, the "commanding heights" of the economy, as Lenin called them—the major industrial enterprises, that is—remained under state control; but even here a measure of independence was given to the managements of such enterprises in order to encourage greater commercial efficiency and certain smaller industries were allowed to revert to private ownership. Furthermore, the currency was stabilised and a State Bank formed. In order to coordinate and oversee the working of both the state and private sectors of the economy a new state planning commission was established, known as Gosplan.

These new measures, dictated largely by the need to come to terms with the grim economic facts of the situation, nevertheless came too late to avert the famine of 1921–1922. But they set in motion processes which were soon to put the Russian economy on its feet again. They also set in motion processes of dissent within the Communist Party. Trotsky, for instance, brilliant though he may have been in organising the Red Army during the civil war, believed that the dictatorship of the proletariat should be dependent upon the strictest discipline in the organisation of trade unions and the management of industry. His dictatorial management of transport had aroused bitter resentment among the rank and file of the Party. When he came out against Lenin's policy of greater liberalisation, he was defeated—a defeat which was to be a portent for the future. Opposition also came from other quarters. A Workers' Opposition, headed by Shlyapnikov, objected to the abandonment of the policy of "workers' control", disapproved of the violations of the elective principle at union committee level and believed that the trade unions should have a greater say in the control of industry. The

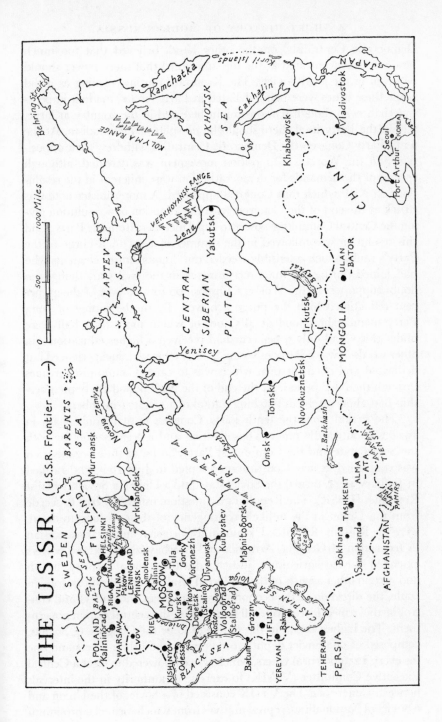

THE U.S.S.R. (U.S.S.R. Frontier —·—·—)

1000 Miles
500
0

Behring Straits
Kamchatka
Kuril Islands
JAPAN
OKHOTSK SEA
Sakhalin
Vladivostok
KOLYMA RANGE
Port Arthur
Seoul
KOREA
CHINA
Khabarovsk
VERKHOYANSK RANGE
Lena
Yakutsk
ULAN-BATOR
L. Baikal
Irkutsk
CENTRAL SIBERIAN PLATEAU
MONGOLIA
Yenisey
BARENTS SEA
Novaya Zemlya
Murmansk
LAPTEV SEA
Ob
Novokuznetsk
Tomsk
URALS
Omsk
L. Balkhash
TIEN SHAN
ALMA-ATA
PAMIRS
Arkhangelsk
SWEDEN
FINLAND
BALTIC SEA
Karelian Isthmus
Ladoga
HELSINKI
TALLIN
Murmansk
Aral Sea
TASHKENT
Bokhara
Samarkand
AFGHANISTAN
Magnitogorsk
Kuibyshev
POLAND
Kaliningrad
WARSAW
RIGA
VILNA
PSKOV
LENINGRAD
MINSK
Smolensk
Kalinin
MOSCOW
Tula
Gorky
Ulyanovsk
Oryol
Kursk
Voronezh
(Stalino)
Volga
KIEV
Kharkov
Dnieper
Donetsk
Don
Rostov
Volgograd
(Stalingrad)
Grozny
KISHINYOV
Odessa
BLACK SEA
Batum
Tiflis
Baku
CASPIAN SEA
YEREVAN
TEHERAN
PERSIA
Lvov

197

Democratic Centralists, on the other hand, believed that too much power was concentrated at the top and urged that more power should be given to the local Soviets. The Kronstadt mutiny, coming as it did while these issues were being debated in Party circles, made it imperative that, even though tensions might be eased in the country at large, within the Party itself there should be no splits or factionalism. At the tenth Party Congress the Democratic Centralists withdrew their opposition and the Workers' Opposition movement was defeated, although certain of the demands for democratisation were inherent in the resolutions on NEP which that Congress approved. A more sinister note was struck at the end of the Congress with the adoption of a resolution giving the Central Committee power to expel members from the Party; and this resolution was followed in the summer of 1921 by a purge of the Party's ranks which ostensibly weeded out "opportunist" elements who had joined during the mass recruitments in the civil war, though no doubt supporters of the Workers' Opposition formed part of the 25 per cent reduction which the purge achieved. By the beginning of 1923 Party membership stood at 485,500, of whom more than half were under thirty and only 5 per cent had received a higher education—in other words, it was a Party of young, poorly educated, inexperienced but dedicated and obedient men which was to carry Communist fortunes through the NEP period. At the end of the NEP period Party membership had almost trebled, reaching a total of 1,304,471 members.

The period from the tenth Party Congress until Lenin's death in 1924 was outwardly one of consolidation and reorganisation for both the Soviet state and the Communist Party. So far as state organisation was concerned, a new Constitution adopted in July 1923 and ratified in January 1924, turned the Soviet state into a Union of Soviet Socialist Republics (USSR). The Republics in question, ostensibly free to secede from the Union in the unlikely contingency of their wishing to do so, were the Russian (RSFSR), Ukrainian, Belorussian and Transcaucasian (a federation of Georgia, Armenia and Azerbaydzhan), whose powers extended only to agriculture, justice, education, social security, health and certain other aspects of their internal affairs. Foreign affairs, foreign trade, the direction of the economy, fiscal matters, the budget and control of the armed forces were all handled by the central Union government. The highest organ in the state was to be the Congress of Soviets, composed of one Soviet deputy for every 25,000 urban voters and one for every 125,000 rural voters, which was empowered to elect a Central Executive Committee (VTsIK) to exercise its authority in the intervals between Congresses. The VTsIK consisted of a Soviet of the Union and a Soviet of Nationalities, representatives from which formed a presidium authorised to act for the VTsIK when it was not in session. The central Union government was the Sovnarkom of the USSR, of which Lenin became the first chairman. But, despite such a paraphernalia of constitutionalism, the Constitution of 1924 did not reveal so much as obscure the mainsprings of power. Reference, admittedly, was made to the state political directorate—or OGPU, as the *Cheka* had been renamed; but no reference was made to the Communist Party.

The exigencies of civil war and the need for centralised control meant that ever greater power in the Party became concentrated in various policy-making and organisational appendages of the Party Central Committee. The Politburo was, of course, the topmost policy-making body, but much power also came to be attached to the Orgburo (Organisational Bureau), a body intended to deal with organisational matters in the Party. In addition, a Secretariat was formed as a means of controlling the Party machine. This last body quickly snowballed, through a multiplication of its various departments and bureaux, into the most powerful section of the Central Committee apparatus, deriving much of its influence from the fact that it exercised control over the Party secretaries who were the key men at every level of the Party hierarchy. From 1921 onwards these Party secretaries became the controlling influences in the local Soviets. In view of this, it is no exaggeration to claim that the Secretariat of the Central Committee of the Communist Party was a government within the government of the Soviet Union. Whoever controlled the Secretariat had his finger upon practically every aspect of the country's life. Such massive bureaucratic power naturally led to abuses, which in turn led to the registering of complaints against the top echelons. To examine these matters a Central Control Commission eventually came into existence in 1922, but this body soon passed into the control of the Party's General Secretary and thus became yet another means of exercising power from above. Who, however, was the General Secretary?

Stalin became General Secretary of the Party in March 1922. Apart from being Commissar for Nationalities, he had also, from 1919, been Commissar of the Workers' and Peasants' Inspectorate.

Stalin, born Joseph Vissarionovich Dzhugashvili in Gori near Tiflis on December 21st 1879, had received his early education in the Tiflis Theological Seminary. He apparently joined the Social-Democratic Party in 1898 and after being arrested in 1902 was exiled to Irkutsk. Early in 1904 he succeeded in escaping, but the actual facts of his subsequent revolutionary activity in Tiflis and Batum are difficult to disentangle from the official Soviet hagiography. He first met Lenin in 1905 and later performed a number of useful "services" for him, the most notable being a raid upon a Tiflis bank in 1907 which gained much-needed roubles for the Bolshevik cause. Arrested in 1908 and exiled to Vologda, he again escaped, was rearrested, escaped again and finally, in 1913, after attending the Bolshevik Central Committee meeting in Cracow, was urged by Lenin to write a pamphlet on *Marxism and the Nationality Question*. He spent 1913–1916 in Siberian exile. When he reappeared in Petrograd in March 1917 he was the senior member of the Central Committee and assumed a somewhat hesitant leadership of the Bolsheviks until Lenin's arrival on April 3rd.

Stalin's story is full of obscurities, like his personality. Lacking both the education and the intellectual precocity of many of his Bolshevik colleagues, he gained Lenin's trust through his willingness to perform the unpleasant tasks which formed a necessary part both of underground political activity and, when Bolshevism had triumphed, of the routine administration of Party affairs. Though dedicated to the cause of revolution, he was a man of consuming ambition who knew how to accumulate power in his hands by a patient and unspectacular manipulation of the Party apparatus. Obscurity chiefly surrounds all that was private in Stalin's life. He assiduously cultivated a public image of himself as the benevolent moustachioed, paternalistic "man of steel", but in the end he seems to hang over Russian history like some nightmarish Cheshire Cat whose grin exudes a calculated and chilling menace. The menace of Stalin's power first became apparent in 1922. By that time he was the only Communist leader to be a member of the Central Committee, Politburo, Orgburo and Secretariat.

In May 1922 Lenin suffered his first stroke and, except for a period during the autumn of that year, took no further active part in public life. But his suspicions of those who had charge of the country's affairs, particularly of Stalin, had been aroused. In a letter of March 5th 1923 he complained of Stalin's "rudeness"; more than this, he composed what has since come to be known as his Testament in which he gave his estimates of his colleagues in the Politburo. The references to Stalin were suppressed in the Soviet Union during Stalin's lifetime and were only made know to a Soviet audience during Khrushchev's denunciation of Stalin at the twentieth Party Congress in 1956. Lenin complained that Stalin, as General Secretary of the Party, had accumulated unlimited power in his hands—"and I am not sure," he wrote, "whether he will always know how to exercise such power with sufficient care". He then suggested that a way should be found of removing Stalin from the post of General Secretary and of appointing in his place "another man, who would be in every respect different from Comrade Stalin with the one overriding condition that he should be more patient, more loyal, more

polite and more attentive to his comrades, less capricious, and so on . . ."
Lenin was dying and his utterances were often disregarded by the Party
leaders in the Kremlin. His Testament, though composed early in 1923,
was not divulged until the thirteenth Party Congress in May 1924 and
then only to a limited number of Congress delegates. Stalin offered to
resign, but in view of Lenin's death on January 21st 1924 it was imperative that an appearance of unity should be maintained in the Party and
Stalin's resignation from the post of General Secretary was not accepted.
He, not Trotsky, had meanwhile become Lenin's successor and the
foremost champion of the dead leader's memory. The cult of Lenin was
initiated at the second Congress of Soviets in January 1924 when resolutions were passed calling for the erection of a Lenin mausoleum on
Red Square and changing the name of the city where Lenin had come
to power from Petrograd to Leningrad.

The struggle for supreme power which ensued between Stalin, Zinovyev, Kamenev and Trotsky after Lenin's death revolved about the
fundamental policy questions which had been raised and debated at the
time of the tenth Party Congress. Towards the end of his life Lenin
insisted that socialism in Russia should be based on a union between the
workers and the peasants. Stalin, Zinovyev and Kamenev, the triumvirate who assumed control of the Politburo during Lenin's illness,
espoused this policy, believing that a prosperous peasantry was an essential prerequisite for the growth of industry. Trotsky, to put it simply,
believed that industry should come first and that the free market of
NEP should be replaced by a planned economy in which industry would
have the dominant role. A premise of Trotsky's argument was that there
had to be a world proletarian revolution before socialism could be guaranteed in Russia. Stalin attacked this notion with his assertion that it
displayed a lack of faith in the Russian Communist Party. In place of
it he enunciated the doctrine of "socialism in one country". Aided by
Zinovyev and Kamenev, Stalin succeeded, early in 1925, in prising
Trotsky loose from his connection with the Red Army and in having
him roundly berated in the Central Committee. Having thus disarmed
his major opponent, Stalin now turned his attention to his erstwhile
supporters, Zinovyev and Kamenev, who had come out in opposition to
his dictatorial methods. Kamenev was demoted to candidate membership of the Politburo and Zinovyev was removed from his controlling
position in the Leningrad Party organisation. Trotsky, Zinovyev and
Kamenev now joined forces in a united opposition to Stalin, but it was
already too late; Stalin's nominees already packed the Central Committee and its various bodies.

The first show-down between Stalin and the new opposition came at a plenum of the Central Committee in October 1926 which removed Trotsky from his seat on the Politburo, displaced Kamenev from candidate membership and robbed Zinovyev of his leading position in the Comintern. The struggle had now become one to the death. The opposition made desperate efforts to retain what little influence remained to them and even went to the lengths of addressing street demonstrations. At a further plenum of the Central Committee in October 1927 the *coup de grace* was administered. Both Trotsky and Zinovyev were expelled from the Central Committee and three weeks later from the Party. In January 1928, less than four years after Lenin's death, Trotsky was sent into exile, first to Alma-Ata, then to Turkey and finally to Mexico where an NKVD agent killed him in 1940. But the fifteenth Party Congress, which opened on December 2nd 1927, not only endorsed the expulsion of Trotsky, Zinovyev and seventy-five supporters of "Trotskyism", it also adopted resolutions increasing the taxation of the *kulaks* and calling for the preparation of a Five Year Plan for the development of industry. In other words, at the moment of getting rid of the opposition, Stalin, it seems, felt it expedient to adopt their policy. Stalin accommodated his policies to whatever course best suited his needs in the struggle for supreme power. By the beginning of 1928 Soviet power was Stalin's power. For the next twenty-five years, until Stalin's death in 1953, there was to be no serious internal opposition to his one-man leadership of the Soviet Union—or so it must be assumed from the evidence at present available.

The struggle in the Politburo and Central Committee between 1924 and 1928, which ended in Stalin's victory over the "left opposition", as it was called, was in many respects a struggle between revolutionaries and bureaucrats. Trotsky was by temperament and character a man who flourished in a revolutionary atmosphere; he enjoyed the grand gesture, the oratorical posture. Stalin, by contrast, a less honest and less brilliant man, preferred a less conspicuous, more devious way of achieving his ends: he worked through the bureaucratic apparatus of the Party machine which he had himself largely created, relying upon a multitude of hand-picked henchmen for support, leavening his words with an implied threat of police reprisals and never committing himself wholly to one or another policy. Stalin inherited Lenin's ruthlessness, but transformed it from revolutionary ruthlessness into the sinister, cloacal ruthlessness of a bureaucracy which was answerable neither to revolutionary justice nor to public opinion. In short, Stalin's defeat of the "left opposition" was a necessary stage in the creation of a totalitarian state system far more authoritarian and arbitrary, especially in its suppression of individual freedom, than Tsarist absolutism.

But the struggle between Stalin and his rivals had not been conducted wholly in a vacuum. Both economic and foreign policy issues had their part to play in determining the outcome, although it would be wrong to ascribe too much importance to these issues at the expense of the simpler issue of personal power. Nonetheless, at the end of the civil war the Soviet government was faced with the paradox that it had come to power as a "dictatorship of the proletariat" in a predominantly peasant country. To many, particularly to the "left opposition", NEP seemed to be a denial of the theory of proletarian revolution; indeed, for a time it was confidently thought in the West that the Soviet government had abandoned Marxism. There was some foundation for this view, since the effect of NEP was to bring about a fairly rapid increase in agricultural production; whereas by 1923 the labour force in heavy industry had reached only 60 per cent of the 1913 total, and industrial production was barely half-way there. As a consequence, industry and agriculture began to get seriously out of step. Prices of industrial goods rose steeply while agricultural prices began to fall—a divergence which, when it was illustrated on a graph by Trotsky at the twelfth Party Congress, resembled a scissors; hence the economic crisis of 1923 became known as the "scissors" crisis. Measures taken in 1924 included lowering industrial prices by as much as 29 per cent and increasing the amount of money in the countryside, aided by the creation of a Central Agricultural Bank and the issue of a new gold-backed currency. The economic crisis was gradually overcome and pre-war production levels in both agriculture and industry had been achieved by 1927. However, in the absence of foreign loans, capital could not be accumulated in sufficient quantity to allow for a rapid expansion of industry. In 1926–1927 80 per cent of all capital funds were used for rehabilitating and enlarging existing plants and only 20 per cent could be allocated to industrial expansion, including the grandiose electrification schemes of the State Commission for the Electrification of Russia which had been created in 1920 for the purpose of putting into effect Lenin's dictum that "Communism is Soviet power plus the electrification of the whole country". Notwithstanding this, the building of the enormous hydro-electric project on the Dnieper was begun in 1927; at the same time the Turksib railway was started (completed in 1930), work began on the first large tractor plant in Stalingrad (formerly Tsaritsyn) and—in an excess of "gigantomania"—enormous metallurgical plants were begun at Kuznetsk in Siberia, Magnitogorsk in the Urals and Krivoy Rog in the Ukraine.

In the countryside during the NEP period the peasantry had become stratified into *kulaks* (barely 4 per cent), middle peasants (almost

70 per cent) and poor peasants (about 20 per cent). Despite the large increase in the number of middle peasants, communes and communal land tenure were still very common; but the influence of the Communist Party as such remained weak. The peasants, having little incentive to sell their produce, preferred to eat it. By late 1927 the inability or refusal of the mass of the peasantry to offer sufficient produce for the urban markets was beginning to have serious effects. The call for sterner measures against the *kulaks* which was made at the fifteenth Party Congress was justified on the grounds that the *kulaks*, in failing to produce more food, were undermining the Soviet economy. Whether or not the *kulaks* were to blame, or whether the threat from them had been cooked up by Stalin as an excuse for his industrialisation programme will never be satisfactorily established; what can be said is that by the beginning of 1928 the days of the independent peasants, whether *kulaks* or not, were numbered.

In Soviet foreign policy the hope of world proletarian revolution was balanced by the fear that the capitalist Powers would unite in order to destroy the socialist Soviet Union. If the one did not materialise, then the other had at all costs to be prevented. One important weapon in the Soviet armoury against the capitalist Powers, or the "capitalist encirclement" as it came to be known, was the Comintern. But though the Comintern could help to spread dissension among the capitalist Powers by promoting international Communist activities, it could do little to enhance Soviet Russia's diplomatic prestige. For this reason, Chicherin, the Commissar for Foreign Affairs, made serious efforts both to protect Soviet frontiers with a series of non-aggression treaties and to enter into diplomatic relations with the major capitalist nations. In 1921 treaties were signed with Persia, Afghanistan, Turkey and Mongolia, and friendly relations established with China. Simultaneously trade agreements were made with Great Britain, Norway, Italy and Austria. The first important victory for Chicherin's diplomacy came in 1922 when, during the International Economic Conference at Genoa, a treaty of friendship and neutrality was signed between Germany and Russia at Rapallo. The two outcast nations of Europe had now joined forces, giving rise to a cooperation in both the economic and military spheres which was to be extremely close until 1925; after that, despite the renewal of the treaty in 1926, relations between the two countries gradually cooled. The Comintern's attempt to provoke a Communist revolution in Germany in 1923 after the French occupation of the Ruhr failed very largely because the Soviet government found it expedient to maintain friendly relations with the Weimar Republic, its only European ally at this time. A Soviet delegation participated in the Lausanne Conference (November 1922–July 1923), but would not accept the resulting Lausanne Convention which permitted the passage of merchantmen and naval vessels through the Straits. However, in 1924, diplomatic relations were established with Great Britain (February 2nd) and, a little later, with Italy, Norway, Austria, Greece, Sweden and Denmark; in May diplomatic relations were renewed with China and in October with France. Soviet Russia had begun to gain recognition among the nations of the world, but the process was by no means easy. A severe strain, for instance, was placed upon relations with Great Britain towards the end of 1924 by the publication of a letter allegedly written by Zinovyev, who was at that time chairman of the Comintern, calling for subversive action during the General Election; the letter caused widespread anti-Soviet feeling in Britain and helped to return the Conservatives to power under Stanley Baldwin. The Locarno agreement of October 1925, which guaranteed Germany's western frontiers under the Versailles Treaty, was interpreted by the Soviet Union as giving Germany a free hand in extending her eastern frontiers; but the already-mentioned Soviet–German treaty of 1926 helped to allay this fear. During 1926 loud Soviet support for the General Strike in Great Britain caused alarm in Conservative circles which assumed the proportions of a war scare in May 1927 when a raid on "Arcos", the Soviet trading organisation in London, brought to light documents allegedly implicating the Soviet Union in espionage and other subversive activities. Great Britain severed diplomatic relations—an act which, in conjunction with anti-Soviet activities in China and the murder of the Soviet ambassador in Poland, created the impression in the Soviet Union that an anti-Soviet crusade by the capitalist Powers was imminent. It is possible that the war scare of 1927 provoked Stalin's decision to embark on the crash programme of industrialisation announced at the fifteenth Party Congress.

The period of NEP saw greater social freedom than probably any other period in modern Russian history. The marriage and divorce laws were so permissive that the family practically ceased to exist as a social unit. Though gangs of homeless boys roamed the streets, symptomatic of the immorality of the period, the Komsomol (the Communist league of youth, founded in 1918) was a counterweight which imbued young people with a sense of dedication to the Party, encouraged them to spy on their "bourgeois" parents and inculcated a new, if rather strait-laced, attitude to moral questions. The church was ruthlessly persecuted, especially by the League of Militant Atheists founded in 1925 for the dissemination of atheistic propaganda, but by the late '20s an uneasy *modus vivendi* had been achieved between church and state. In the educational sphere great efforts were made to eradicate illiteracy, new universities were opened and much emphasis was laid on the teaching of science. Organised sport and other "cultural" activities became extremely popular. Social insurance for injury, unemployment and old age was introduced, as was free medical care.

As a result of the mass emigration of "bourgeois" intellectuals after the October revolution, practically all the older generation of writers — including, incidentally, Maxim Gorky — had left Russia by 1921. In the NEP period the cultural scene was dominated by a younger generation whose aim of breaking with the past gave rise to much colourful, if naïve, experimentation. It was a period of ferment, of many different currents and isolated examples of brilliance, of lively academic criticism (particularly the work of the Formalists) and bitter literary polemics. The failure, for example, of Bogdanov's attempt to foster an exclusively proletarian literature with the Proletcult opened the way for the emergence of a number of literary groupings, such as "Lef", "On Guard" and the "fellow-travelling" writers of the group known as the "Serapion Brothers". The attempt by the proletarian writers of the "On Guard" group to gain a hegemony in literature failed in 1925 when the Central Committee of the Communist Party resolved not to interfere in literary matters. Such freedom permitted satire and humour to flourish, chiefly in the work of Zoshchenko and Ilf and Petrov. As with the literature, artistic developments were as novel as any in Western Europe, but probably the most striking innovations occurred in the cinema. Eisenstein's use of the technique of "montage" in his famous Odessa steps sequence from *Battleship Potyomkin* (1926) was one example.

But despite the virtually non-existent censorship, which was only to become repressive after 1928, intimations of what was to come were discernible even in this springtime of literary freedom. Zamyatin's *We* (1921), a satire on the Utopian state which anticipated Aldous Huxley's *Brave New World*, was banned in the Soviet Union (and has never been published there); and one of the most remarkable novels of the period, Olesha's *Envy* (1927), about the problem of intellectual readjustment to Soviet conditions, received a lukewarm reception in official circles. The poetry illustrated the difficulties of literary independence more keenly than did the prose of the period. The dominant figure was Mayakovsky (b. 1893), whose "loud-speaker" poetry celebrated the proletarian revolution and Soviet achievement in such major works as *150,000,000*, (1920) about a duel between President Wilson and Ivan, the representative of Russia's "liberated" millions; in *Vladimir Ilyich Lenin* (1924), a solemn hymn to Lenin's memory; in *Good* (1927), a eulogy on the tenth anniversary of the revolution; and in many shorter poems. If, on the surface at least, Mayakovsky seemed to be committed wholeheartedly to the Soviet cause, then his contemporary Yesenin (b. 1895), a poet of peasant extraction, could not come to terms with Soviet reality and turned his more conventional, lyrical poetry into a touching lament for the disappearance of the peasant Russia which he had known in his childhood. In 1925, a victim of alcoholism and depression, he committed suicide. Mayakovsky criticised him for this act of despair, but five years later, in 1930, he also took his own life. The reasons for this suicide by one who in so many ways seemed to epitomise Soviet faith in the future are obscure; the tragedy of it served to illustrate the tragedy facing all original talent at the onset of the Five Year Plan period. In the final reckoning, however, if one excludes such fine works as Pasternak's *Lofty Illness* (1923) or the poetry of Mayakovsky and Yesenin, NEP was a period not so much of great achievements as of great beginnings by many young writers of promise. But the later fruit was not destined to fulfil the high hopes of the ripening.

The Third Revolution

THE first Russian Revolution was that of 1905–1907 which forced the Tsarist autocracy to grant a constitution; the second Revolution of 1917 overthrew the Tsarist autocracy and, in October, brought into being Lenin's "dictatorship of the proletariat" under the guise of a union between the proletariat and the poorer peasantry; the Third Revolution of 1928–1936 transformed Russia, in the course of two Five Year Plans, from a predominantly agricultural country into an industrial Power of the first magnitude.

The expression—"a third revolution"—was coined by Bukharin who, along with Tomsky, the trade union leader, and "Papa" Kalinin, the nominal President of the USSR, and Rykov formed what came to be known as a "right opposition" in the Politburo in the latter half of the 1920s. Bukharin, who had become a member of the Politburo after Lenin's death, advocated the view that the peasantry should be given every encouragement to increase their standard of living. In this way they would provide a stable internal market for the growth of industry. Stalin, having rid himself of the Trotskyite "left opposition" but having appropriated their views on the pre-eminence of industry, turned his attention in 1928 to the so-called "right opposition". His new plan for rapid industrialisation naturally depended for its success upon making the peasantry play a secondary role in the economy. Bukharin's views had in consequence to be branded as anathema. At the sixteenth Party Conference, in April 1929, approval was given to the optimal Five Year Plan, as prepared by Gosplan, for rapid industrialisation and the collectivisation of agriculture. The adoption of this new policy gave Stalin grounds for attacking the "right opposition" in earnest. Tomsky lost his place as trade union leader and Bukharin was removed from the chairmanship of the Comintern's executive committee. After public recantations of their views, Bukharin was expelled from the Politburo (November 1929) and Tomsky and Rykov were given severe warnings. "Papa" Kalinin was too popular, inoffensive and amenable a man for Stalin to take his "deviation" too seriously. The defeat of the "right opposition" marked the beginning of the adulation of Stalin as supreme leader of the Soviet people. The Third Revolution was to become Stalin's Revolution, more ruthless and far-reaching in its changes than any that preceded it.

The effects of this economic revolution were felt most keenly in the countryside. The Five Year Plan adopted in April 1929 envisaged the collectivisation of four to five million peasant households throughout the USSR. The initial idea was to encourage the poorer peasantry to form themselves into cooperatives for the joint working of the land. These cooperatives quickly became the nuclei of collective farms, or *kolkhozy*. Instead of working scattered strips of land and using such few, usually primitive, implements or draught animals (if indeed he had any) that might belong to him, the peasant who entered a *kolkhoz* was called upon to surrender his land and his implements, etc., to the *kolkhoz* for the benefit of the collective as a whole. Each *kolkhoz* was presumed to be a self-sufficient economic unit with its own management consisting of a chairman and a farm committee. A *kolkhoz* member could earn only as much as the *kolkhoz* could afford to pay him— which was usually very little in view of the fluctuating harvests and the low state prices offered for *kolkhoz* produce. It must be stressed that the *kolkhozy* were supposed to be independent of the state, as opposed to the *sovkhozy* or "state farms" run supposedly on factory lines in which each worker received a fixed wage. No *kolkhoz* could own its own tractors. Tractors were to be provided by state-owned machine tractor stations, with which the *kolkhozy* had to negotiate contracts for mechanised ploughing, etc.; and in the summer of 1929 a start was made with the establishing of these stations. The *kolkhozy* were therefore to have a two-fold aim : economically, by getting rid of the previous demarcations between the various strips of peasant land, they were to provide a basis for large-scale mechanised agriculture; politically, by concentrating many households in one collective farm, they were to make it simpler for the state to extract the compulsory deliveries of foodstuffs from the peasantry. The success of the *kolkhoz* system was to be dependent very largely upon the supply of tractors, combine harvesters, etc., but at the beginning of collectivisation Soviet industry was incapable of producing such equipment in sufficient quantity (and even at a most liberal estimate there were not more than 35,000 tractors in the USSR by the end of 1929). Success was also dependent upon preventing too great a disruption of the country's agricultural economy, but peasant resistance to the obligatory surrender of their implements and particularly their livestock caused such severe tensions that there became almost the equivalent of open civil war between the peasants and the authorities responsible for enforcing collectivisation.

For a peasant household a cow or a horse was at least as important as an able-bodied worker. The surrender of such important livestock, with the resulting loss in potential yield of milk or meat or horse-power for ploughing, might represent the difference between poverty and starvation. In the summer and autumn of 1929 peasant opposition to collectivisation became intense. By this time large numbers of poorer peasants had already been formed into *kolkhozy* and concerted efforts were being made to attract or coerce the mass of the middle peasantry to follow this example. A class war developed in the countryside. Almost simultaneously with the final humiliation of the "right opposition", in late 1929, Stalin decided to intensify the class war by calling for the liquidation of the *kulaks* (*kulaks* in fact meant all peasants opposed to collectivisation). This involved the brutal expropriation of about 1,250,000 *kulak* households, the enforced destitution, deportation and death of more than 10,000,000 people. The process of mass collectivisation gathered momentum throughout the winter of 1929–1930. In desperation, rather than give up their livestock, the peasants slaughtered their cows and horses; or, in the enthusiastic belief that collectivisation betokened the coming of the millenium, they slaughtered their cattle to make a Roman holiday. By March 1930 more than half of all peasant households in the USSR had been collectivised, though much of this collectivisation had occurred on paper only. More effort had been expended on liquidating the *kulaks* and a section (possibly as much as 20 per cent) of the middle peasantry than on organising new *kolkhozy*. Consequently, on March 2nd 1930 Stalin called a halt to the mass collectivisation process, explaining away the excesses of the previous five months by asserting that the authorities had become "dizzy from success". Such relaxation sent the collectivisation process rapidly into reverse. In the Moscow region, for instance, the 73 per cent collectivisation achieved by March 1st 1930 had dropped to 7·5 per cent by May 1st. Though one may justifiably doubt the value of such percentages, they give some indication of the resistance offered by the peasantry. In the end, though a significant start had been made with universal collectivisation, the real "success" had been the gratuitous destruction of millions of valuable livestock and the impoverishment of millions of peasants.

The Five Year Plan in industry was designed to provide such an industrial expansion that, in ten years or so, socialist Russia would be able to catch up with and overtake the major capitalist nations. Three things were necessary to achieve this. Firstly, an enormous investment programme : 64·5 milliard roubles were to be invested in industry during 1928–1932 (by comparison with only 5·2 milliard roubles in the preceding five-year period); and late in 1929, when it appeared that the growth norms were being met, these were upgraded one-and-a-half times. Secondly, patriotic enthusiasm on a nationwide scale had to be engendered. Intensive propaganda for the building of socialism was accompanied by patriotic appeals to the Russian people to create a stronger Russia. A feature of this process was the formulation of workers' shock brigades who engaged in enthusiastic "socialist competition", each one more eager than the next to be the first to storm the heights of the production targets. Thirdly, there had to be an increase in the enforcement of discipline at all levels of society. The eradication of the *kulaks* and the "Nepmen" speculators who had oiled the wheels of the internal market during NEP, in addition to the disasters accompanying the first hurried stage of the collectivisation process, led to the introduction of food rationing and an internal passport system. Soviet Russia was literally placed on a war footing. Every human activity, whether in the economic, social or cultural sphere, was to be made to serve the needs of the state and the Communist Party. Arrest, imprisonment or deportation to labour camps were to be the penalties for criticising the state or failure to meet the plan norms. Exemplary show trials, such as those of industrial saboteurs and Mensheviks in 1930–1931, were staged as a means of unmasking "enemies of the people".

The Herculean labours of the first Five Year Plan were often rendered largely useless through lack of technical knowledge. One instance will suffice. The energies of an enormous labour force were deployed in building the Stalingrad tractor factory in record time, but after the first Stalingrad tractor had been produced, as promised, in time for the opening of the sixteenth Party Congress on June 26th 1930, lack of technical knowledge meant a delay of between four and five months before a second Stalingrad tractor could be produced. It was a year before the enormous plant was able to produce more than ten tractors a day. But in the end, by dint of hard work, incredible sacrifices, and large-scale purchases of equipment from abroad, chiefly from Germany and America, the difficulties of such rapid industrialisation were gradually overcome. By the end of 1932 it was officially claimed that the first Five Year Plan had been completed in four years. Industrial production had increased 2·7 times by comparison with 1913 and a large number of new industrial plants producing such items as trucks, tractors, aircraft and many types of complex industrial machinery, most of which were previously imported from abroad, had laid the basis for the independence of the Soviet Union as an industrial Power. The success of the first Five Year Plan, it was officially claimed, abolished unemployment—an important propaganda claim in view of the widespread unemployment in the West caused by the depression—and started Russia on the road from capitalism to socialism.

The triumphant claims made by Soviet propaganda for the first Five Year Plan should not be allowed to diminish the great achievements of the years 1928—1932. It is equally important not to overlook the failures. The Five Year Plan norms were not fulfilled in coal production or in the output of ferrous metals, crude petroleum and cotton textiles. Although it was officially claimed that more than 60 per cent of all peasant households had been collectivised my mid-1932 and almost 150,000 tractors were established in 2,446 stations, against this must be set the famine of 1932 which was caused not only by drought but also by the government's policy of forcing the peasantry to make compulsory sales of their produce at artificially low state prices. The government of course needed the grain in order to pay for imports and to ensure supplies for the urban industrial areas. The cost of this policy in terms of peasant suffering was incalculable but immense. The cost of collectivisation in terms of loss of livestock has been officially calculated as almost half the horned cattle (from 60,000,000 in 1928 to 33,000,000 in 1933) and almost half the horses (from 32,000,000 in 1928 to 17,000,000 in 1933). It must also not be forgotten that the emphasis in the first Five Year Plan was upon heavy industry. There was a consequent severe shortage of consumer goods, a catastrophic housing shortage in the major industrial centres and a marked decline in the general standard of living. Discipline in factories and state and collective farms became much stricter. Absenteeism and other infringements of factory discipline, including any attempt to strike, were punishable by instant dismissal or deportation to the increasing number of forced labour camps run by the NKVD (the People's Commissariat for Internal Affairs which, after 1934, took over the duties of the former

OGPU). In the *kolkhozy* farm workers were organised into brigades and fixed norms of work were established for the various branches of agriculture and animal husbandry. Though discipline in the collective farms became a little less strict in 1934–1935 with the introduction of *Kolkhoz* Statutes which gave each *kolkhoz* household a right to a private allotment and regularised the sale by *kolkhoz* members of their surplus produce in "free" *kolkhoz* markets, even this—the only "capitalist" sector permitted in an otherwise socialist economy—was ringed about by controls and savagely exploited by the state. It is probably no exaggeration to claim that the first Five Year Plan, the first and most crucial stage in Stalin's Third Revolution, represented a declaration of war by the state machine against the workers and peasants of the USSR who were subjected during this period to greater exploitation than any they had known under capitalism.

Immediately after the fulfilment of the first Five Year Plan in 1932 a second Five Year Plan was launched covering the years 1933–1937. This second Plan envisaged capital investments in industry more than two-and-a-half times greater than those projected in the first Plan and a doubling, by 1937, of the 1932 production levels. The planned increases were more realistic than were the impossibly high targets set for the first Five Year Plan. The second Five Year Plan figures were approved at the seventeenth Party Congress (January 26th–February 10th 1934), which came to be known as the Congress of Victors. But whose was the victory? Admittedly, by 1934 the economic improvement, especially in agriculture, was undeniable and there was therefore some justice in the claim that the Communist Party had achieved a victory. However, Stalin, in the conviction that the increasing industrialisation of the USSR would lead to an aggravation of the class war and a tightening of the capitalist encirclement, was not prepared to allow any relaxation of tension in the country as a whole. Faced with the emergence of Hitler's Nazi dictatorship in Germany and with murmurings of discontent against his own dictatorship inside the Communist Party, Stalin began to lay plans for his own victory over the Party machine. There has been much speculation about Stalin's motives for the ensuing purges, but in the absence—so far—of first-hand evidence and in view of the fact that practically all the people who could have provided such evidence were liquidated, it is idle to assume at present that the full facts of 1934 (not to speak of subsequent years) are, or will ever be, known. Stalin seems to have covered his traces, for which reason alone history is unlikely to look favourably upon him.

On December 1st 1934, Kirov, the popular secretary of the Leningrad Party organisation, was assassinated while working in his office at

Smolny. Simultaneously a decree emanating from the Kremlin rendered anyone accused of acts of terrorism an outlaw, and a secret instruction demanded that all so accused should be executed without delay and without right of appeal against their sentence. The "preparation" of acts of terrorism could now be used by the NKVD investigators as a pretext for liquidating any Soviet citizen. Any pretence of legality was waived; mass executions—without trial or as a result of "confessions" elicited under torture—became the order of the day. The first prominent Party members to suffer from this new wave of terror were Zinovyev and Kamenev (who had been readmitted to Party membership in 1928 after the expulsion of Trotsky). According to an announcement by the deputy state prosecutor, Vyshinsky, in January 1935, they were to be tried for attempting to create a "Trotsky-ite" opposition centre; and after a secret trial they were sentenced, along with their collaborators, to terms of imprisonment. Meanwhile, the Party, whose membership had topped the 2,000,000 mark by the time of the sixteenth Party Congress in 1930, had undergone a serious purge in 1933 (800,000 expulsions) and a further, though less serious, purge in 1934. New names had begun to appear in the top echelons : Yezhov became a secretary of the Central Committee in 1935, along with Zhdanov, appointed a year earlier; Malenkov, in the Secretariat, became closely involved in purging the Party cadres; and on March 9th, 1935, it was announced that N. S. Khrushchev had been appointed first secretary of the Moscow Party organisation.

As the second Five Year Plan progressed, the face of Russia saw gigantic changes. The completion of the Dnieper hydroelectric project in 1932 was an important step in ensuring that by 1935 Lenin's plan for the electrification of the country should have been overfulfilled three times. In 1933 the White Sea–Baltic canal was completed—largely with the help of forced labour; and that year also saw the completion of the Uralmash plant. In 1934, through the construction of giant new plants in the Donbass, the production of pig-iron increased by almost one-third; and in 1935 the first line of the Moscow Metro was opened. A good harvest in 1933 and better harvesting arrangements in 1934 permitted the gradual abolition of food rationing in 1935. Money began to play an increasing role in the economic life of the country and the promise of higher wages became an important inducement to higher productivity. Yet, despite a general lowering of the prices of foodstuffs in state shops in October 1935, food remained scarce and was not even plentiful in the higher-priced *kolkhoz* markets. An attempt to increase Party control over agriculture by establishing political sections in the *sovkhozy* and machine tractor stations was not successful, though it may have contributed to the general improvement in agricultural productivity which occurred in 1933–1934. The increase in the amount of machinery available for *kolkhoz* use made collectivisation appear to be a more attractive proposition; and by 1935 it was officially claimed that 83 per cent of peasant households had been collectivised. On the industrial front a young mine-worker, Aleksey Stakhanov, succeeded in exceeding his shift norm for coal production by fourteen times. This success led, in the last months of 1935, to the growth of a nation-wide "Stakhanovite" movement in which Stakhanovite workers, either individually or in brigades, set themselves the task of achieving outputs far in excess of the planned norms. Though many genuine successes were recorded, Stakhanovism soon began to get out of hand, too much attention being paid to the star Stakhanovite worker while the mass of his work-mates were overlooked and more often than not failed to achieve even the minimal production rates.

Industrialisation on the scale envisaged in the first two Five Year Plans naturally demanded the training of thousands of new specialists. 460,000 such new specialists were trained during the first Five Year Plan and by the end of the second the USSR could claim to have a student population in universities and university-level institutions of more than 600,000 (by comparison with 127,000 before 1917). In 1930 steps were taken to introduce universal compulsory education for children of eight years and above. Four-year school courses were introduced in country districts and seven-year courses in the towns and industrial areas. Experimental school curricula, which had flourished during the NEP period, were abolished in 1932. The new school programmes laid emphasis upon acquiring the basic rudiments of reading and writing, a knowledge of the sciences, the maintenance of class discipline and respect for the authority of the teacher. In 1934, the teaching of history, which had previously been dominated by the "vulgar Marxist" approach of Pokrovsky, was re-orientated towards a glorification of Russia's national past. New history textbooks were introduced in secondary schools and new history faculties were created in the universities. The Third Revolution may have brought much suffering in its wake, but due credit must be given to the Soviet government for the great changes that were wrought in the educational sphere. The rapid increase in the number of primary and secondary schools, training centres, technical institutes and universities, though it naturally formed part of the process of political indoctrination, was an educational revolution which probably had a greater effect on Russia's backwardness than any other feature of the industrialisation programme.

The reinterpretation of history along more traditional, less sociologically Marxist, lines was a consequence of the general reinterpretation of socialist principles which occurred during the Five Year Plan period. Socialist "egalitarianism" suffered a gradual erosion. More people began to become significantly more equal than others—the industrial worker more equal than the *kolkhoz* worker, the skilled worker more equal than the unskilled, the technician more equal than the skilled worker, the factory manager more equal than the technician. Hierarchical ranks, privileges and pay-scales in industry, the armed forces, the bureaucracy —in every aspect of Russian life—meant a return to the traditions of the past. Not so surprisingly, perhaps, the ostensible building of socialism involved an increasing *embourgeoisement* of Russian tastes and habits.

Culturally this change manifested itself in a return to traditional forms in literature, music and the arts. Literary tastes underwent a dramatic transformation. The attempt to dragoon writers into serving the aims of the Five Year Plan—an attempt which began in 1928 with the enforced enrolment of all Soviet writers in an organisation known as RAPP (Russian Association of Proletarian Writers)—was abandoned in 1932 when it was discovered that writers were not machines capable of producing great literature to order. With the exception of a few outstanding novels such as Katayev's *Forward, Time!* (1933), a couple of novels by Leonov and the first part of Sholokhov's *Virgin Soil Upturned* (1933), the work produced during the RAPP era was singularly arid. Moreover, the RAPP era witnessed the first deliberate persecution of writers who would not conform : Zamyatin, for instance, was forced into emigration and Pilnyak is supposed to have been liquidated by the NKVD. After 1932 and the dissolution of RAPP all writers, Communist and non-Communist, were invited to join a Union of Soviet Writers. At the first Congress of this Union in 1934, Soviet literature was given the task of conforming to the doctrine of Socialist Realism, a major tenet of which was that a writer should offer "a truthful, historically concrete depiction of reality in its revolutionary development". Party control over Soviet writers, though less obvious than under RAPP, now became more insidious. Experimentation was virtually banned. What emerged was a consciously national literature informed by a spirit of "togetherness with the Party" and couched in didactically realistic terms. Big historical novels, such as Aleksey Tolstoy's *Peter the First*, became the fashion; long epic novels about the civil war and the emergence of Soviet Russia (Sholokhov's *Quiet Flows the Don*, Aleksey Tolstoy's *Road to Calvary*) set the tone for the period; great popularity was enjoyed by Nikolay Ostrovsky's *How the Steel was Tempered* (1934) which described the development of a new type of Soviet hero. Heroic themes from both past and present, and the dominance of prose rather than poetry, were hallmarks of the new concern for tradition, continuity and self-consciously national achievement which accompanied the building of "socialism in one country". Gorky's return to the Soviet Union in 1928 after seven years of voluntary exile in Italy helped to give Soviet literature a sense of living connection with past values. The classic works of nineteenth-century Russian literature, relatively neglected during the NEP period, were re-issued in enormous editions for a vastly enlarged, newly-literate public avid for first-hand knowledge of their literary heritage.

In music efforts were made to create a specifically Soviet opera, though the young Shostakovich (b. 1903), already well known for his symphonic works, had trouble with his *Lady Macbeth of Mtsensk* which was banned by Stalin after having received considerable praise from lesser critics. Prokofyev (1891–1953), who returned to the Soviet Union in 1932, produced his very popular *Peter and the Wolf* in 1936, but found difficulty in composing the kind of "monumental" works officially approved by Soviet musical law-givers. Monumentalism, whether in the debased form of innumerable representations of Lenin and Stalin or the slightly worthier form taken by the sculptural ornamentation in the early Metro stations, was the criterion of "great" art in this period. Abstract or experimental forms of any kind were banned as "decadent".

So far as foreign relations were concerned, it was during the period of the first two Five Year Plans that the Soviet Union gained recognition as a world Power. One of the first steps of Litvinov, who succeeded Chicherin as Commissar for Foreign Affairs, was to arrange for the signing in 1929 of what came to be known as the East Pact—or the Litvinov Protocol to the Kellogg–Briand Pact for the renunciation of war—by the USSR, Poland, Roumania, Latvia, Estonia, Lithuania, Turkey, Persia and the Free City of Danzig. Finland alone refused to participate in this new security system. In 1929, after the return of Ramsay MacDonald's Labour government to power, diplomatic relations were renewed with Great Britain. In the Far East, Chinese interference with Russian officials of the Chinese Eastern Railway led, in October 1929, to the invasion of Manchuria by Red Army troops, but under a Sino–Soviet protocol signed at Khabarovsk in December the former arrangements for the administration of the Railway (agreed upon in 1924) were formally endorsed. From 1932 onwards the Soviet government gave considerable material and moral support to the Chinese Red Army which had been created in the Province of Kiangsi. Meanwhile, Japan had taken over Manchuria. This new threat to Russian influence in the Far East was countered by the signing of a non-aggression pact between the USSR and the Chinese government in Nanking. In the same year, 1932, non-aggression pacts were signed between the USSR and Finland, Latvia, Estonia, Poland and France. Relations with Great Britain became strained in January 1933 when six Metro-Vick engineers and their Russian associates were put on trial for alleged sabotage. Of greater consequence for the future was Hitler's rise to power in Germany. The Rapallo Treaty with Germany was hastily ratified again in April 1933, though there can be little doubt that the Soviet government had seriously miscalculated the importance of Hitler. Originally it had been supposed that Hitler's rise to power would be the prelude to a Communist take-over in Germany; as Hitler's *Mein Kampf* anti-Communist sentiments began to be translated into reality, Soviet foreign policy had to be reshaped. Towards the end of 1933 the Soviet diplomatic *rapprochement* with capitalism reached its final stage when the United States, under Roosevelt's new Democratic administration, agreed to recognise the USSR. By this time it was clear that the most serious threat to the Soviet Union came not from the bourgeois-democratic capitalist nations of the West, but from the new dictatorships—and particularly serious was the new German threat underlined by the Polish–German ten-year non-aggression pact of January 1934 which seemed to point to German territorial ambitions in the Ukraine. Admitted to the League of Nations in 1934 and given a permanent seat on the Council, the Soviet Union began to pose as the leading opponent of Hitler. This new policy achieved its first notable success with the signing of the Franco–Soviet mutual assistance treaty in May 1935, which was shortly afterwards expanded into a tripartite treaty including Czechoslovakia, with the proviso—of great and tragic significance in view of future developments—that mutual aid would only be effective if France came to the assistance of one of the other signatories. A period of "popular fronts" ensued in which Communists allied themselves with other left-wing parties in order to defeat the rising pro-Nazi movements in the Western democracies. In the Far East the Japanese seizure of Manchuria was followed, in March 1935, by the Soviet agreement to sell to Japan the Chinese Eastern Railway at a fraction of its cost. Despite all its vociferous denunciation of the appeasement of aggressors, in its attitude towards Japanese aggression the Soviet government was to be among the first of the appeasers and in its later attitude towards Nazi aggressiveness it was to carry appeasement to the lengths of active cooperation with its mortal enemy.

CHAPTER VII

1936 – 1953

The Stalin Constitution and the Purges

THE Stalin Constitution, submitted for public discussion in June 1936 and finally approved in December, can be said to have had the threefold aim of proclaiming, in constitutional form, the existence of socialism in the USSR, of appearing to give the Communist dictatorship an aura of democratic respectability and of announcing to the world at large, especially to the Western democracies, that the Soviet Union was a bulwark of freedom in the struggle against Nazi, Fascist and Japanese tyranny. As subsequent events were to show, the Stalin Constitution, for all its declaration of "rights" and "freedoms", was designed not so much to protect the individual Soviet citizen as to act as a propaganda façade of legitimacy, ideal socialist promises and egalitarianism, behind which all manner of violations of human dignity could be committed with impunity. On the face of it the Constitution seemed to conform to Soviet reality in its assertion that the USSR was a "socialist state of workers and peasants", other antagonistic classes having been eradicated with the end of NEP and the liquidation of the *kulaks*. The supreme organ of power in the state was to be the Supreme Soviet of the USSR, comprising a Soviet of the Union, deputies to which were to be directly elected by secret ballot on a ratio of 1 deputy to every 300,000 inhabitants, and a Soviet of Nationalities, to which elections would also be direct and secret on a ratio of 25 deputies to each republic, 11 to each autonomous republic, 5 to each autonomous region and 1 to each national area. The Supreme Soviet, elected for four-year terms, was empowered to elect a Presidium with a chairman to act as titular head of the state. The government of the USSR was to be, as before, the Sovnarkom. Power, though appearing to be federalised, in fact remained as centralised as ever. The Constitution recognised eleven union republics–the Russian (RSFSR), Ukrainian, Belorussian, Azerbaydzhanian, Georgian, Armenian, Turkmen, Uzbek, Tadzhik, Kazakh and Kirgiz, all of which had the right to secede from the USSR if they wished. Provision was also made for a judicial system, though no attempt was made to draw a distinction between the judiciary and the executive. The cement for the whole constitutional edifice, referred to on two occasions in the document of the Constitution, was of course the Communist Party. In this respect the Stalin Constitution of 1936 was more candid than its predecessor of 1924; in practically every other respect it was a recital of constitutional *desiderata* which would have to await the withering away of the Communist Party rather than the withering away of the state in order to become effective. It was Stalin's aim to ensure that neither should wither away save at his own behest.

During the course of 1936, while the new Constitution was under public discussion, Stalin set in motion the machinery of a new purge. Initially it seems that he was striking at the Old Bolsheviks (those who had joined the Party before October 1917) and their associates. Sinister portents in 1935 had been the sudden death of Kuibyshev, a member of the Politburo since 1927 (and, on the face of it, one of Stalin's staunchest supporters), and the dissolution of the Society of Old Bolsheviks. But the purge quickly began to acquire all the features of a new "terror" aimed at renovating the Party and the entire administrative personnel of the country. The Party underwent the first stage of its new purging in the early months of 1936. In August Kamenev and Zinovyev and fourteen of their supporters were suddenly put on public trial for allegedly organising a "terrorist centre" under the direction of Trotsky. All confessed to the charges and were immediately shot. Their evidence had, moreover, implicated other former opponents of Stalin, such as Bukharin and Radek (who had, incidentally, been members of the Commission appointed to draft the new Constitution and who were to learn at first hand how ineffective were the guarantees of individual freedom which it contained). In addition, the finger had been pointed at Tomsky and Rykov.

In September 1936 Yagoda was replaced as People's Commissar for Internal Affairs by Yezhov and a new period in the "terror" began, known as *Yezhovshchina*. During the height of the *Yezhovshchina*, in 1937 and 1938, many millions of Soviet citizens were arrested, interrogated, tortured, forced into making false confessions and then shot or despatched to forced labour camps run by the NKVD. It is impossible to estimate how many quite innocent people were, as Khrushchev and Soviet history books put it, "repressed" as a result of what are politely called the "excesses associated with the cult of personality". So much is hidden, unknown or has been deliberately erased from the records. Outwardly the *Yezhovshchina* manifested itself in a series of show trials at which prominent Party members, under the diabolically skilful cross-examination of Vyshinsky, made grovelling confessions to charges that were for the most part transparent fabrications. "Conveyor belt" methods of interrogation, involving prolonged and intensive bouts of questioning by a succession of interrogators, which deprived the victim of sleep and "brain-washed" him into confession, or the use of drugs aimed at weakening the central nervous system, or the employment of physical torture, or a combination of these methods, produced results which deceived many eminent foreign observers—and, presumably, many members of the Soviet public—into believing that the confessions were genuine. But in fact the period of *Yezhovshchina* gave the lie to the high-sounding declarations of the Stalin Constitution.

During 1936 and 1937 Gorky died mysteriously (June 18th 1936), Tomsky committed suicide, and Ordzhonikidze, a member of the Politburo and People's Commissar for Heavy Industry, is believed to have shot himself. In January 1937 Radek and sixteen other prominent defendants were put on public trial. The charges on this occasion involved not only complicity with Trotsky in attempting to overthrow the Party leadership, but also conspiring with Germans and Japanese in order to dismember the Soviet Union. These charges, combining anti-Party and anti-state activity, treason and industrial sabotage, were designed both to arouse patriotic revulsion against the defendants and to provide scapegoats for the shortcomings of the Five Year Plan. Although Radek, who confessed with a theatrical flourish, was not sentenced to death, nothing concrete is known of what happened to him subsequently; the majority of the defendants were shot. In March 1937 it was announced that Bukharin and Rykov had been arraigned before a plenum of the Central Committee and expelled from the Party. It is possible that there may have been opposition in the Central Committee to Stalin's ruthless methods. Yet, if there was such opposition, it had little effect, for one consequence of the *Yezhovshchina* was that about 70 per cent of the full members and candidate members of the Central Committee elected at the seventeenth Party Congress in 1934 were either liquidated or eliminated in one form or another. Stalin did not stop at half-measures in purging the Party; nor did he stop at the Party. By the spring of 1937 it was the turn of the army.

A press announcement in June 1937 stated that Tukhachevsky (already implicated in the Radek trial) and a group of high-ranking officers had been arrested. They were charged with spying for Germany and Japan, plotting to undertake a Trotskyist *coup d'état* and planning the dismemberment of the Soviet Union. It is not known whether they were tried, but it was announced that they had all been shot. There followed widespread arrests, involving chiefly the older officers in the higher command posts. In the end, after two successive waves of arrests during 1937 and 1938, the officer corps was probably depleted by as much as half its total complement. Such a weakening of the military command was to be a crucial factor three years later during the Nazi invasion, when the military unpreparedness of the Soviet Union became painfully evident. Stalin must be held directly to blame for this state of affairs, since it is unlikely that the reduction in the number of experienced officers would have been so sweeping had not Stalin himself personally approved such a drastic purge.

In March 1938 the *Yezhovshchina* reached its climax with the final show trial of Bukharin, Rykov, Yagoda and eighteen further defendants accused of plotting with Trotsky, of conspiring to overthrow Stalin, of espionage for Germany and Japan, of sabotage and of planning to dismember the Soviet Union. Yagoda was further charged with having poisoned Gorky, Kuibyshev and the former OGPU chief, Menzhinsky. One of the defendants, Krestinsky, withdrew his confession, but subsequently recanted his disavowal. With the exception of three lesser lights, all the defendants were sentenced to death. Though these men confessed to crimes of ludicrous enormity and covered themselves with odium, they did so no doubt as a consequence of the interrogations and tortures to which they were subjected by the NKVD. Other prominent Party members named by Khrushchev in 1956—Kosior (Politburo member), Chubar, Rudzutak, Postyshev, Eykhe (all Politburo candidate members) and Kosarev (secretary of the Komsomol) presumably did not confess, but perished into anonymity along with many other innocent victims of the purges. By mid-1938, however, the *Yezhovshchina* had come to an end. Yezhov was replaced as head of the NKVD by Beria, the mass arrests ceased and Yezhov's henchmen in the NKVD apparatus found themselves despatched to the forced labour camps to which they had earlier sent so many of their victims. By the end of the purges the labour force in the NKVD camps and enterprises probably exceeded seven million and may have reached twenty million. With the help of forced labour the Moscow–Volga canal was completed in 1937; and forced labour was used on many other industrial projects in remote areas of the Soviet Union where it would have been uneconomical to use ordinary labour. The purges, especially the *Yezhovshchina*, ensured that the Soviet economy received the substantial supplies of slave labour upon which Stalin's servile Russia had become increasingly dependent.

The purges undoubtedly had the effect of slowing down economic growth. The removal of so many senior personnel in industry and at key points throughout the economy caused a lowering of production rates and seriously impaired managerial efficiency, initiative and responsibility. Although it was officially claimed that by the end of the second Five Year Plan, in 1937, gross industrial output had increased more than twice by comparison with 1932, short-falls were admitted—and it is more than probable that the figures were doctored for propaganda purposes in order to hide the true extent of underfulfilment—in coal and pig-iron production and generally throughout light industry. Ferrous metallurgy continued to drag its feet during the third Five Year Plan, which was launched in 1938 and planned for completion by 1942. During the three years prior to the Nazi invasion pig-iron and steel production increased by only 3 per cent. The "gigantomania" of the previous Five Year Plans, which involved the construction of vast metallurgical plants to which the raw materials had to be carried over hundreds of miles of railway track, was partly responsible for the lack of planned increase in the metallurgical industry. "Gigantomania" was repudiated during the third Five Year Plan in favour of the construction of smaller, more rationally and strategically sited plants. Even so, bureaucratic inefficiency, serious abuse of the "decade" system of working (a month's work norm would be divided into three periods of ten days or "decades"; workers would work slowly during the first two "decades" and then attempt to "storm" the production target in the final "decade", thereby giving rise to uneven production rates and slipshod workmanship), the transfer of certain sections of the consumer goods industry to arms production—such factors meant that the output of capital goods increased by little more than 50 per cent (in rouble value) during the three years prior to 1941, representing only a quarter of the planned increased for the full Plan period. Nevertheless, it could be claimed that the Soviet Union was second only to the United States in total oil production, the world's third largest steel-producer and fourth largest producer of coal; that by 1940 the volume of heavy industrial production was 12 times greater, and machine-building 35 times greater than in 1913.

The Stalin Constitution, though parading as the manifesto of a workers' paradise, was hardly the signal for the introduction of a more leisured life for the proletariat and the peasantry. On the contrary, labour discipline became markedly tighter. From 1939 onwards all workers had to possess "work books" giving a record of their employment; employment was conditional upon the possession of such a book and violations of labour discipline, such as late arrival at work, quitting work, unduly long meal-breaks, slacking on the job, could be punished, if committed three times in one month and four times in two successive months, by dismissal for absenteeism. In June 1940 an eight-hour day and six-day week, with Sunday as rest day, became obligatory throughout Soviet industry; workers were forbidden to leave their place of work, the penalty for doing so without proper authorisation being up to four months' imprisonment. Absenteeism now became punishable by compulsory labour and a 25 per cent cut in wages. Hooliganism and the theft of state property could lead to a year's imprisonment; and sentences of five to eight years' forced labour could be passed on absentees in the defence industries. Later in 1940 a State Labour Reserve was created which conscripted up to a million boys between fourteen and seventeen for industrial training. As against such repressive measures, inducements to higher productivity were offered in the shape of graduated wage scales, bonuses, Stalin prizes, the title of Hero of Socialist Labour and various medals for heroic or meritorious work.

By 1940 about 97 per cent of all peasant households had been gathered into about 250,000 *kolkhozy* (*sovkhozy* now occupied only a fractional part of the agricultural scene). A record grain harvest in 1937 gave a much-needed fillip to the morale of the collectivised peasantry, but drought in 1938 caused a sharp drop in harvest yield. The right to a personal allotment and to private livestock, granted under the *Kolkhoz* Statute of 1935, made working for oneself seem more attractive to the *kolkhoz* worker than working for a collective which could only offer, even in the so-called "millionaire" *kolkhozy*, relatively meagre returns. In order to combat this tendency, the Party and the Soviet government jointly issued a resolution in 1939 imposing severe penalties for the unlawful possession of *kolkhoz* land and prescribing a minimum number of "labour days" per year to be worked by each *kolkhoz* member, regardless of sex, on the collectivised land. Failure to comply with these regulations was punishable by banishment from the collective farm. As procurement agencies and as a means of controlling the peasantry, the *kolkhoz* could no doubt be considered successful. In terms of agricultural production, though the sown area was about one-third greater in 1940 than in 1928, productivity and yields—with the exception of a record year such as 1937—were by no means proportionately as great. Depending upon the quality of the land, the efficiency of the *kolkhoz* chairman and the ability of the machine tractor stations to fulfil their ploughing, sowing and harvesting contracts, *kolkhozy* differed widely one from another. Generally speaking, the collectivised peasants enjoyed a standard of living below, sometimes far below, the standard of the middle peasantry under NEP. The position was particularly deplorable in animal husbandry. By the end of 1940, with a population of 193,000,000 (by comparison with a pre-1917 population of 139,000,000), the Soviet Union possessed fewer head of horned cattle than did imperial Russia in 1916.

Stalin's power was everywhere on the increase. At the eighteenth Party Congress, in March 1939, Stalin specifically rejected the Marxist concept of the withering away of the state. He could hardly do otherwise : the Soviet state was largely of his own making. So, for that matter, was the Party. The purges had swept away practically all the Old Bolsheviks and all the members of Lenin's Politburo with the exception of Stalin himself. During the *Yezhovshchina* 850,000 Party members had been purged and the total of full members had fallen below the 2,000,000 mark. About half the delegates at the eighteenth Party Congress were under thirty-five. For want of a more democratic procedure, the purges can therefore be said to have produced a rejuvenation of the Party cadres, but this rejuvenated Party was to be a dull, cowed, obedient, Stalin-worshipping machine, geared to fulfil Stalin's orders and not equipped to move of its own volition. The new Politburo was also composed of faithful Stalinists: Stalin, Molotov (Foreign Affairs),* Voroshilov (Defence), Kalinin (President), Kaganovich (Transport and Industry), Andreyev (Agriculture), Mikoyan (Trade), Zhdanov (Cultural Matters) and Khrushchev (First Secretary, Ukraine). There were two candidate members: Malenkov and Beria. Such were the Party leaders destined to carry Russia through the fateful next half-dozen years. Yet Stalin frequently, it seems, by-passed or did not consult the Politburo on important matters and much of his power was exercised through the agencies of the NKVD which, under Beria, acted as Stalin's ears and eyes and a dutiful scourge of his enemies at every level throughout the length and breadth of Russia. Not content with mastery over the present, Stalin saw to it that history was rewritten to glorify his role in the revolution: particular instances are Beria's account of Stalin's pre-revolutionary activities in Georgia and the official *Short Course* on the history of the Party. Lenin faded into the background, dwarfed by the lustrous image of Stalin who was everywhere proclaimed the "leader, teacher and friend" of the Soviet people.

Fear of war brought about an increase in the armed forces. By 1934 the Red Army had been increased to 1,300,000 men; in 1939 universal military conscription was introduced for all who had reached the age of nineteen—a two-year term for ground forces, three years for the air force and five years for the navy. In addition, much reliance was placed on the civilian military organisation *Osoaviakhim* (originally created in 1927), which by 1939 had a membership of more than 12,000,000. After the purge of the armed forces rates of pay were substantially increased, discipline was tightened and the officer corps acquired new status and prestige. The Party succeeded in maintaining a tight hold over the armed forces both by ensuring that a high proportion of officers were Party members and by a system of joint command between military commanders and political commissars, though this system was abolished after the Russo–Finnish War and the commissars were replaced by assistant commanders for political affairs.

* The bracketed headings are the Sovnarkom posts or Party responsibilities allocated to Politburo members.

Culturally the period of the third Five Year Plan, opening as it did at the height of the *Yezhovshchina*, was barren of any works of real literary or artistic merit. Many writers disappeared during the purges, notably Babel and Pilnyak, and a great many of those who survived embarked on an "inner emigration" in which they wrote inoffensive children's books or devoted themselves exclusively to translation. There was a spate of novels dealing with industrial wreckers and *kolkhoz* life and there were several on historical themes. 1940 saw the completion of Sholokhov's *Quiet Flows the Don* and in 1941 Aleksey Tolstoy finished the third part of his *Road to Calvary*. Eisenstein's *Alexander Nevsky, Lone White Sail* (based on Katayev's novel) and Donskoy's *The Youth of Maxim* were successful films of the period. Though the spiritual life of Russia was stifled by an enormous weight of anti-religious propaganda, by the persecution of the clergy and by the closing of churches, it is noteworthy that even the League of Militant Atheists was obliged to estimate, however circumspectly, that almost half of the population were still believers.

Russian foreign policy in the years immediately preceding the Nazi invasion combined the pursuit of expedients with loud protests against Fascist aggression and Anglo–French appeasement. Such a policy was merely a projection into foreign relations of the brazen hypocrisy which characterised Stalin's management of Russia's internal affairs. Stalin could sanctimoniously admit that "mistakes" had been committed in Russia during the purges without fear that a servile public opinion would ever dare to question his responsibility for them; but in foreign relations such "mistakes" could not be glossed over. And Russian foreign policy stumbled from error to error in face of the increasing power of Nazi Germany. Litvinov's attempts to construct somewhat limp collective security systems, involving cooperation between the Soviet Union and the Western democracies, proved of little effect, since even during the "popular front" period the smiling face of Soviet policy could change overnight into the grimace of Comintern subversion. With the outbreak of the Spanish Civil War in 1936, Soviet support in the shape of armaments and volunteers was forthcoming for the Republican cause after Hitler and Mussolini had given their support to Franco, but even such Soviet aid as was provided had to be accompanied by the infiltration of NKVD agents and the purging of alleged Trotskyists among Communists fighting on the Republican side. Antonov-Ovseyenko, for instance, though made officially responsible for such activities in Spain, was recalled to Moscow in 1937 and liquidated. However, in 1938 when Hitler, after the seizure of Austria, began to make demands on Czechoslovakia, the Soviet Union once again found itself isolated.

Relations between the USSR and the Franco–British coalition were strained. Stalin's efforts to achieve a Communist take-over in Spain and the weakening of the Red Army during the purges gave the British and the French good reason for believing that the Soviet Union, despite its protestations to the contrary, was not to be relied upon as an active opponent of Nazi Germany. In the subsequent negotiations with Hitler during the Munich crisis of September 1938, the British and French governments disregarded the Soviet Union. Such an attitude no doubt contributed to the paradoxical, and in the last resort tragically mistaken, re-orientation of Soviet foreign policy which was to occur between September 1938 and September 1939.

In the Far East, after the Chinese Red Army under Mao Tse-tung had made its famous "Long March" from Kiangsi to Yenan in Shensi Province near Soviet-controlled Mongolia (in 1934), the Chinese Communist Party, following the "popular front" policy advocated by Moscow, joined in a coalition with Chiang Kai-shek's nationalist government (in February 1937) in order to present a united front to the Japanese invasion. Incidents soon occurred between Soviet and Japanese troops along the Mongolian border. But a non-aggression treaty with the Chinese government in August 1937 and agreement over the Mongolian question with the Japanese in September 1939 safeguarded the Soviet Far Eastern borders at a time when the Soviet government was preoccupied with events in the West.

The Soviet change of heart towards Nazi Germany may perhaps have been discernible in the Soviet reaction to Anglo–French appeasement of Hitler at the time of Munich. When, as a result of the Munich agreement, German troops marched into the Sudetenland areas of Czechoslovakia, this could be construed as a threat to the Soviet Union deliberately engineered by the Western Powers. French reluctance to support the Czechs invalidated the Franco–Soviet–Czech treaty arrangements of 1935 and it no doubt seemed expedient to the Soviet government to look elsewhere for allies. At the time of the German seizure of Czechoslovakia in March 1939 Soviet reaction was comparatively mild. Despite this, it was generally assumed that the Soviet Union remained as hostile as ever to the Berlin–Rome axis and the anti-Comintern alignment of Germany and Japan. Behind the scenes the new approach to Germany was probably initiated by the appointment of Molotov as Commissar for Foreign Affairs in May 1939. Although British and French overtures were made to Moscow throughout the spring and early summer of 1939, the Soviet government demanded a greater say in determining the Soviet borders with the Baltic states and Poland than the British and French were ready to allow. By August military negotiations on arrangements for safeguarding the borders of the Baltic States and Poland were taking place in Moscow, but Voroshilov's demand that the Red Army be allowed right of passage through Poland and Roumania met with resistance from the British and French delegations. In any event, these negotiations were being conducted under duress of Soviet propaganda threats to the effect that the British and French were endeavouring to use the discussions with the Soviet government as a means of disguising their true purpose. The true aim of the Western allies, according to Soviet propaganda, was to achieve agreement with Nazi Germany. This myth—or so one must assume it to be for want of better evidence—has since become enshrined in Soviet history books; it can be regarded as a face-saving device for excusing the gravest "mistake" ever committed by Stalin. For on August 19th 1939 a trade agreement was signed with Germany and Stalin agreed that Ribbentrop, the German Foreign Minister, should fly to Moscow for negotiations. Ribbentrop arrived on August 23rd and in a matter of hours agreement was reached on a ten-year non-aggression treaty between Germany and the Soviet Union. Secret clauses of this treaty laid down that Poland should be divided between the two Powers, Estonia and Latvia were to become Soviet spheres of influence and Lithuania a German sphere; Bessarabia was left to the mercy of the Soviet Union. The treaty became effective at once and was ratified on August 31st, the day before Hitler's troops entered Poland and four days before Great Britain and France declared war on Germany in defence of Polish interests.

The Hitler–Stalin Pact caused an instantaneous lowering of Soviet prestige throughout the world. Soviet duplicity and opportunism were now evident for all to see. Although Stalin might later justify this act with the argument that it allowed the Soviet Union eighteen months' respite before the Nazi invasion, there was no reluctance on the Soviet part to fulfil its side of the bargain in scrupulous detail. To all outward appearances the Soviet Union became the ally of Nazi Germany, condoned and benefited from Nazi aggression, entertained hopes of sharing the spoils of a Nazi victory over the Western allies and greedily anticipated that the whole of Europe, maimed and rent by strife, would soon fall an easy prey to Communist subversion. For a while the Hitler–Stalin Pact may have seemed to be a diplomatic victory from which the Soviet Union had nothing to lose and everything to gain. But in the longer term it served to create a profound mistrust of Soviet intentions in the democratic West—a mistrust which no amount of later cooperation could allay and which will no doubt be present, like an ominous spectre, at every conference of Soviet and Western statesmen during the twentieth century.

The first gain achieved by the Soviet Union from its new-found alliance was a large area of Eastern Poland. On September 17th 1939, when the German *Blitzkrieg* against Poland had virtually ended all resistance, Soviet troops invaded the Polish rear and appropriated the areas designated, in Soviet parlance, as the Western Ukraine and Western Belorussia. These were swiftly incorporated into the Ukrainian and Belorussian Soviet Socialist Republics. A Soviet–German agreement of September 28th transformed most of Lithuania into a Soviet sphere of influence in return for the withdrawal of Soviet troops from the Vistula to the Bug. These simple operations netted for the Soviet Union an additional population of 13,000,000. Almost simultaneously mutual aid pacts were concluded with Estonia, Latvia and Lithuania which gave the Soviet Union the right to station troops in those countries. Only Finland resisted Soviet demands. As a result, at the end of November Soviet troops attacked Finland with the aim of seizing the Karelian Isthmus.

The Russo–Finnish War or "Winter War" of 1939–1940 caused a further loss of Soviet prestige. Apart from being expelled from the League of Nations, the Soviet Union suffered the more serious humiliation of being forced to demonstrate to the whole world its military inefficiency. All attempts to open a breach in the Finnish defence system known as the Mannerheim Line proved ineffective. The Finns showed themselves to be adept at winter warfare and inflicted enormous losses upon the ill-trained and ill-equipped Soviet troops. It was only when Marshal Timoshenko took charge of the Soviet forces in February 1940 and launched a series of massive attacks, supported by an overwhelming superiority in fire-power, against the Mannerheim Line that Finnish resistance was broken. In mid-February the Finns were obliged to sue for a truce. The Karelian Isthmus, Vyborg and other areas along the Finnish border were ceded to the Soviet Union. The Hangoe peninsula was leased to the Soviet Union for a thirty-year period.

The German invasion of Denmark and Norway in April 1940 and the subsequent collapse of the Anglo–French armies in northern France, culminating in the British evacuation from Dunkirk and the French surrender on June 16th, gave the Soviet Union an opportunity to extend its hold over the Baltic states. During June Communist-controlled governments were established in Estonia, Latvia and Lithuania and at the beginning of August these countries were officially incorporated into the Soviet Union as Republics. In July Soviet troops entered Bessarabia and northern Bukovina and these territories were transformed, also in August, into the Moldavian SSR. Such annexations, though officially declared to be in conformity with "the will of the people", were accompanied by rigged elections, purges, liquidations, mass deportations, enforced collectivisation of agriculture and other customary features of Sovietisation. The total effect of such an enlargement of Soviet territory was to bring under the hegemony of Moscow all the areas, with the exception of Finland and western Poland, which had been formerly within the borders of the Russian Empire. More than this, such annexations may be regarded as the start of a new empire-building process which was to carry Soviet power into the heart of Europe.

In the spring of 1940 Soviet–German relations had begun to deteriorate. German unwillingness to supply the military equipment demanded by the Soviet government and Soviet reluctance to supply raw materials resulted in an *impasse* which Molotov's visit to Berlin in November 1940 could not overcome. By this time Hitler had no doubt already decided to attack Russia. Fobbed off by Hitler with suggestions that the Soviet Union might expand towards Persia and India, Stalin and Molotov might at this point have realised that it would have been wise policy to join with Great Britain before Germany, temporarily held at bay by Britain's lone stand, turned eastwards. As it was, Great Britain remained alone in opposition to Hitler for a year from June 1940. Outwardly the Soviet government gave no appearance of anticipating Hitler's intentions. The German invasion of Jugoslavia and Greece in April 1941 may have sounded the warning note that had already been present in the German pacts with Hungary and Roumania of November 1940 and the pact with Bulgaria of March 1941. At this juncture the Soviet Union signed a neutrality pact with Japan (April 1941) which was to guarantee the Soviet borders against attack in the Far East. But Soviet military preparedness in the West was not, it seems, considered a matter of urgency. Rumours of an impending German invasion were discounted. Therefore, on June 22nd 1941, when Hitler's "Barbarossa" plan for the invasion of Russia was put into effect, the attack came, it appears, as a complete surprise to the Soviet government and it was a fortnight before Stalin could bring himself to admit the fact to the Soviet people.

The Great Patriotic War

THE 170 or so German divisions which invaded the Soviet Union in June 1941 were divided into three army groups of the North, Centre and South. Their respective objectives, in what was confidently assumed would be a short, victorious war, were the Baltic territories, Pskov and Leningrad in the north, Smolensk and Moscow in the centre, and Kiev and the Caucasus in the south. Saturation bombing of airfields, troop concentrations and inhabited areas in the path of the invading forces quickly disorganised the Soviet defences; and swift "pincer" movements by German tank columns, especially those commanded by General Guderian in the centre, cut off large numbers of Soviet troops who had been deployed too close to the border regions. By mid-July the Germans had surrounded and captured more than 300,000 troops in the region of Minsk. By September, after heavy fighting outside Kiev (captured September 20th), a further 600,000 troops had been surrounded and an equivalent number fell into a German trap outside Vyazma in October. The Soviet forces, commanded in the north by Voroshilov, in the centre by Timoshenko and in the south by Budyonny, retreated all along the front, frequently in panic but usually leaving in their wake a "scorched earth" of empty townships and burning crops. The same policy was adopted towards Hitler as had been adopted towards Napoleon : the enemy's advance was countered by retreat in an effort to avert the possibility of a decisive engagement.

By the beginning of October Hitler claimed that victory was imminent. In the light of subsequent events it is more likely that by this time victory was no longer feasible. If Hitler in July had permitted an all-out advance towards Moscow, as Guderian advised, instead of turning Guderian's tanks southwards to support the advance of von Rundstedt's southern army group in the Ukraine, the course of the war might have been decisively different. But Hitler's miscalculations were political as well as military. He had anticipated that an attack on Russia would become an anti-Communist crusade which such capitalist nations as Great Britain and the United States would be unlikely to oppose. In fact, immediately after the German invasion Winston Churchill, Prime Minister of Great Britain since May 1940, pledged British support for the Soviet Union regardless of the ideological or other differences which may previously have divided the two countries. Similarly, President Roosevelt within a week of the invasion made arrangements for United States "lend-lease" aid to be extended to the Soviet Union. In the ensuing months of 1941 until the Japanese attack on Pearl Harbour (December 7th) and in the remaining war years, when the United States was a co-belligerent of the Soviet Union, American aid assisted the Soviet war effort to the tune of more than eleven billion dollars. Much of this aid was transported through Persia; but a considerable proportion was also shipped in British convoys to Murmansk which suffered grievous losses from German air force and submarine attacks. Such aid, though never fully acknowledged by the Soviet government, contributed in no small measure towards preventing the collapse of the Soviet Union after the Germans had occupied, by the end of 1941, practically the whole of European Russia, containing more than 40 per cent of the population and almost two-thirds of Soviet industry.

The Soviet government's immediate reaction to the German invasion was to establish a State Defence Committee consisting of Stalin, Molotov, Voroshilov, Beria and Malenkov. On August 8th Stalin, who had already become Chairman of the Sovnarkom in May, assumed supreme command of the armed forces, though the actual military leadership was in the hands of an HQ presided over by General Shaposhnikov, and later by General Vasilevsky. Apart from inspiring in the Soviet people a patriotic hatred of the invader (who, it should be remembered, had been represented until the eve of invasion as the Soviet Union's staunchest ally), Stalin called for a "scorched earth" policy and the destruction of whatever industrial or military equipment could not be evacuated. In the course of the first three months of the war 1,360 factories were evacuated to the Soviet rear and were often, through the superhuman efforts of the workers, operational within three or four weeks of transfer to the new sites. Such examples of patriotic self-sacrifice by the civilian population were matched by countless acts of heroism in the face of the enemy : the heroic last-ditch defence of the Brest fortress, for example, of Odessa, Borisov and Smolensk. Though there were many instances of readiness to welcome the Germans as "liberators", particularly in the Ukraine and the Baltic Republics, and some sections of the population displayed an apathetic indifference, the majority of the Soviet people threw themselves into the struggle against Hitler with an enthusiasm and dedication due less to love for Communism than to hatred of a cruel and rapacious enemy. It became a case of Russians fighting for their Russian homeland rather than of Soviet citizens fighting for Communism; patriotic feeling dominated all ideological allegiances.

By October the German advance had reached its climax. More than fifty divisions were concentrated on Moscow, but stubborn Russian rearguard actions at Mozhaysk, Kalinin and Tula slowed down the German forward thrust though they could not prevent advance German units from penetrating to the outlying suburbs of the capital by late November. By this time, however, German units were 50 per cent under strength, exhausted by heavy fighting and beginning to suffer from the intense winter cold. As early as October the tide of German advance towards Leningrad had been halted, though this did not prevent the city from being besieged. Then, on December 6th, in a temperature of 40 degrees below zero, Red Army troops under Generals Zhukov and

Konev and Marshal Timoshenko launched a counter-offensive which drove the Germans back over one hundred kilometres from Moscow, recapturing Klin and inflicting enormous losses in dead and wounded on the retreating enemy. Simultaneously Rostov-on-Don and, shortly afterwards, Kerch and Feodosia in the Crimea were wrested from the invaders. It had become clear not only that Hitler's hopes of a short, victorious war were shattered, but also that he had seriously under-estimated Russian military potential. The German retreat was only pre-vented from becoming a rout, it seems, through Hitler's personal inter-vention—intervention, however, which did not come soon enough to save the cream of the German army from destruction outside Moscow.

German policy in the occupied territories betrayed all the worst features of Nazi racialist theories. The systematic killing of Jews was accompanied by determined efforts on the part of Rosenberg, *Reichs-leiter* for the Eastern Territories, to colonise the native Slav populations. Brutal reprisals against Communists and non-Communists, mass execu-tions, the indiscriminate taking of hostages and enforced labour recruit-ment were all designed to suppress any form of anti-German resistance; but no effort was made to foster anti-Soviet sentiment by encouraging religion or disbanding the collective farms. When attempts were made later in the war to support an anti-Soviet movement, led by Andrey Vlasov, Hitler himself, it is believed, scotched the idea; in any event, it came too late. As soon as the German administration in the occupied territories revealed that it was concerned only to reduce the Russian population to the status of slaves, widespread partisan activity began to develop which continually harassed the German rear and seriously impaired German military effectiveness.

Soviet relations with the Western allies were close, though not always amicable. If, on the one hand, the Soviet government gave its support to the United Nations, entered into a twenty-year treaty of alliance with Great Britain in May and a further aid agreement with the United States in June 1942, then on the other it displayed ill-concealed hostility towards the Polish government-in-exile in London, demanded recognition of the Soviet annexation of the Baltic republics (a recognition, by the way, which the Western allies have not so far felt ready to grant) and pressed for the opening of a second front in Europe. Western reluctance to open such a front was due, apart from the enormous military difficulties involved, to a fairly natural scepticism about the Red Army's capacity for survival after the tremendous defeats of 1941; but by the end of 1942 such scepticism was no longer justified and Stalin's demands for active Western support grew correspondingly more strident and captious.

The German summer offensive of 1942, under Hitler's personal direction, was carefully prepared but more limited than the large-scale offensive of the previous year. Moreover, although the Germans had wiped out all Soviet resistance in the Crimea by mid-July, the main offensive towards the Volga and the Caucasus was delayed by Marshal Timoshenko's bold counter-attack in the Voronezh region in May. When the German offensive finally gathered momentum, it began to head towards Stalingrad, leaving the Soviet troops north of Voronezh free to regroup. Hitler's aim, it seems, was to capture Stalingrad and then to advance up the Volga towards Moscow while other German units invaded the Caucasus and seized the oil wells. Throughout the late summer massive German attacks were launched against Stalingrad —attacks which were resisted foot by foot until the whole city was a heap of rubble. Meanwhile, the German advance into the Caucasus petered out before reaching Grozny. At this point Hitler, deprived of the possibility of capturing either Moscow or Leningrad, showed a frenzied and lunatic determination to seize Stalingrad no matter how great the cost. An army of 300,000 troops under General Paulus was given this unenviable task. But before the Germans could reach the Volga Red Army troops under General Zhukov launched an enveloping movement on November 19th which soon cut off the German retreat to the Don. Despite counter-attacks by General Manstein and efforts to fly in supplies, the position of General Paulus's army became so desperate that at the beginning of February 1943 he, his staff and 90,000 surviving troops were forced to surrender. The Russians swept forward and captured Kharkov, but German counter-attacks in March recaptured the city. However, Stalingrad had been relieved and for the first time in the war the initiative had clearly passed to the Soviet side—an initiative which, coupled with the German defeat in North Africa, was to show the way to eventual victory.

Winston Churchill's visit to Moscow in August 1942 contributed little towards improving relations between Stalin and his Western allies. Though it was agreed that the war should only end with the unconditional surrender of the Germans, Stalin insisted upon the opening of a second front in Europe and was not satisfied with Churchill's substitute plans for Anglo-American operations in the Mediterranean. The Soviet conduct of the war had meanwhile become marked by a return to Tsarist traditions which involved the introduction of epaulettes for officers, military awards, the strict enforcement of hierarchical ranks and official acknowledgement of the importance of the Orthodox Church. In 1943 the Comintern was dissolved. The NKVD, instead of suppressing opposition to the Soviet state, began to play an important part in organising partisan activity against the Germans in the occupied territories. Most important of all, despite the awful privations of wartime, the Soviet people began to evince a new spirit of confidence and Soviet international prestige, after the victory at Stalingrad, reached such heights that Stalin had good reason for behaving as the senior partner in the anti-German alliance.

The summer of 1943 was well advanced before large-scale operations began on the Russian front. In anticipation of a Russian offensive, the Germans on July 5th launched an attack in the Kursk region, but on this occasion Soviet troops under General Vatutin stood their ground and after ten days' heavy fighting were able to embark on the first Soviet summer offensive of the war. In August Oryol and Kharkov were liberated; a month later Smolensk was recaptured, the Donbass was cleared of Germans and Soviet troops reached the Dnieper south of Kiev; in October the Germans were driven from the Taman peninsula and in November they abandoned Kiev, surrendering by the end of the year almost two-thirds of the Soviet territory captured earlier in the war. This succession of Soviet victories proved to be a useful bargaining point for Stalin at the first Summit Conference between the leaders of the Anglo–Soviet–American alliance. Churchill, Stalin and Roosevelt met in Teheran on November 28th 1943 and on December 1st issued a joint declaration about their complete agreement on the scope and timing of future military operation and their determination to work together in the ensuing peace. The declaration concealed the fact that Stalin had won a major diplomatic victory in obtaining the rejection of Churchill's plan for an invasion through the Balkans and in gaining recognition of the Curzon Line for Poland's eastern frontier. Another Soviet gain at Teheran was the ice-free port of Koenigsberg. Poland was to be compensated for the loss of territory in the east by being given East Prussia. But Soviet–Polish relations had worsened considerably in the spring of 1943 after the Germans had announced the discovery of the corpses of thousands of Polish officers in the Katyn Forest outside Smolensk. According to the Germans, the massacre of the Polish officers had occurred in 1940, before the German invasion. This charge, supposedly substantiated by later investigations though denied by the Soviet government, led Stalin to break off relations with the exiled Polish government in London.

Stalin's diplomatic victories were soon backed up by Soviet military successes. In January 1944 the blockade of Leningrad, which had lasted 900 days, was finally broken. In the course of the next few months Krivoy Rog, Odessa and the Crimea were cleared of the enemy and Soviet troops began the invasion of Roumania. With the Anglo–

A SHORT HISTORY OF MODERN RUSSIA

American invasion of Normandy on June 6th the Red Army increased its pressure on the eastern front by capturing Vilna, Lvov and Kishinyov, inflicting terrible losses on the Germans in the process. Roumania collapsed and Bulgaria surrendered on September 8th almost simultaneously with the Soviet invasion of Estonia and Latvia. By the end of the year all Soviet territory had been liberated, Russian troops had entered Jugoslavia and had begun the defeat of the Germans in Hungary. Only in Poland was the general picture of success marred by the Soviet refusal either to offer direct aid or to permit allied aid for the uprising of the Polish right-wing resistance movement in Warsaw, which was eventually brutally crushed by the Germans in October. In Soviet eyes a committee composed of Polish Communists which had been established in Lublin in July was to be the new provisional government of Poland.

The final year of the war opened with Soviet offensives on the eastern front which helped to relieve the pressure on the Anglo–American forces during the German attack in the Ardennes. Red Army troops entered Warsaw on January 17th 1945, liberated Budapest a month later and embarked on the invasion of East Prussia, capturing Koenigsberg in April. It was at this point in the war, during the Yalta Conference of the "Big Three", held in the Crimea between February 1st–10th, that fateful decisions were taken which have since had a profound effect upon both the European and the world political scene. Firstly, it was agreed that Germany should be divided into British, American, Soviet and French occupation zones with four-power control of Berlin. The anomaly of Berlin as an international outpost surrounded by the Soviet occupation zone was not apparent at the time; but it was to prove to be a tragic bone of contention in subsequent East–West relations. Secondly, the very division of the world into East and West was inherent in the Yalta agreement that Eastern Europe, with the exception of Greece, and all the Far Eastern Russian territories ceded to Japan since 1904 should become Soviet spheres of influence. Thirdly, agreement was reached on Soviet participation in the United Nations Organisation on the condition that the Ukrainian and Belorussian Republics were admitted separately. Fourthly, the Lublin committee, with an admixture of unspecified "democratic" elements, was recognised as the government of Poland. Such thorny questions as Poland's western borders and the amount of German reparations were left unsolved. Roosevelt, already a sick man, made concessions to Stalin in the hope that future cooperation between the allies would ensure a stable peace; the more sceptical Churchill tended to regard such concessions as merely adding fuel to Stalin's imperialist ambitions. By the time of

Roosevelt's death on April 12th Anglo–American opposition to Soviet demands was beginning to harden. However, Stalin's shrewd and calculating vitality had won the day for him at Yalta, just as Soviet troops under Zhukov and Konev were winning the war against Germany by storming their way towards Berlin. At the end of April Berlin was surrounded. Though advance units of the American and Russian forces met on April 25th, the actual capture of Berlin was a Soviet affair. On April 30th Hitler committed suicide and on May 2nd the Berlin garrison capitulated. The war in Europe finally ended on May 7th with the unconditional surrender of the German provisional government.

The Soviet contribution to the defeat of Nazi Germany was, whether viewed in terms of military effort, casualties or economic disruption, appreciably greater than the contribution of either Great Britain or the United States. The valour and military effectiveness of the Red Army as a fighting machine were unquestionable; also undeniable was the policy of disregarding the losses provided the desired objective was attained. The ruthlessness which had characterised the domestic policies of the Soviet government before the German invasion proved even more effective when employed against the invader. At the time Western opinion unanimously approved such ruthlessness, since it was directed against the common enemy; but a similar ruthlessness was also displayed by the Soviet government in its treatment of the Crimean Tatars, the Volga Germans and other national minorities. The Soviet leopard did not change its spots, and with the Soviet conquest of most of Eastern Europe such ruthlessness became an instrument of policy for ensuring the "Sovietisation" of Roumania, Bulgaria, Hungary, Poland and the Soviet zone of Germany. In many respects such "Sovietisation" quite simply involved the extension to these non-Russian territories of a Russian domination which, if not more efficient, was more far-reaching than the former German domination. It is small wonder that Stalin, at a Kremlin celebration on May 25th 1945, proposed a toast to the Russian people. The Russian people, of all the nations of the Soviet Union, had made the greatest contribution to the defeat of Nazi Germany; they, in turn, would reap the greatest fruits of the victory. This Greater Russian predominance was cultivated both by stressing the superiority of the specifically Russian advances in military technology (the new "Yakovlev" fighter planes, "Ilyushin" bombers, Stalin tanks, etc.) and by emphasising in art and propaganda the sufferings and gallantry of the Russian people. Soviet literature during the Great Patriotic War extolled the heroism and self-sacrifice of the partisans, as in Fadeyev's *The Young Guard* (1945), which was later emended to give more prominence to the role of the Party; it also stressed the humour and valour of the ordinary Russian soldier, as in the poem *Vasily Tyorkin* by Tvardovsky (*b.* 1910) and, as in *Days and Nights* by Simonov (*b.* 1915), it celebrated the defence of Stalingrad. In music the greatest contribution was made by Shostakovich, who dedicated his seventh symphony to the heroic city of Leningrad.

The Potsdam Conference (July 17th–August 2nd 1945) was attended by Stalin, Churchill and Truman (who had succeeded to the US presidency after Roosevelt's death), though on July 26th Churchill was replaced by Prime Minister Attlee after the Labour victory in the British elections. The fact that Stalin was the only member of the original "Big Three" to participate in the conference from start to finish not only emphasised the peculiar rigidity of Soviet democracy but also helped to ensure the acceptance by the conference of most of Stalin's proposals. These included the ceding of Koenigsberg, since renamed Kaliningrad, and a part of northern East Prussia to the Soviet Union and the transference of German territory east of the Oder–Neisse line, including the free city of Danzig, to Poland, despite Anglo–American insistence that such territorial arrangements were to be provisional pending a general peace settlement. This settlement was to be worked out by a permanent Council of the Foreign Ministers of the Soviet Union, the United States, Great Britain, France and China. The conference agreed to establish allied control commissions in Berlin and Vienna, but there was no specific agreement on the means of exacting reparations from Germany. If the Western allies appeared to accept Stalin's territorial and political arrangements in Eastern Europe, then they did so because they were really in no position to do otherwise, whereas in dealing with matters over which they had some control, such as opposition to Communism in Greece or Soviet bases in the Mediterranean, they were able to offer firm resistance to Stalin's demands. History may well judge that the Potsdam Conference, though outwardly concerned with dividing the spoils among the recent victors, was equally if not more concerned with a redistribution of spheres of influence among old enemies.

The Soviet Union finally declared war against Japan on August 8th 1945. This Soviet move, ostensibly undertaken in fulfilment of promises to Roosevelt, was probably prompted by the fact that on August 6th a new and incalculable factor had appeared in international relations with the dropping by an American aircraft of the first atomic bomb on Hiroshima. A day after the Soviet declaration of war the second atomic bomb was dropped on Nagasaki and by August 14th the Japanese had surrendered. The official Soviet view upholds that it was Soviet intervention in the Far East which forced Japan to capitulate. In fact, Soviet intervention came just in time to ensure that the Russians could occupy

South Sakhalin, Port Arthur and the Kuril Islands and regain a half interest in the Chinese Eastern Railway. By this means Soviet Russia retrieved the losses of the Russo–Japanese War of 1904–1905 and achieved a position of unprecedented power in the Far East.

Stalin's Last Years and Death

AFTER Potsdam hopes for cooperation between the Soviet Union and her Western allies quickly began to fade into an era of "cold war". Though the world was a better place once Nazism, Fascism and Japanese tyranny had been defeated, it remained divided into the two camps of capitalism and socialism, separated from one another by opposed ideologies, political systems and geopolitical interests. Both the Soviet Union and the Western allies proclaimed "democracy" as their aim, but in the difference between the Soviet concept of democracy as unopposed rule by a Communist party and the Western belief that democracy involved majority rule curbed by minority opposition lay the real division between East and West. There was much ignorant wishful thinking about Western hopes of cooperation with Soviet Russia; the subsequent disillusionment in the immediate post-war years obliged Western statesmen to remind themselves of such disagreeable facts as the Hitler–Stalin pact and to accept the not very palatable truth that it was their judgment of Stalin, not Stalin's judgment of the West, which had proved to be at fault. Stalin had gained for Russia positions of unprecedented power both in Europe and the Far East. Equally significant was the fact that this increase in Russian power involved an expansion of the socialist camp and a corresponding contraction of the capitalist world. In the final estimate, the Second World War ended by producing a world situation in which two Super-Powers, the Soviet Union and the United States, confronted each other; and the difference between them, in terms of real power, was that the United States possessed a temporary monopoly of the atomic bomb.

Soviet hostility towards the West took the form of aggressive non-cooperation on such important issues as the international control of atomic energy and arrangements for a peace treaty with Germany. The Soviet Union would not participate in the United Nations Atomic Energy Commission; and in the United Nations Security Council the Soviet delegation made persistent use of the veto. Though there was Soviet cooperation over the de-Nazification of Germany and the Nuremberg trial of the Nazi leaders in 1946, the Soviet Union would not agree to a peace treaty with Germany or to unification of the country. The fusion of the British and American zones of occupation in December 1946 was interpreted by the Soviet government as a deliberate attempt to make the division of Germany permanent, though in fact it was obviously designed to promote some degree of unification. Although in February 1947 in Paris, as a result of protracted negotiations with twenty-one participating states, the Soviet Union signed peace treaties with Italy, Hungary, Roumania, Bulgaria and Finland, gaining incidentally the lease of the Porkkala base from Finland and the annexation of the Carpatho–Russian or Ruthenian area from Czechoslovakia, the Soviet government insisted that there could be no peace treaty with Austria until a German peace settlement had been reached. The Soviet Union also refused to participate in the Marshall Plan of 1947 and in September of that year resurrected the Comintern in the shape of the Cominform, an agency set up in Belgrade ostensibly for the dissemination of information among the Soviet satellites though in reality designed to coordinate the activities of the European Communist Parties. In 1948 Soviet relations with the Western allies reached crisis-point over the Soviet decision to close the autobahn route to Berlin. The Soviet attempt to cut off West Berlin and thus to obliterate this outpost of capitalism in the middle of the Soviet occupation zone would have been successful had not the Americans and British mounted an enormous air lift of supplies, beginning in June 1948, which eventually forced Stalin to end the blockade in May 1949.

Hostility towards the West was accompanied by Soviet consolidation in Eastern Europe. The presence of large Soviet armed forces and the activities of Soviet agents ensured the establishment of left-wing governments which were soon dominated by local or Moscow-trained Communists. By 1948 Communist régimes had gained control in Poland, Hungary, Roumania, Bulgaria and Albania. In Czechoslovakia, where free elections in May 1946 had given the Communists 38 per cent of the vote, a Communist *coup* in February 1948 finally brought that country within the Soviet orbit. Politically and economically, through treaties and close economic links (the creation of the Council for Mutual Economic Assistance, Comecon, in January 1949, for example), these countries, together with the Soviet zone of Germany, were welded into what has since come to be known as the Soviet bloc, subservient in many aspects of its internal affairs and in every aspect of its international relations—at least during Stalin's lifetime—to the dictates of Moscow. Only Jugoslavia, where Communism had acquired a strongly nationalistic character under the guidance of Marshal Tito, refused to accept

Soviet policies and in June 1948 an open breach occurred over the issue of collectivisation. Tito, unimpressed by Stalin's threats, adopted an independent or "Titoist" line which tended nonetheless to bring Jugoslavia into closer alignment with the West. In 1949 the American monopoly of the atomic bomb was broken when the Soviet Union became a nuclear power. From this point forward the world political scene began to be dominated not so much by the issue of nuclear ascendancy in the relationship between the two Super-Powers as by the need to maintain a nuclear power balance.

The Western answer to Soviet hostility, at first somewhat lamely indignant, very soon took a more positive form. In January 1946 the United States brought pressure on the Soviet Union to withdraw Russian forces from northern Iran. In March of that year Winston Churchill, in his famous speech at Fulton, Missouri, declared that an "Iron Curtain" had fallen across the European continent. The United States soon began to adopt a policy of "containment" towards the Soviet Union on lines recommended in an anonymous article by the American Russian expert, George F. Kennan. One manifestation of this new policy was the Truman Doctrine of extending aid to countries threatened by Russia. In March 1947 such aid was offered to Greece and Turkey. In June 1947 the more ambitious Marshall Plan, named after the American Secretary of State, led to the setting up of the Organisation of European Economic Cooperation for distributing American aid to countries striving to revive their post-war economies. The Soviet blockade of Berlin provided a new stimulus to Western unity which resulted in the creation of NATO (North Atlantic Treaty Organisation) in March 1949. The United States, Great Britain, France, the Benelux countries, Italy, Portugal, Denmark, Norway, Iceland and Canada joined forces under a Supreme Headquarters, Allied Powers, Europe (or SHAPE, organised in 1951) under the command of General Eisenhower. Closely connected with the formation of NATO was the merging of the three Western occupation zones in Germany and the establishment of the German Federal Republic with its capital in Bonn (May 1949). The Soviet answer was the creation of a German Democratic Republic in the Soviet occupation zone (October 1949); and the Soviet answer to NATO came in 1955 with the Warsaw Pact which involved a pooling of military resources by the Soviet Union, Poland, Czechoslovakia, the German Democratic Republic, Roumania, Bulgaria, Hungary and Albania.

A position of stalemate having been reached in Europe, Soviet attention was turned to the Far East. In 1949 Nationalist China, led by Chiang Kai-shek, was defeated by the Communist armies of Mao Tse-tung and a Chinese People's Republic was proclaimed in Peking. Chiang Kai-shek's government transferred from the Chinese mainland to the island of Formosa. American opposition to Mao Tse-tung's régime in China and the refusal to allow the Chinese Nationalist seat in the UNO Security Council to be taken by a Red Chinese delegate precipitated a walk-out by the Soviet delegation in January 1950. When, in June 1950, Communist North Korea invaded South Korea, there was no Soviet delegate in the Security Council to veto the resolution that the United Nations should actively intervene in Korean affairs. Under the flag of the United Nations American troops, aided by contingents from other member nations, landed in South Korea and had succeeded by November 1950 in pushing the North Korean force back to the Chinese border. At this point Chinese Communist "volunteers" crossed into Korea and the United Nations troops were forced to retreat. After bitter fighting and subsequent protracted negotiations at Panmunjon, peace terms were finally agreed in July 1953.

The Soviet Union, though giving military aid to North Korea and Communist China, had not participated directly in the hostilities. A Peace Campaign launched in 1949 aimed to depict the Soviet Union as a steadfast guarantor of peace throughout the world; but it was to be peace only on Stalin's terms. Naturally, within the Soviet bloc only Stalin's views were permitted to prevail: hence the vilification and ex-communication of Tito. The arrest of Gomulka in Poland in 1948 and the visit of the Bulgarian leader, Dimitrov, to Moscow in January 1949, from which he never returned, were similar manifestations of Stalin's determination to suppress all forms of centrifugal movement away from Moscow's hegemony within the Communist camp. Relations with the non-Communist world became increasingly cold and embittered in the early 1950s. The Deputy Foreign Ministers of the Soviet Union, United States, Great Britain and France, meeting in Paris during March–June 1951, could not agree on a policy towards Germany. The uncooperative attitude of the Soviet Union led the United States and other Western Powers to sign a separate peace treaty with Japan in September 1951. Eisenhower's victory in the 1952 United States presidential election and John Foster Dulles's talk of "rolling back" Soviet power and "liberating" the Soviet satellites produced spasms of nervousness in the Soviet government, which reached a climax with the convulsion of Stalin's death in March 1953.

At the end of the Second World War the Soviet Union consisted of sixteen Soviet Socialist Republics (reduced to fifteen in 1956 with the demotion of the Karelo–Finnish SSR to the status of an autonomous republic within the RSFSR). Officially 7,000,000 Soviet citizens had been killed during the war, but actual deaths were probably closer to 20,000,000. One-quarter of Soviet industrial potential had been destroyed. It was estimated that in 1946 there were 29 per cent fewer able-bodied *kolkhoz* workers than before the war. So far as livestock was concerned, losses in horned cattle amounted to 17,000,000. The total or partial destruction of 1,710 towns, 70,000 villages and 32,000 factories, not to speak of enormous losses in houses, railways, rolling-stock, tractors, etc., represented a blow to the Soviet economy from which recovery seemed at best uncertain. Nevertheless, the rebuilding of the war-devastated areas was initiated in August 1945, when plans were set in motion for a fourth Five Year Plan and a special directorate was created for rebuilding Stalingrad and fifteen of Russia's oldest cities. The State Defence Committee was dissolved and replaced by the Sovnarkom. In 1946, however, the Sovnarkom was renamed Council of Ministers, the Narkoms (Peoples' Commissariats) became Ministries and the Red Army became the Soviet Army—changes in nomenclature which, apart from indicating certain unimportant organisational differences, were appropriate to the Soviet Union's new role as leader of the Soviet bloc. But 1946 also witnessed a drought in Moldavia, south-western and northern Ukraine, the central black-earth belt and the lower Volga region; and industrial production, rather than rising as the fourth Five Year Plan anticipated, actually fell due to the change-over from wartime to peacetime production.

Signs of economic recovery began to be apparent in 1947 when intensive efforts were made to combat the effects of the drought by increasing the output of tractors and by devoting 67 per cent of all capital investment to intensified development of heavy industry, electrical power and transport. As a result, it was officially claimed that in 1947 industrial production reached 93 per cent of pre-war. Some of the increase must have been due to reparations from Germany, Bulgaria and Roumania, which frequently involved the transference of whole factories and specialist personnel to the Soviet Union. The eight-hour day, six-day week remained obligatory throughout Soviet industry. Though rationing was abolished, rationing by price took its place; and a currency reform, which substituted one new rouble for ten old roubles, caused widespread dissatisfaction by virtually wiping out many people's wartime savings. Further evidence of the Soviet government's doctrinaire attitude towards its own subjects was provided in 1947 by the enactment of a decree forbidding marriages between Soviet citizens and foreigners; this decree was only rescinded after Stalin's death.

By 1948 industrial production was 18 per cent above pre-war and continued to increase rapidly until, by 1952, at the beginning of the fifth Five Year Plan, industrial production was claimed to be 2·3 times greater than in 1940. Agricultural production, however, had only increased by 10 per cent. During the last years of Stalin's life agriculture became the Achilles heel of the whole Soviet economy. In the immediate post-war years, under the guidance of Andreyev, a certain leniency was shown towards the peasantry, despite the strict enforcement of regulations against the dispersal of *kolkhoz* land, despite the purging of *kolkhoz* administrations and the fact that low procurement prices left the peasant with little incentive to increase his production rates. In general the standard of living of the average *kolkhoz* worker was abysmally low and hardly above starvation level. Yet until 1948–1949 the "link" system of work, which encouraged the peasants to work in family or other groups containing about ten members, made allowances for individual initiative. After 1949 a "brigade" system was introduced. Large numbers of *kolkhoz* workers were now organised in quasi-military brigades to undertake field work on the collective farms. Such a new organisational procedure no doubt proved effective in view of the increasing mechanisation, but it could also be justified on the grounds that it provided a better basis for exercising Party control over *kolkhoz* work and because, with the rapid amalgamation of *kolkhozy*, larger work units were obviously more suitable on the enlarged collective farms. This change of policy was accompanied by the downfall of Andreyev and the emergence of Khrushchev, who had been transferred from the Ukraine to Moscow in late 1949, as the leading Party spokesman on agricultural matters. The amalgamation of the collective farms was his idea, as was the more grandiose plan for building "agro-cities"; but this latter plan apparently encountered considerable opposition in the Politburo.

In the last years of Stalin's life a generally low standard of living, estimated at below the pre-1928 level or even the pre-1914 level, served as a background to various grandiose schemes for transforming Russia. Such were Stalin's scheme for transforming nature by planting windbreaks in the drought-prone areas of the eastern Ukraine and the lower Volga, the construction of enormous hydroelectric power stations near Kuibyshev and Stalingrad on the Volga and at Kakhovka on the Dnieper, the linking of the Volga to the Don (the Volga–Don Canal was completed in 1952) and the erection in Moscow of various multi-storey buildings, such as the skyscraper tenement on the Kotelnicheskaya Embankment or the Lomonosov University building on the Lenin Hills. There was a similar concern for monumentalism in the realm of theory. Academician Lysenko's claim to be able to change the heredity of plants received the approval of the Party, since by implication it tended to suggest a grandiose vision of Communism changing the nature of man. Similarly, in the controversy over linguistics, Stalin, in June 1950, came out in opposition to the philologist Marr (1864–1934), who had claimed that language was part of the superstructure of society, by asserting that language was independent of the superstructure but that the superstructure itself was "the greatest of active powers" in transforming society. In speaking of the superstructure Stalin undoubtedly had in mind the machinery of Soviet power and Party control by which he governed not only the Soviet Union but also the new Soviet empire in Eastern Europe. A corollary, therefore, of Stalin's standpoint on linguistics was that, if the Russian language was independent of, or above, the superstructure, then Soviet Russia would exert a similar independent domination over the socialist camp.

The glorification of Stalin himself, of the Party and Soviet achievement formed part of that Greater Russian nationalism which had grown up during the war. A further symptom of such nationalism was the stress laid on specifically Russian contributions to scientific knowledge. Exaggerated claims were made for Russian inventors and their works, usually with the aim of demonstrating Russian priority over Western achievements. Greater Russian nationalism, however, acquired a more sinister aspect during the period 1946-1953 under the influence of Zhdanov. On August 14th 1946 a Party decree attacked the Leningrad journals *Zvezda* (*The Star*) and *Leningrad*, the latter being banned. Zhdanov, who had been Party boss of Leningrad during the war, also attacked the humorous writer, Zoshchenko, and the poetess, Anna Akhmatova. The burden of all such attacks was that literature, in grovelling before the West, could be regarded as morally injurious to Soviet youth. Zoshchenko and Akhmatova were expelled from the Union of Soviet Writers, other writers were clearly directed to toe the new Party line and further decrees were issued about the new line to be followed in the theatre and the cinema. The West, particularly America, now became the object of a scurrilous campaign of vilification. One feature of this anti-Western policy was that the Soviet Union became increasingly isolated from the West in terms of taste, cultural standards and intellectual attitudes. Works of art, plays, novels and films avoided all "conflict" in their depiction of Soviet life; Babayevsky, for instance, who won a Stalin Prize for his novel *Cavalier of the Golden Star* (1949), offered a deliberately uncritical, idealised picture of life on a collective farm. Soviet literature went through its darkest period, lightened by only one or two works of interest, such as *Fellow Travellers* (1947) and *Kruzhilikha* (1948) by Vera Panova (*b.* 1905) or Fedin's *Unusual Summer* (1948). Another feature of the anti-Western campaign was a concerted attack on "rootless cosmopolitans", launched in 1949, which contained a none-too-subtle admixture of anti-Semitism. In this oppressive climate Soviet culture almost ceased to exist. It is worth remarking in this connection that on the occasion of Stalin's seventieth birthday in 1949 the Pushkin Museum of Fine Arts in Moscow was given over to a tasteless display of Stalin's birthday presents : Soviet culture had become a series of birthday presents to Stalin.

On August 31st 1948 Zhdanov died. His influence lived on, but several of his associates—Voznesensky (full Politburo member since 1947, after the death of Kalinin in the previous year), Kuznetsov (a secretary of the Central Committee) and Rodionov (chairman of the RSFSR Council of Ministers)—were arrested and shot in what came to be known as the "Leningrad case", an anti-Zhdanov plot hatched, according to Khrushchev's 1956 speech, by Beria. It must be assumed that Stalin either promoted or at least condoned this fabricated case, and that Malenkov played a leading part in executing it. For the outcome of it was that Malenkov, who had been somewhat put in the shade by Zhdanov, succeeded in recouping his fortunes and regaining his place as Stalin's successor. It was Malenkov who delivered the main address at the nineteenth Party Congress in October 1952. This congress, the first since 1939, adopted new Party statutes, proposed by Khrushchev, which altered the name of the Party from "All-Union Communist Party (Bolsheviks)" to the simpler "Communist Party of the Soviet Union". Apart from offering the customary adulation to Stalin, who deliberately dissociated himself from his Politburo colleagues, the congress called for "self-criticism" and ended by substituting for the Politburo and Orgburo an enlarged Presidium consisting of twenty-five full members and eleven candidate members. There was every indication that "self-criticism" would involve a purging of some of Stalin's older colleagues and the introduction of younger men into the Party leadership.

Moreover, on the eve of the congress Stalin stole much of its thunder by publishing his pamphlet *Economic Problems of Socialism in the USSR*. As a Christian monarch might have invoked God, Stalin invoked Marxist economics as a means of ensuring his immortality. He prophesied an imminent crisis of world capitalism and foresaw that the so-called "imperialists" would rather fight among each other than attack the Soviet Union. Stalin's mental senility, his hypochondriacal suspiciousness and fondness for duplicity made themselves felt in the obscurantist threats about "capitalist remnants", the need for vigilance and so on which filled each *Pravda* editorial during this period. Throughout the winter of 1952–1953 the atmosphere in Moscow was extremely tense. On January 13th 1953 *Pravda* announced the arrest of nine Soviet doctors, the majority of whom were Jews, accused of murdering Zhdanov and plotting the death of leading military figures. According to Khrushchev, this "doctors' plot" was fabricated by Stalin. Whatever the motives for this curious affair may have been, they became pointless on March 4th when it was announced that Stalin had had a stroke. He died on the evening of March 5th.

Serious disorders broke out in Moscow on the evening of March 6th, after Stalin's remains had been placed in the Hall of Columns for the lying-in-state. Despite attempts by security and other troops to cordon off the central areas of the city, crowds swarmed unchecked through many of the city's streets or tried to fight their way through the barricades. Long queues formed outside the Hall of Columns. But there was little overt grief for Stalin, unlike the universal bereavement which was displayed at Lenin's funeral. Stalin's funeral on March 9th was accompanied by much pomp and lip service was paid to his greatness, but his was not the kind of greatness to give cause for sincere mourning. His embalmed remains, when placed beside those of Lenin in the mausoleum on the Red Square, were testimony to a "cult of personality" about which most of his colleagues and contemporaries preferred to forget.

Epilogue

1953 – 1964

The Era of Khrushchev

THE era of Khrushchev opened, it seems, with a struggle between the Party and the state machine in which Khrushchev and the Communist Party soon gained the ascendancy. The era of Khrushchev also involved the "de-Stalinisation" of the Party and the reassertion of what were called "Leninist principles" of majority rule and socialist legality in the policy-making activities of the Party Presidium and the Central Committee. Khrushchev also enunciated, and pursued, a policy of peaceful coexistence with the capitalist "imperialists", chiefly with the United States of America, which was based on the assumption that war between socialism and capitalism would not be inevitable. Such an assumption resulted as much from considerations of practical expediency as from a fundamental reinterpretation of Marxism, since full-scale war in a nuclear age would most likely involve the destruction of friend and foe alike. War was to be replaced by economic competition between the two systems. In domestic affairs the Khrushchev era witnessed the first serious attempts to embark on the transition from socialism to Communism. So far as the world Communist movement was concerned, disagreement between Khrushchev and Mao Tse-tung gradually led to a growing, and apparently irreconcilable, rift between the Soviet Union and the Chinese People's Republic and their respective supporters.

The era of Khrushchev did not begin immediately after Stalin's death, but the stage was set for his rise to power within a matter of days of the late dictator's funeral. Malenkov, who was apparently the senior partner, together with Molotov and Beria, in the collective leadership proclaimed on March 7th 1953, relinquished his post in the Party Secretariat on March 14th and relied on his position as Chairman of the Council of Ministers to exercise effective government. Khrushchev was now given a free hand in the Party Secretariat and used this power, as did Stalin three decades earlier, to gain control of the Party apparatus. The enlarged Party Presidium created by the nineteenth Party Congress was meanwhile reduced to ten members: Malenkov, Beria, Molotov, Voroshilov, Khrushchev, Bulganin, Kaganovich, Mikoyan, Pervukhin and Saburov. The new administration quickly introduced such palliative measures as the granting of an amnesty to certain categories of prisoners in the slave labour camps and an increase in the output of consumer goods. But the apparent unity of the collective leadership was soon shattered. In July 1953 it was announced that Beria had been expelled from the Party and in December that he had been shot. The power of Beria's secret police and the MVD (Ministry of Internal Affairs) which he had headed was greatly reduced by the creation of a Committee of State Security.

During 1954 Khrushchev, as First Secretary of the Party Central Committee, began to play an increasingly prominent part in the country's affairs. He became the leading exponent of a new, realistic agricultural policy and launched a much publicised campaign for ploughing up one hundred million acres of virgin land in Kazakhstan. He added further to his prestige and influence when, in February 1955, Malenkov was forced ignominiously to resign from the post of Chairman of the Council of Ministers and was replaced by Bulganin. In May 1955 Khrushchev and Bulganin took the initiative in healing the rift with Tito by making a visit to Jugoslavia. Molotov, the Minister of Foreign Affairs, who had been closely associated with Stalin's anti-Tito policy, was conspicuous for his absence on this occasion. If the Geneva Summit Conference in July 1955 between the leaders of the Soviet Union, the United States, Great Britain and France achieved nothing in terms of solving outstanding international problems, then it at least served the purpose of demonstrating to the Soviet public and the world at large that Khrushchev and Bulganin were now the new leaders of Russia. This was again demonstrated in November and December 1955 when, during state visits to India, Burma and Afghanistan, they became the first Soviet leaders to visit non-Communist countries.

It was also left to Khrushchev to initiate the process of "de-Stalinisation". On February 24th–25th 1956, at a closed session of the twentieth Party Congress in the Kremlin, Khrushchev gave a secret speech—probably carefully prepared and edited some time before—in which he denounced Stalin's one-man rule, his "cult of personality", his sadism, bloodthirstiness, cowardice, military incompetence, his deliberate fabrication of cases against loyal Party members—the case of Eykhe figured prominently in this connection—and his invention of the term "enemy of the people" to denote anyone whom he considered to be in need of liquidation. The denunciation also broached such matters as Lenin's appraisal of Stalin's character, Stalin's possible complicity in the assassination of Kirov, the mass deportations of the Chechen–Ingush people and other national minorities which were undertaken on Stalin's orders, Stalin's fabrication, with Beria's help, of the "Leningrad case" and the "doctors' plot" and, finally, Stalin's suspiciousness and his ignorance of the true state of affairs in Soviet Russia (the last time he visited a village,

Khrushchev claimed, was in January 1928). The speech concluded by calling for the re-establishment of Leninist norms of consultation and majority rule in order to prevent the arbitrary use of power by one individual and to ensure socialist legality.

Though never published in the Soviet Union, the speech has percolated down, through Party secretaries and other delegates of the Congress, to all sections of the Soviet population. It has clearly become a bone of contention in the conflict between Khrushchev and Mao Tsetung. So far as one can judge, however, its real purpose was to refurbish the Party's image in its own eyes and to rekindle a sense of purpose and initiative among the Party's rank and file which Stalin's tyranny had almost extinguished. Yet what it left unsaid, particularly in relation to Khrushchev's role as one of Stalin's loyal henchmen, must inevitably have given rise in many Communist minds to doubts about the integrity and efficacy of the Communist system. The ideological shock caused by these revelations about Stalin was a contributory factor in the unrest which seized the Soviet satellite empire later in 1956—the Poznan riots in Poland which brought Gomulka to power and the Hungarian uprising (October 23rd–November 4th). But Khrushchev survived these tempests and in June 1957 succeeded in defeating the "anti-Party group" of Malenkov, Molotov, Kaganovich and their associates who had opposed him in the Party Presidium. They were expelled by a plenary meeting of the Central Committee in which Krushchev could count on massive support. After expulsion they were given unimportant posts (Malenkov was supposed to have become director of a power plant in the Urals and Molotov was sent as ambassador to Ulan-Bator in Mongolia). Similarly, in October 1957, Marshal Zhukov, who was supposed to have been one of Khrushchev's chief supporters in the struggle with the "anti-Party group", was accused of attempting to create his own "cult of personality" in the armed forces and replaced as Minister of Defence by Marshal Malinovsky. The final step in Khrushchev's rise to power occurred in March 1958 when Bulganin, who had been associated with the "anti-Party group", resigned from the Chairmanship of the Council of Ministers. Khrushchev took his place and thus gathered into his hands control over both the Party and the state machine.

No one could have been more unlike Stalin in temperament and manner than his denunciator and heir, Nikita Sergeyevich Khrushchev. He was born in 1894 in the settlement of Kalinovka in Kursk province, the son of a miner. In 1909 or 1910 he went to the Donbass, where he took a variety of jobs until in 1918 he was admitted to full membership of the Party and distinguished himself as a Bolshevik leader during the

Civil War. In 1922 he enrolled at a Party secondary school (*Rabfak*) and later became Party secretary of the Petrovo-Marinsky region of the city of Stalino (since renamed Donets) in the Ukraine. In 1929 he was moved to the Stalin Industrial Academy in Moscow. His rise was now meteoric. By March 1935 he had become first secretary of the Moscow Party organisation. As a close associate of Kaganovich, he was concerned with constructing the Moscow Metro and he must also have been connected with the Party purges. In 1938 he became first secretary in the Ukraine and a candidate member of the Politburo. At the eighteenth Party Congress in March 1939 he was made a full member of the Politburo and during the war he organised the defence of the Ukraine against the Germans. In the immediate post-war period he managed to survive attempts by Malenkov to oust him from power within the Ukrainian Party machine. Brought back to Moscow in 1949, he soon became well known as the exponent of a new line in agriculture. It seems that he achieved his meteoric rise in the Party hierarchy and survived purges and intrigues through a combination of hard work, toughness, sagacity and buoyancy. Ebullient, opportunistic, superbly resilient, a devotee of quick panaceas and quick profits but not averse to cutting his losses, basically a small-time politician who could act big when the big time demanded it, impetuous and fallible and therefore likeable after his own rough-hewn fashion, Nikita Sergeyevich Khrushchev could be relied upon always to be interesting if not always predictable.

Under his aegis the Party prepared the way for the transition to Communism at the twenty-first Party Congress in 1959. This process appears to have involved more clearing of the ground in preparation for the future, for at the twenty-second Party Congress in October 1961 further attacks were made on the "anti-Party group" of Malenkov, Molotov, Kaganovich, Bulganin, Pervukhin, Saburov, Shepilov and Voroshilov, and Stalin's ghost was finally laid when his remains were removed from the mausoleum on Red Square and Stalingrad was renamed Volgograd. In order to distract public attention from such an unedifying interment of the past, Khrushchev offered a new Party programme which promised that by 1970 the Soviet Union would overtake the United States in terms of food production and that by 1980 the Soviet people would have created the material and technical basis for Communism. Communism was described as

"a classless social system with one form of social ownership of the means of production and full social equality of all members of society; under it, the all-round development of people will be accompanied by the growth of the productive forces through continuous progress in science and technology, all sources of public wealth will gush forth abundantly, and the great principle 'From each according to his ability, to each according to his needs' will become a reality."

In more practical terms, what Communism promised for the Soviet people was the highest standard of living in the world, the abolition of the difference between the town and the country and the disappearance of the intelligentsia as a separate social stratum. The Party, with a membership of 10,000,000, was to lead the transition to Communism. Viewed in this light, the process of "de-Stalinisation", the removal from leading positions of practically all Stalin's major associates—with the exception of Khrushchev and Mikoyan—and the rehabilitation of so many of Stalin's victims (in October 1962 Bukharin, Rykov, Tomsky, Pyatakov and Radek were rehabilitated) were not only measures designed to cleanse the Party of the less salubrious aspects of its past but seemingly very necessary stages in the transition from a Stalin-proclaimed socialism to the beginnings of a Khrushchev-proclaimed Communism which, it must be assumed, will be the peak of Soviet achievement in the twentieth century.

Economically the Soviet Union made great strides forward under the Khrushchev administration. The pro-consumer policy of Malenkov was replaced in 1955 by renewed emphasis on heavy industry and in 1956, after the successful completion of the fifth Five Year Plan, a sixth such Plan was announced. However, in March 1957 sweeping changes were made in the organisation of industry. The top-heavy Stalinist system of central ministries was scrapped : of fifty-two All-Union central ministries twenty-five were abolished, four were merged to form two ministries and twenty-three were retained with modifications. Control of industry was delegated to ninety-two regional economic councils distributed throughout the USSR. The only All-Union central ministries to be concerned with industry were the Ministries of the Aircraft Industry, Shipbuilding, Radio, Chemicals, Medium Machine-Building (concerned with atomic energy), Transport Machinery, Foreign Trade, Defence, Merchant Marine, Railways and Power Stations. The sixth Five Year Plan quickly ran into difficulties and in 1958 a Seven Year Plan, destined to run from 1959 to 1965, took its place. Further reorganisation in May 1961 divided the USSR into seventeen large economic areas and in November 1962 the supervisory functions of Gosplan were transferred to a National Economic Council and a new State Planning Committee was made responsible for long-term planning. A somewhat sinister feature of the 1962 changes was the creation of a Party and State Control Committee, headed by the former chief of the security police, Shelepin, and intended to supervise fulfilment of Party and state directives. At the same time Party committees for industry and agriculture were to be established in various regions and territories of the USSR. The number of regional economic councils was reduced, but the new councils were given greater powers, as were factory directors, and employees were encouraged to participate more actively in production planning. In March 1963 a Supreme Council of the National Economy was created for the overall management of industry.

If, at the time of Stalin's death, Soviet production was only 33 per cent of US production, then ten years later it had reached 65 per cent. It was officially claimed that the national income of the USSR had increased 2·3 times in the same ten-year period and there had been a 93 per cent production increase per head of population. There were indications, however, that the rate of production increase, which would have to be annually between 9–10 per cent if the demands of the 1961 Party programme were to be met, had begun to slacken.

In agriculture the picture was less happy. Khrushchev's plans of 1954 for increasing the production of maize for fodder and his virgin lands project, though initially successful, began to pay diminishing dividends. The yield of wheat per acre, especially in the virgin lands, was subject to wild fluctuations; and the poor harvest of 1963 obliged the Soviet government to make large purchases of grain from Canada, Australia, and the United States. In other respects, reorganisation and rationalisation gave the *kolkhozy* incentives to increase production and very marked improvements were recorded. The most important organisational change was the transference in 1958 of the machine tractor stations to the *kolkhozy* and the introduction of new, and much more favourable, compulsory state purchase prices for *kolkhoz* produce. Continuing amalgamations reduced the number of *kolkhozy* to about 45,000 and the number of *sovkhozy* rose to about 7,400. The Russian peasant was generally richer than at any time in his history, but the problem of creating a sound agricultural base for the Soviet economy remained unsolved.

Probably the most important socio-economic change to occur during the Khrushchev era was the dismantling of Stalin's slave economic empire. In 1963 the population of the USSR had reached more than 225,000,000 (52 per cent urban, 48 per cent rural); and it was a population materially better off and universally better educated than at any time during the Soviet period. In 1958, for instance, a compulsory eight-year education programme had been introduced in the schools, with emphasis on a close connection between formal education and factory work. By the mid-1960s more than 70,000,000 Soviet citizens could boast of a secondary or higher education and more than 65,000,000 were in regular attendance at some kind of educational institution. But old habits died hard. The slave empire might be dismantled and the administration of criminal law might be improved, but savage penalties, including the death penalty, were introduced for certain kinds of speculation, for bribe-taking by officials, rape and attacks on the police. The judiciary was not independent of the state, nor were judges free from Party interference. Anti-Semitism, often officially encouraged, remained as deep-rooted as ever.

Before Stalin's death the outside world had tended to discount the achievements of the Soviet technological revolution. When the first sputnik or artificial earth satellite was launched in October 1957, the Soviet Union offered convincing proof of its lead in rocketry. The military as well as the technological implications of this fact came as a shock to the West. Enormous American expenditure succeeded in reducing the Soviet lead, but the Soviet Union could still claim that it was the first country to put a man into orbit round the earth. Major Yury Gagarin orbited the earth on April 12th 1961 and on August 6th Major German Titov made seventeen orbits; a year later Major Nikolayev and Lt.-Col. Popovich made sixty-four and forty-eight orbits respectively; and on June 14th 1963 Col. Bykovsky completed eighty-one orbits, to be followed two days later by the first woman in space, Valentina Tereshkova, who orbited the earth forty-eight times. These achievements, though accompanied by none of the frank publicity of American space launchings, were a justifiable source of national pride to the Soviet people, made them more confident of their capabilities and made it clear that, at least in this respect, Soviet Russia was indisputably the most advanced country in the world.

Culturally, particularly in literature, the ten years since Stalin's death were a period of short-lived "thaws" and longer "freezes". The publication in 1954 of the short novel *The Thaw* by Ilya Ehrenburg (b. 1891), whose best work was probably the satirical novel about Western culture, *Julio Jurenito*, written in the 1920s, marked the beginning of the first "thaw". By the time of the second Congress of Soviet Writers (December 1954), Aleksey Surkov and other conservative elements in the Writers' Union had gained the upper hand and Soviet literature was again "frozen" into the conformist mould of Socialist Realism. After the twentieth Party Congress in February 1956 there was a brief period of freedom marked by the appearance of Dudintsev's *Not By Bread Alone*, probably the most outspokenly critical novel ever published in the Soviet Union, and the second volume of a literary almanac called

Literary Moscow which contained several very critical stories, articles and poems. By this time such young poets as Yevtushenko (b. 1933) and Voznesensky (b. 1933) had begun to publish more candid, sincere and experimental poetry than any since the death of Mayakovsky. Of the older generation of writers Boris Pasternak was the only one to publish a major work. His novel *Doctor Zhivago*, after its completion in 1955, was rejected by the journal *Novy Mir* (*New World*) and first published in Italian translation in 1957 and in English a year later. Awarded the Nobel Prize for literature in 1958—an act which the Soviet government regarded as a deliberate political provocation—he was expelled from the Union of Writers. His great novel, the most important literary work to be written since the revolution, was banned from publication in the Soviet Union for failing to conform to the tenets of Socialist Realism.

During the 1960s such young writers as Aksyonov (*Ticket to the Stars*), Voinovich, Kazakov, Tendryakov and Nagibin introduced new zest and freedom into Soviet prose literature. But the most famous work to appear was Alexander Solzhenitsyn's *A Day in the Life of Ivan Denisovich* (1962) which described, in frank and very harsh terms, the experiences of a prisoner in a concentration camp during the Stalin period. Comparable with Dostoyevsky's *House of the Dead*, more interesting for its documentary than its literary value, it recorded at first hand truths which had never before been publicly admitted about the methods of Stalin's tyranny.

In the sphere of foreign affairs the Soviet government made tentative efforts to reduce tension with the West after Stalin's death. Coexistence was proclaimed as the new policy. The rancour in the Soviet satellites, so long suppressed or hidden when Stalin was alive, expressed itself in serious riots in Pilsen, Czechoslovakia, and in the East Berlin uprising (June 1953) which had to be put down by Soviet tanks. Soviet military might, however, continued to increase : in August 1953 it was announced that the Soviet Union had exploded its first hydrogen bomb. The meeting, though fruitless, of the Council of Foreign Ministers in Berlin early in 1954, the subsequent Soviet decision to join UNESCO and the International Labour Organisation and the ending of the war in Indo-China were signs of Soviet willingness to negotiate, if not to agree, with the West. During 1955, with the Geneva Summit Conference and the Khrushchev–Bulganin visit to India, Burma and Afghanistan, prospects for peace seemed brighter—an impression confirmed by the conclusion of the long-delayed Soviet peace treaty with Austria and the return of the Porkkala base to Finland.

The visit of Khrushchev and Bulganin to Great Britain in the spring of 1956, after Khrushchev's denunciation of Stalin, was chiefly remarkable for chants of "Poor old Joe!" from Oxford undergraduates and an acrimonious quarrel between Khrushchev and members of the Labour Party. By the autumn of the year unrest in Eastern Europe had assumed the proportions of revolution. The abolition of the Cominform in April 1956 and the Poznan riots in June were followed by a revolt in Hungary in October. A new coalition government under the moderate Communist, Imre Nagy, withdrew Hungary from the Warsaw Pact and called for help from the West. Thousands of Hungarians took advantage of the collapse of the former police régime to flee across the border into Austria. But at the moment of Hungary's greatest need world attention was diverted by the ill-conceived Franco–British attack on the Suez Canal. Soviet troops invaded Hungary and, after bitter street fighting in Budapest, succeeded in restoring order. The tragedy of Hungary proved to be for many Communist sympathisers in the West and elsewhere a salutary reminder of the inhuman brutality of the Communist régimes in Eastern Europe; for the West it was a moment of truth in which exponents of "brinkmanship" recognised that they could do nothing for Hungary short of involving the world in total nuclear war; and for the Soviet and other Eastern European governments it was the writing on the wall, warning them that they would have to adopt a more flexible and humane course in future if they were to retain control.

Rapprochement with the West came a little closer in 1959 when Khrushchev paid a visit to the United States and met President Eisenhower at Camp David. But "the spirit of Camp David" could not lessen Khrushchev's anger at the violation of Soviet airspace by an American U2 plane which was shot down a fortnight before the projected Paris Summit Conference of 1960. After a series of angry conferences the Summit Conference was abandoned. Khrushchev carried his indignation with him to the New York headquarters of the United Nations in September of that year and delivered a hostile diatribe against the UN Secretary-General, Dr Hammarskjöld. In 1961 tension between East and West increased considerably. Though Khrushchev met the new American President, John F. Kennedy, in Vienna in June, by August a crisis had developed over the Soviet insistence upon signing a separate peace treaty with the German Democratic Republic which would have had the likely effect of isolating West Berlin. The construction by the East German authorities of the notorious wall dividing East from West Berlin reduced the tension though it did nothing to solve the problem of a divided Germany. Almost simultaneously the Soviet Union resumed nuclear testing (temporarily suspended during the Geneva disarmament talks) and on September 10th exploded a fifty-megaton super-bomb in the region of Novaya Zemlya. The Soviet armed forces, previously slightly reduced, were again increased.

More Soviet nuclear tests occurred in 1962 and Khrushchev claimed early in the year that the Soviet Union possessed a global rocket which would render useless the elaborate Western defence system. Soviet complaints about American rocket bases, reiterated over several years, dramatically acquired a new meaning in October when aerial reconnaissance showed that Soviet rockets were being installed in Cuba. President Kennedy's deft handling of the ensuing nuclear confrontation between America and Russia averted the possibility of world war, but world war was closer during this period than at any time since 1945. The American naval quarantine of Cuba obliged Khrushchev to agree to the withdrawal of the rockets, though he may also have been prompted to refrain from further action by the Chinese invasion of northern India on October 20th. One apparent effect of this crisis over Fidel Castro's pro-Communist Cuba was to create a temporary stalemate in the chess game of power politics which could be reduced to the formula that if Soviet Russia took the pawn of West Berlin, the United States would take the pawn of Cuba. Another effect of this crisis was the establishment in June 1963 of a direct telephonic link, or "hot line", between Moscow and Washington—the beginning, perhaps, of a new and much more direct form of contact between the leaders of the two countries. Also, after protracted negotiation, a nuclear test-ban treaty covering all nuclear tests except those held underground was concluded in July 1963 between the Soviet Union, the United States and Great Britain. But the possibility of further agreement between the two "Ks", Kennedy and Khrushchev, was ended on November 22nd in Dallas, Texas, when John F. Kennedy was needlessly and wantonly assassinated by a gunman of allegedly pro-Communist sympathies.

A marked feature of Soviet foreign policy in the post-Stalin period was the attempt to increase Soviet influence abroad by providing long-term loans and military and economic aid to the underdeveloped countries. Though this could be regarded as part of a general strategy of world domination, it tended to have the boomerang effect of placing a heavy strain on Soviet resources, especially in the case of Soviet support for Cuba and Egypt. It also tended to promote a conflict of interests with China.

Sino–Soviet relations in the ten years since Stalin's death underwent a progressive deterioration. The thirty-year treaty of friendship, alliance and mutual assistance, signed between the USSR and the Chinese People's Republic in February 1950, returned to China the Chinese Eastern Railway and Port Arthur. It also opened the way for the stationing in China of more than 70,000 Russian military and civilian advisers. During the period of the Malenkov government relations between the two countries were on the surface extremely amicable, but Khrushchev's unilateral modification of the fundamental Marxist doctrine about the inevitability of war between capitalism and socialism at the twentieth Party Congress in 1956 aroused Chinese animosity. During 1957 the Chinese called for unity, cohesion and equality in the world Communist movement. The rift between the two countries and their respective points of view had now clearly opened. No doubt the Chinese were smarting from the indignity not only of having to be dependent upon the Soviet Union for their industrialisation programme but also of having to play second fiddle to the Russians in the Communist camp and in the alignment of world Powers because of the Russian refusal to share their nuclear secrets. The Chinese countered by attempting to find a short-cut to Communism through a system of communes and other far-fetched projects which were politely sneered at by Khrushchev in July 1960. Meanwhile, the Chinese Minister of Defence, Marshal Peng, apparently obtained Soviet backing for an attack on the Chinese leadership at a plenary meeting of the Central Committee of the Chinese Communist Party in August of the same year. In September and October, after his visit to Eisenhower, Khrushchev met Mao Tse-tung in Peking. To all appearances this was not a happy occasion. Mao Tse-tung's anti-Western militancy, his demand that the stability of the capitalist system should be tested, his possible demand for nuclear weapons and the fact that the Russians had made attempts to oust him from power left little room for cordiality with a Khrushchev fresh from a successful and outwardly friendly tour of the United States.

In 1960 the Soviet advisers began to leave China in a massive homeward migration and Chinese trade with the Soviet Union declined sharply. An attempt was made at a meeting of Communist bloc leaders in Bucharest in June to reassert Soviet control of the Communist movement. A further meeting of Communist leaders in Moscow in November gave rise to a series of embittered exchanges. Enver Hoxha of Albania, for example, who had refused to accept the denunciation of Stalin and had become a supporter of the Chinese attitudes, made a violent attack on Khrushchev. The differences between the two sides were becoming irreconcilable. Chinese militancy was based on the assumption that the world was divided into two hostile camps of capitalism and socialism; it was therefore necessary to increase the pressure against the "imperialists". The Russian attitude assumed that imperialism had changed and that nuclear war would only bring total destruction. A highly ambiguous agreed Statement issued after the Moscow conference did not bring the sides any closer.

The decision by Chou En-lai, the Chinese representative at the twenty-second Party Congress in October 1961, to lay a wreath at the feet of Stalin may have provoked the anti-Stalin speeches at that Congress and the resolution to remove Stalin's remains from the mausoleum. By 1962 the conflict was out in the open. Like two computers engaged in a polemic, *Pravda* and the Peking *People's Daily* embarked upon lengthy editorial filibusters at the end of 1962 and the beginning of 1963. The call for bilateral talks between the Russian and Chinese Communists was accompanied by further mutual recriminations, culminating in the breaking of display windows outside the Chinese embassy in Moscow and the expulsion of Chinese students. The meeting between the two Communist Parties in July proved to be little more than a face-saving device.

The real issues in the Sino–Soviet conflict were those of personality and status. In background, experience and manner Khrushchev, the Party manager rather than the revolutionary leader, was quite unlike Mao Tse-tung, the militant Communist hardened by a long struggle for power. Moreover, Soviet Russia was one of the "have" nations, whereas Communist China, despite its enormous man-power and conventional military potential, was one of the "have-nots". Russian obduracy and Chinese pride, as well as the more obvious issues of race and geography, had a conspicuous role in fomenting this disagreement, which may well prove to be one of the climactic episodes in twentieth-century history.

During the course of 1964 Khrushchev paid visits to Egypt and Scandinavia, and to all appearances he was the acknowledged leader of the Soviet Union; but on October 16th it was suddenly announced that he had been released from his responsibilities at his own request. Such a request had obviously been made only under extreme pressure from his colleagues in the Central Committee. The official excuses of advanced age and failing health, coupled with references to his "harebrained schemes" and the wilfulness of his behaviour, could not be taken at their face value. Personal animus against him within the Central Committee and undue self-confidence on his own part would probably be closer to the truth; and the almost simultaneous explosion by the Chinese of a low-yield nuclear device may have contributed. Khrushchev's successors, Leonid Brezhnev as boss of the Party and Aleksey Kosygin as Chairman of the Council of Ministers, were quick to indicate that they sought friendlier relations with China, though in other foreign policy questions they reiterated the Khrushchev line of peaceful coexistence. Rapprochement with Mao Tse-tung's China, however, was not likely to prove an easy matter.

Khrushchev's period of high office—approximately from February 1955 until October 1964—were years when Soviet Russia turned its face against Stalinism without submitting to an equivalent Khrushchevism. When the merits and weaknesses of his rule are finally weighed in the balance, it may well transpire that his refusal, or inability, to cast himself in the role of absolute ruler was of greater moment than the many other changes associated with his name. For by instinct, it seems, despite his bombast and his caprices, he was more of a democrat than an autocrat, and that instinct tended to inform his actions. He travelled more widely than any other Soviet leader; he was closer to the people than any ruler of Russia since Peter the Great; and he created precedents in the sphere of government, industrial organisation and agricultural policy, in foreign relations and in regard to Communist China, which no future Soviet government can afford to overlook. He exerted an influence on Russia and the world which many may have found disagreeable, but few could condemn as valueless. After his own fashion he was an honourable man, gifted with broad humanity and a capacity for friendliness that demonstrated the essential Russian-ness of his Communism. History may well accord him the honour of acknowledging that he not only did less evil than his predecessors, but also more good than his own time was prepared to expect of him.

Conclusion

Conclusion

VAGUE patterns may be discerned in Russian history, as if the centuries, like successive winds making the wheat on the steppe bend in unison, troubled the surface of Russia more conspicuously at their coming than at their going. The troubles at the beginning of the seventeenth century were followed by relative calm towards the century's end; the dramatic changes of the Petrine era at the opening of the eighteenth century gave way to the conservative policies of later rulers; the Napoleonic invasion, which brought Russia into the limelight of world events, served only to emphasise, as the nineteenth century progressed, the backwardness and traditionalism of Russia in the century's closing decades; and in the twentieth century the changes produced by revolution and civil war have gradually evolved into a familiar pattern of territorial expansion and conservative government.

The history of Russia is a history of ever-increasing territorial expansion. It is hardly surprising, therefore, that the history of government in Russia should be a story of the ever-increasing power of the central administration. The crises in Russian history have occurred when the continuum of the central rule has been disturbed. For continuity and permanency are essential to government in Russia, just as they are essential elements in a Russian's concept of himself, his ideals and his achievements. Changes, when they occur in Russian history, have a brevity, splendour and miracle-working impact similar to the effect of spring thaw after a winter's snow; but Russian history is really a story of unchangeability, a story of snow. The landmarks in it are easily discernible; less readily discernible perhaps is the pervasive grip of the snow itself like the power of government on Russia. Rulers of Russia have not so far been in the habit of retiring; they have either died in office, been killed, or forced to resign. Nor have they been chosen to rule by any process so human or fallible as the nationwide casting of a vote. Like the snow, they are the result of Russia's political climate which demands that government power should come as if from heaven.

The foreigner to Russia, if he has been educated in Western democratic principles, may well be appalled both at the political ingenuousness of the Russian attitude to government and at the ingenuity with which both government and governed in Russia excuse the conspiracy which apparently unites them. To all intents and purposes, government in Russia during the period with which this history is chiefly concerned has been a conspiracy of the rulers against the ruled. During the years 1801–1964 Russia had only eight rulers (excluding the Provisional Government of 1917; the short-lived triumvirates after the deaths of Lenin and Stalin; and the collective leadership following Khrushchev's departure); not one of these rulers gained power through a process of democratic election or ruled by popular mandate. It may be argued that Lenin was "elected" by the second All-Russian Congress of Soviets, although his Party was clearly not given a majority in the Constituent Assembly. However, Lenin's attitude to government was always that of the conspirator who, when he gained power as a result of the Bolshevik *coup d'état*, ruled Russia through the conspiratorial Bolshevik Party which he had himself created.

Soviet Russia has made great advances under the leadership of the Communist Party. Its present position as a great world Power is largely due to such Communist leadership. But the advances made during the Soviet period have been the result of a dictatorship which, though initially declared to be a "dictatorship of the proletariat", has always proved to be more para-military, chauvinistic and narrowly tyrannical in character than genuinely international, socialist or proletarian. The Party remains an essentially para-military organisation; and the Party rule of Russia may well end by becoming an obvious military dictatorship. Yet there is more direct popular participation in the country's affairs, whether through Soviet or Party organisations, than there was under Tsarism or there is in many other countries at the present time. Popular support for the Communist Party should not be underestimated; but it would also be wrong to forget that the Communist Party achieved power by conspiratorial means, that it has conspired to rule Russia, that it regards all opposition as conspiratorial in character and fears nothing so much as a conspiracy of the proletariat against its rule. It might be said that with the denunciation of Stalin's "cult of personality", and the transition to Communism, a minor democratic revolution has occurred in the Soviet Union. But the denunciation has since been employed against the denunciator, and there is no guarantee that in the future some other leader's cult may not need to be denounced in its turn. It would be unwise to overlook the fact that there has never been a time in modern Russian history when government policy has not involved enforcement and democracy has not involved agreement with the government.

What is precious in Russian history is not the activities of Tsars, General Secretaries or Chairmen of Councils of Ministers. History, as

Pasternak's Yury Zhivago has said, "cannot be seen, just as one cannot see how the grass grows". Though one may discern the vague successive patterns which the changing winds of the centuries make in the wheat on the steppe, the precious wisdom of Russian history lies deeper. It is to be discerned only in the life-giving processes within the soil which continually refertilise each season's seed. Such wisdom speaks to us from the sermon of Ilarion, from the *Lay of Igor's Raid* and the simple spirit of Avvakum; it is in the clarity and sanity of Pushkin, the gentle stoicism of Turgenev, Tolstoy's majesty and Dostoyevsky's saintliness; it is in the soft-voiced humour of Chekhov and the stridency of Mayakovsky; its voice is always robust, deep, inquiring, unsettled. The history that cannot be seen in the official annals, or which official Russia dare not recognise, is the vital source of all that is true and good in Russian life. Pasternak's Yury Zhivago is the unseen grass growing beneath the official statuary and ponderous architecture of Soviet Russia. This is the secret history of Russia, created out of a love of freedom and God and humanity which continually replenishes the Russian spirit and cannot be extinguished by political conspiracies; it makes the grass grow; it is the soil of Russia, the source of Russian greatness.

Select Bibliography

This select bibliography of works available in English represents both an acknowledgement of some of the sources used in the writing of this history and a guide to further reading, special emphasis being given to recently published or reprinted studies. It omits specialist works on social or economic questions, institutions, particular historical episodes, individual Russian authors, non-Russian nationalities, etc. in favour of works of a more general character. Many of the works listed below offer extensive bibliographies, but of particular value for bibliographical reference is D. Shapiro's *A Select Bibliography of Works in English on Russian History 1801–1917*, Blackwell, 1962. Places of publication, unless otherwise indicated, are L. (London) and N.Y. (New York); (P) indicates that a work is known to have been issued in paperback form.

General Histories
(first published, reprinted or revised since 1953)

1. Charques, R., *A Short History of Russia*, L. 1956, 2nd ed. 1962, E.U.P. abridgement 1958.
2. Clarkson, J. D., *A History of Russia*, N.Y. 1961, L. 1962.
3. Florinsky, M. T., *Russia, A History and an Interpretation*, 2 vols., N.Y. 1953, several reprintings.
4. Kliuchevsky, V. O., *A History of Russia* (trans. from Russian) L., N.Y. 1911–1931; reprinted N.Y. 1960.
5. Kochan, L., *The Making of Modern Russia*, L. 1962, L. (P) 1963.
6. Mazour, A. G., *Russia, Tsarist and Communist*, Princeton 1962.
7. Pares B., *A History of Russia*, L. 1926; revised ed. L. 1955, L. (P) 1962.
8. Riasanovsky, N. V., *A History of Russia*, N.Y. 1963.
9. Sturley, D. M., *A Short History of Russia*, L. 1964.
10. Sumner, B. H., *Survey of Russian History*, N.Y. 1943, L. 1944, 2nd ed. L. 1947, L. (P) 1961.
11. Vernadsky, G., *A History of Russia*, Yale 1929, latest revised ed. 1961, Yale (P) 1961.

(1, 5 and 9 are short general histories, the last being intended primarily for schools; 2, 6, 8 and 11 are more advanced histories by American scholars intended for university students; 7 and 10 are by eminent British historians but both works are rather dated; 3 is the best survey of Russian history from the beginnings to 1917; 4, despite the inadequate translation, is a classic work of Russian history to the beginning of the nineteenth century.)

Modern Russian History

Chapter I 1801–1825

Mazour, A. G., *The First Russian Revolution, 1825*, California 1937, 2nd ed. Stanford 1961.
Paléologue, M., *The Enigmatic Czar* (trans. from French) L., N.Y. 1938.
Raeff, M., *Michael Speransky*, Hague 1957.
Strakhovsky, L. I., *Alexander I of Russia*, N.Y. 1947, L. 1949.
Tarlé, E., *Napoleon's Invasion of Russia* (trans. from Russian) L., N.Y. 1942.

Chapter II 1825–1855

Bowman, H. E., *Vissarion Belinsky*, Harvard 1954.
Custine, Marquis de, *Journey for Our Time* (trans. from French) L., N.Y. 1951. (Originally published as *The Empire of the Czar*, 3 vols. L. 1843.)
Hare, R., *Pioneers of Russian Social Thought*, O.U.P. 1951.
Malia, M., *Alexander Herzen and the Birth of Russian Socialism*, Harvard 1961.
Riasanovsky, N. V., *Russia and the West in the Teaching of the Slavophiles*, Harvard 1952.
— — *Nicholas I and Official Nationality in Russia*, California 1959.

Chapter III 1855–1881

Almedingen, E. M., *The Emperor Alexander II*, L. 1962.
Billington, J. H., *Mikhailovsky and Russian Populism*, O.U.P. 1958.
Footman, D., *Red Prelude*, L. 1944.
Mosse, W. E., *Alexander II and the Modernization of Russia*, L., N.Y. 1958.
Petrovich, M. B., *The Emergence of Russian Panslavism 1856–1870*, N.Y. 1956.
Robinson, G. T., *Rural Russia under the Old Régime*, N.Y. 1932, reprinted 1949.
Sumner, B. H., *Russia and the Balkans*, O.U.P. 1937, reprinted L. 1962.
Venturi, F., *Roots of Revolution* (trans. from Italian) L. 1960, N.Y. 1961.
Yarmolinsky, A., *Road to Revolution*, L. 1957, N.Y. 1959.

Chapter IV 1881–1905

Fischer, G., *Russian Liberalism*, Harvard 1958.
Haimson, L. H., *The Russian Marxists and the Origins of Bolshevism*, Harvard 1955.
Keep, J. L. H., *The Rise of Social Democracy in Russia*, O.U.P. 1963.
Kindersley, R., *The First Russian Revisionists*, O.U.P. 1962.
Seton-Watson, H., *The Decline of Imperial Russia*, L., N.Y. 1952, 4th printing 1960, L. (P) 1964.
Treadgold, D. W., *Lenin and His Rivals*, N.Y., L. 1955.
Troyat, H., *Daily Life in Russia under the Last Tsar* (trans. from French) L. 1961.

Chapter V 1905–1917

Almedingen, E. M., *The Empress Alexandra*, L. 1961.

Charques, R., *The Twilight of Imperial Russia*, L. 1958, N.Y. 1959.

Deutscher, I., *The Prophet Armed, Trotsky 1879–1921*, L., N.Y. 1954.

Florinsky, M. T., *The End of the Russian Empire*, Yale 1931, N.Y. 1961.

Futrell, M., *Northern Underground*, L. 1963.

Hare, R., *Portraits of Russian Personalities between Reform and Revolution*, O.U.P. 1959.

Kerensky, A., *The Crucifixion of Liberty* (trans. from Russian) L. 1934.

Kokovtsov, V. N., *Out of My Past* (trans. from Russian) Stanford 1935.

Maynard, J., *Russia in Flux*, L. 1941, N.Y. (P) 1962.

Mazour, A. G., *Rise and Fall of the Romanovs*, N.Y. (P) 1960.

Pares, B., *The Fall of the Russian Monarchy*, L., N.Y. 1939, N.Y. (P) 1961.
— — *Russia between Reform and Revolution* (ed. F. B. Randall) N.Y. (P) 1962.

Wallace, D. M., *Russia on the Eve of War and Revolution*, N.Y. (P) 1961.

Wolfe, B. D., *Three Who Made a Revolution*, N.Y. 1948, several reprintings, N.Y. (P) 1960. L. (P) 1966.

Zernov, N., *The Russian Religious Renaissance of the Twentieth Century*, L. 1963.

Chapter VI 1917–1936

Baykov, A., *Development of the Soviet Economic System*, C.U.P. 1950.

Beloff, M., *The Foreign Policy of Soviet Russia, 1929–1941*, 2 vols., L. 1949.

Carr, E. H., *The Bolshevik Revolution*, 3 vols. L., N.Y. 1950–1953.
— — *The Interregnum 1923–1924*, L. 1954.
— — *A History of Soviet Russia: Socialism in One Country, 1924–1926*, Vol. I, L. 1958; Vol. II, L. 1959; Vol. III Pts. 1 and 2, L. 1964.

Chamberlin, W. H., *The Russian Revolution*, 2 vols., N.Y., L. 1935, N.Y. 1952.

Deutscher, I., *Stalin*, L., N.Y. 1949.
— — *The Prophet Unarmed, Trotsky 1921–1929*, L., N.Y. 1959.
— — *The Prophet Outcast, Trotsky 1929–1940*, L., N.Y. 1963.

Dobb, M. H., *Soviet Economic Development Since 1917*, N.Y. 1949.

Fainsod, M., *How Russia is Ruled*, Harvard 1953, new ed. 1963.

Footman, D., *Civil War in Russia*, L. 1961.

Jasny, N., *The Socialized Agriculture of the USSR*, Stanford 1949.

Kolarz, W., *Religion in the Soviet Union*, L. 1961.

Maynard, J., *The Russian Peasant and Other Studies*, L. 1942, N.Y. (P) 1962.

Pipes, R., *The Formation of the Soviet Union*, Harvard 1954.

Rauch, G. von, *A History of Soviet Russia* (trans. from German) L., N.Y. 1957, N.Y. (P) 1963.

Reed, J., *Ten Days that Shook the World*, N.Y. 1919, several reprintings.

Schapiro, L., *The Communist Party of the Soviet Union*, L. 1960, L. (P) 1963.
Serge V., *Memoirs of a Revolutionary* (trans. from French) L. 1963.
Treadgold, D. W., *Twentieth-Century Russia*, Chicago 1959.
Trotsky, L., *The Russian Revolution* (trans. from Russian) L., N.Y. 1932, N.Y. (P) 1959.

Chapter VII 1936–1953
Conquest, R. *The Soviet Deportation of Nationalities*, L. 1960.
Dallin, A., *German Rule in Russia, 1941–1945*, L. 1957.
Erickson, J., *The Soviet High Command*, L. 1962.
Fainsod, M., *Smolensk under Soviet Rule*, N.Y. 1958, L. 1959.
Mackintosh, J. M., *The Strategy and Tactics of Soviet Foreign Policy*, O.U.P. 1962, reprinted 1963.
Seton-Watson, H., *Pattern of Communist Revolution*, L. 1953.

Epilogue 1953–1964
Armstrong, J. A., *The Politics of Totalitarianism: The Communist Party of the Soviet Union from 1934 to the Present*, N.Y. 1961.
—   —   *Ideology, Politics and Government in the Soviet Union*, N.Y. (P) 1962.
Floyd, D., *Mao against Khrushchev*, N.Y., L. (P) 1964.
Leonhard, W., *The Kremlin since Stalin* (trans. from German) L. 1962.
Paloczi-Horvath K., *Khrushchev: The Road to Power*, L. 1960.
Pistrak, L., *The Grand Tactician*, N.Y., L. 1961.
Wolfe, B. D., *Khrushchev and Stalin's Ghost*, N.Y. 1957.
Zagoria, D. S., *The Sino–Soviet Conflict 1956–1961*, O.U.P. 1962.

Other Works
Black, C. E., ed., *The Transformation of Russian Society: Aspects of Social Change since 1861*, Harvard 1960.
Bourdeaux, Rev. M., *Opium of the People*, L. 1965.
Brown, E. J., *Russian Literature since the Revolution*, N.Y. (P) 1963.
Curtiss, J. S., *The Russian Church and the Soviet State, 1917–1950*, Boston 1953.
Gunther, J., *Inside Russia Today*, N.Y. 1958, 2nd ed. 1962, L. (P) 1964.
Jelavich, B., *A Century of Russian Foreign Policy 1814–1914*, N.Y. (P) 1964.
Kirchner, W., *History of Russia*, 3rd ed. N.Y. (P) 1963.
Kohn, H., *Basic History of Modern Russia*, N.Y. (P) 1957.
Kornilov, A., *Modern Russian History* (trans. from Russian) N.Y. 1943.
Lampert, E., *Studies in Rebellion*, L., N.Y. 1957.
—   —   *Sons against Fathers*, O.U.P. 1965.
Leonard, R. A., *A History of Russian Music*, L. 1956, N.Y. 1957.
Lyashchenko, P. I., *A History of the National Economy of Russia* (trans. from Russian) N.Y. 1949.

Masaryk, T. G., *The Spirit of Russia* (trans. from German) 2 vols., L. 1915, reprinted L., N.Y. 1955.

Mirsky, D. S. *A History of Russian Literature*, L., N.Y. 1949.

Pushkarev, S., *The Emergence of Modern Russia, 1801–1917*, N.Y. 1963.

Riha, T. ed., *Readings in Russian Civilization*, 3 vols., Chicago (P) 1964.

Rice, T. T., *Russian Art*, L. 1949, L. (P) 1963.

Simmons, E. J., ed., *Continuity and Change in Russian and Soviet Thought*, Harvard 1955.

Slonim, M., *The Epic of Russian Literature*, N.Y. 1950.

—   —   *Modern Russian Literature*, N.Y. 1953.

—   —   *Russian Theater*, N.Y. 1961, L. 1963.

Utechin, S. V., *Everyman's Concise Encyclopaedia of Russia*, L. 1961.

Weidlé, W., *Russia Absent and Present* (trans. from French) L. 1952.

Westwood, J. N., *A History of Russian Railways*, L., 1964.

Zenkovsky, V. V., *A History of Russian Philosophy* (trans. from French) 2 vols., N.Y. 1953.

Index

This index omits all references to the names of fictional characters and to the titles of individual literary, artistic, musical, scientific, political or other works mentioned in the text with the exception of news journals.